Framing Somalia

Framing Somalia

Beyond Africa's Merchants of Misery

Abdi Ismail Samatar

THE RED SEA PRESS
Trenton | London | New Delhi | Cape Town | Nairobi | Addis Ababa | Asmara | Ibadan

THE RED SEA PRESS
541 West Ingham Avenue | Suite B
Trenton, New Jersey 08638

Copyright © 2022 Abdi Ismail Samatar

All rights reserved. No part of this publication may be reproduced, stored in a retrieval system or transmitted in any form or by any means electronic, mechanical, photocopying, recording or otherwise without the prior written permission of the publisher.

Book design: Dawid Kahts
Cover design: Ashraful Haque

Cataloging-in-Publication Data may be obtained from the Library of Congress.

ISBNs: 9781569027882 (HB)
       9781569027899 (PB)

Dedication

This volume is dedicated to all Somali children, including Tutu and Yama. May Allah bless your struggle for renewal, and in your engagement with all the other "worthy causes," as Tutu reminded me recently.

To Hussein Kahin, our beloved principal at Amoud Secondary School whose wit, energy, intelligence, and care inspired me during my first year. His "funny" football team made us laugh hilariously at the end of each term. May Allah bless his soul eternally.

May Allah Bless Somalia and Somalis struggling for justice.

Table of Contents

Preamble & Acknowledgements	1
Ways of Seeing Somalia: Challenging Orthodoxy	25
Reframing Democratic Politics	59
Reframing Islam	123
Reframing Piracy	159
Liberating Somalia Studies	189

Preamble and Acknowledgments

In late June 1986, I attended my first International Somali Studies Conference in Rome, Italy, as a novice assistant professor of geography and urban and regional planning at the University of Iowa. I was excited to meet all known scholars of Somali society in one place. However, my enthusiasm soured on the opening day of the conference when I realized that the German leading and coaching a gathering of the major Somali figures was not a senior scholar, but a development practitioner whose credentials were that he controlled a fund, from the German Technical Cooperation Agency (GTZ), earmarked for the conference. The German fund paid the conference expenses of scholars and professionals from the mother country. Somalis needed this support because the twin curses of incompetent dictatorial mismanagement, and of structural adjustment programs imposed by the International Monetary Fund and the World Bank, had destroyed the economy. Such conditions created humiliating vulnerabilities for Somali scholars and professionals that compelled them to operate under the tutelage of this type of sponsorship.

Unbeknownst to some of us who came from the United States, the conference patron expected all of us to be "good Somalis," grateful for the opportunity to be in Rome, and to obligingly go through the motions of scholarly presentations.[1] Two assistant professors upended those expectations when they challenged the theoretical and methodological foundations of some of the papers presented by Somalis and non-Somalis. Two presentations commanded much attention on the first day. A senior Somali scholar delivered the inaugural paper, and the German development expert presented the other later in the day. In the question-and-answer session following the second paper, several younger Somali academics questioned the ways in which both papers framed the issues. A fundamental concern was that the papers' descriptive narrative of the economy and society was outdated or Orientalist in approach and paid little attention to the conceptual and methodological advances in African studies and development thought over the previous two decades. The German author was shocked and visibly annoyed. He had not expected such a searing critique. In contrast, the senior Somali scholar reacted more moderately, but still defensively, in his responses.

The next three days of presentations went as scheduled. The panel I was on took place on the last morning of the conference. The room was full in anticipation of what the younger scholars comprising the panel would offer. Our German colleague donned dark sunglasses and was sitting in the front row. I imagined he was hoping to see us fall flat on our faces, but as we presented our work, we instead sensed his increasing discomfort. We countered the prevailing scholarship on Somali society, but he did not challenge our theory, method, or evidence (Samatar and Samatar 1988). In retrospect, this encounter signaled the opening shot of a scholarly challenge to the functional anthropology in Somali studies, dating back to colonization and particularly preponderant since the late 1950s.

The genesis of the intellectual framework reflected in this volume goes back much further than that fateful conference in Rome. As a freshman undergraduate student at the University of Wisconsin–La Crosse, I had the unbelievable opportunity to read books and articles about Africa and Somalia—all new to me, and impossible for me to have envisaged just a year earlier as a factory worker in England. One of the first volumes I read was Alex Haley's book on Malcolm X (Haley 1964), which I discovered accidentally. Although the book had little to do with Somalia or Africa, more broadly, it nevertheless offered a critical dissection of US society that was new to me. This encounter with Malcolm X's America prompted me to think differently about the materials published by non-Somalis on Somalia.[2] The first book I read on Somali society was Richard Burton's travel essays, *First Footsteps in East Africa* (1894). I was curious about his characterization of Somalis he encountered on his travels, but I found the pretentious title of the book most offensive. I subsequently read two books by the British social anthropologist I.M. Lewis, *Pas-*

toral Democracy (1961) and *A Modern History of Somalia* (1965). Although I understood the paradigmatic link between Burton's work and those of Lewis, I lacked the necessary training to figure out what it was about them that intellectually perturbed me, other than the absence of any Somali voice in these works.

Meanwhile, I was the only person of African heritage enrolled in a class of eighty students in physical geography during that semester. Because of my accent, my professor realized that I was not American, and inquired where I was from, to which I replied, "Somalia." A few days later, the professor came back to me and said that he had checked the *Encyclopedia Britannica* and learned a few facts about Somalis. I was curious to hear what he had read. He stated that the encyclopedia identified two characteristic features of Somalis: "They are good servants and liars." Shocked to hear this, I had to think of a suitable retort. Malcolm X and his responses to similar denigrating comments came immediately to mind, and I reflexively responded that I was neither. This incident compelled me to re-read Lewis's and Burton's works with the professor's misconceptions in mind. I arrived at the realization that they essentially represented Somalis as exotic. I decided to take courses on Africa, reading whatever critical literature on the continent and the Third World I could find. Nevertheless, my undergraduate years ended without much clarity of thought.

During my graduate studies at the Urban and Regional Planning program at Iowa State University, my brother Ahmed suggested that I read Dennis Goulet's book provocatively titled *The Cruel Choice: A New Concept in the Theory of Development* (1981). Goulet's cogently laid-out ideas opened my mind's eye to competing development paradigms, quickly leading me to the discovery of dependency theory. Thereafter, I read the key works of the leading African political economist, Samir Amin (1972, 1974, 1976), who was one of the principal architects of dependency and underdevelopment theories. Those ideas grounded my master's thesis, which dealt with urbanization in Africa.

My advisor and thesis supervisor, Professor Riyad Mahayni, called me into his office after he read the thesis. He was surprised by my use of radical development theory, and gave me a good scolding over lunch. Despite his reservations about my choice of theory, he was not hostile to my scheme. His bigger concern was my professional progress and well-being, because I had an aspiration for academe. When I was admitted to the doctoral program at the University of California, Berkeley, he counseled me to be very careful, convinced that my radical intellectual predisposition might attract hostilities that could block career opportunities in the academy. His concern for my well-being was moving, and I left for Berkeley, mindful of his advice.

Even armed with predictions, I found Berkeley to be quite a different place from Ames, Iowa. Among the first things that struck me was the diversity of the student population, as well as the normality of progressive scholarship and teaching. Within a few weeks of arriving there, I immersed myself in reading courses to make up for the deficit in my theoretical and philosophical training.

My first full year at Berkeley was dizzying intellectually. Cody's bookstore on Telegraph Avenue became a most exciting place to hang out. A group of graduate students in geography organized an informal evening reading group where we studied the theoretical classics like Marx's *Capital*. In the second week of our reading group, I discovered, in the footnotes of the text, the name of the steel factory, Firth Brown, in Scunthorpe, England, where I had worked as immigrant laborer.

In addition to the reading group, I registered for a tutorial with Professor Michael Watts. The course concerned recent developments in Africanist political economy. This involved reading a book per week. Among the authors whose works I read were Samir Amin (1974), John Saul (1979), John Iliffe (1978), Gavin Kitching (1980), Henry Bernstein (1979), Mahmood Mamdani (1976), Nicola Swanson (1980), Walter Rodney (1981), Issa Shivji (1976), and Michael Watts (1979), among others. This foundational course enabled me to realize how disconnected the works on Somalia were from African studies debates.

During the second quarter, I took two reading courses and a regular seminar. The reading courses were with Jack Potter and dealt with China's rural economy before and after the revolution. Through these readings, I saw parallels with Africa's rural economic crisis.

Another graduate seminar I registered for was with Alain de Janvry. It was on agrarian change in Latin America, and enabled me to consolidate my grasp of development theory. By the end of the first year, I had a clear understanding of my previously instinctive discomfort with most of the expatriate-dominated literature on Somalia and Somalis. By the end of the second quarter, I had found my theoretical home in political economy and social history.

Fundamental to political economy and social history is the nature and use of power in all its dimensions. This paradigm avers that it is not possible to understand the nature and the dynamics of development and politics without considering them in relation to capitalist accumulation and colonialism. My studies at Berkeley gave me the tools I needed to recognize that the literature on Somalia was fundamentally implicated in colonial and postcolonial power relations. Thus, my doctoral dissertation and first book examined how colonialism and capitalism qualitatively restructured the Somali world, as well as how Orientalist scholarship represented political life in the country (Samatar 1989). The Somali elite who had some education did not grasp the implications of this scholarship, even though some were aware of global inequality and the underdevelopment legacy of Italian and British colonialism. Thus, Orientalist writers and conventional development experts had free rein in setting the scholarly agenda in the 1960s, without Somali checkmates.

The attitudes of Somalis toward expatriates who peddled this worldview ran into problems in the early years of the military regime, in the 1970s, when scientific socialism and Soviet influence were at their peak. Crude Marxism imported from the Soviet regime, and shorn of historical and cultural moorings, was the dominant ideology. After the Somali regime broke relations with the Soviet Union in 1977, US and Western aid agencies and nongovernmental organizations (NGOs) flooded the country. It was clear then, that Somalis had gained minimal critical intellectual capital from the association with Soviet communism. Instead, mismanagement of the public sector and the economy during the height of scientific socialism had left the terrain fertile for unfiltered Western influence.

Most Somalis welcomed this shift from Soviet to Western influence without discerning what its costs might be, such as the economy going into a tailspin as international donors, led by the International Monetary Fund and the World Bank, demanded austerity policies (Samatar 1993). Austerity policies eviscerated the public sector, sending it into freefall as salaries and incomes precipitously dwindled, inflation rose dramatically, and corruption became rampant. Professional and skilled public sector workers fled public service, flocking to new avenues of employment, such as aid agencies and NGOs. Neoliberal policy under a ruthless and rudderless dictatorship instigated a chaotic political economic environment riddled with conflict and bereft of national civic ethos, ultimately leading to the political calamity of state collapse in 1991.

The absence of a national government to protect the collective interests of the people, and the persistence of sectarian conflicts, produced a humanitarian catastrophe of Quranic proportions.[3] As a result, the lack of civic institutions made it possible for *political tribalism and opportunism to become the opium of the people*. Survival and a narrow self-interest, rather than a national vision and moral order, became the norm for most people. Statelessness for many displaced Somalis meant becoming not only homeless (Samatar 1994), but also political orphans (Samatar 1989). The education system in the country collapsed and literacy rates plummeted, and life expectancy shrank dramatically. Thus, NGOs, the United Nations (UN), and development agencies became the preferred employers of many professional Somalis.

Given these circumstances, actors of the so-called international community became the agenda setters for *framing* and *defining* the country's problems. Further, they decided the country's priorities and who would implement the programs they sponsored. This created lopsided power relations between most Somalis and international overlords.[4] The new merchants of misery, to riff on Graham Hancock's *Lords of Poverty* (1989), had unchallenged sway. By "merchants of misery," I mean UN agencies and other members of the international political establishment whose livelihoods depend on the continuation of crisis. They earn hardship allowances in the comfort of their offices and homes in places like Nairobi, Kenya, while occasionally parachuting into safe locations inside Somalia[5], at phenomenal cost to international taxpayers. Beyond these are consultants (academics or others) who advise and *frame* Somali issues for the establishment, write reports for which they receive heftier fees than what they could earn in their home countries, and publish articles or books. Others are with international NGOs and feed on the largesse of donors as program managers or project implementers.

A cohort of mostly diasporic Somalis play a compliant role to these merchants of misery. Abetting all, is the dysfunctional Somali political class who take part in the ritual humiliation of their people by dancing to the political tunes of choreographers shamelessly masquerading as national or regional authorities. These ways of thinking and doing development still prevail and produce two groups of people: groups whose merchandise is the misery of the indigent Somali people, and impecunious Somalis.

The overwhelming power of aid agencies, NGOs, and their intellectual comrades is such that they rarely ever employ Somali consultants to carry out studies that depart from their *weltanschauung*. I have been witness to their dominance over the last two decades. My encounters with the merchants of misery are too numerous to catalog in this short preface. Six of my experiences suffice to illustrate the relationship between Somalis and the merchants of misery.

The first example is a revealing encounter I had in 2001, with the then-guru of Somali studies, the late Professor I.M. Lewis. A group of Somali journalists who accused the British Broadcasting Corporation (BBC) of illegally terminating their contracts with the BBC Somali Service hired him as an expert witness. These journalists claimed that the BBC Somali Service manager discriminated against them based on their genealogy. The BBC engaged me as its expert witness. The task of the British tribunal was to determine whether Somali genealogical groups ("clans," as Lewis preferred to call them) constitute different racial and cultural groups, and how genealogy affects Somali political identity. Lewis, in his report, asserted that Somali political identity is set at birth through the genealogy of the father, and that each Somali clan has cultural mores that differ from others. My response demonstrated that political identity formation was a complex process that was not based on a single variable (Samatar 2010), and that most Somalis shared the same cultural values. Lewis rebutted with the following: "As a Somali...Professor

Samatar naturally has direct personal experience of Somali culture and social organization, which informs his writing. His position... is similar to that of any other member of the Westernized Somali elite."[6] Lewis's calculated intention was to disqualify, through innuendo and mischaracterization, any Somali scholar who dared to interpret Somali political history differently than he.

I was amused by Lewis's inability to explain how he, the Westerner who barely spoke any Somali, could have an inside understanding of any Somali's way of thinking, politically or otherwise. The judges detected his flawed reasoning and partisanship in the case, and declared, "We accept Lewis is an eminent authority in the field, but the above-quoted remarks do cause us some concern when considering the objectivity of the evidence," presented by Lewis (ibid. p. 76). Dismissal of the case against the BBC marked the first defeat of functional anthropology and its dominance of Somali studies.

My second encounter with the merchants of misery came in 2003 and 2004, during the Somali Reconciliation Conference in Kenya. The conference brought together all the major warlords, who had brutalized the population for nearly twelve years, under the aegis of the Intergovernmental Authority on Development (IGAD), the regional organization whose members are Ethiopia, Kenya, Sudan (and now South Sudan), Uganda, Djibouti, Somalia, and Eritrea. However, the funding for the conference came mainly from the European Union, with some support from the United States.

I went to the conference as an academic observer, and to my surprise, was invited to a dinner organized by the EU representative and the US diplomat responsible for Somalia on the second day of the conference. Agents of the warlords populated the dinner, in addition to one other scholar. At the dinner, the two diplomats announced the conference's agenda and declared the forum's objective was to produce a transitional federal government for Somalia by bringing all the factions together. Surprised by the emphasis on the *federal*, I asked them where their mandate for federalism came from. The startling response was that Somalis consist of "clans," and therefore the new federal order must reflect that reality! The logical follow-up, which I raised, was where were the "clan" leaders who supposedly represent those stakeholders? The two diplomats could not answer the question, and it was apparent from their body language that they regretted inviting me.

Leaders of IGAD lectured Somalis during the plenary gathering of the conference the next day. The Ethiopian and Kenyan leaders offered vacuous platitudes, but President Yoweri Museveni of Uganda made the most memorable remark. He scolded the Somali leaders for letting their people down and behaving as if they were colonial creatures. He ended his remarks by dramatically telling the Somali crowd of several hundred people that "they are the shame of Africa."

The reconciliation conference dragged on for an excruciating eighteen months. Midway through, it had become clear that the warlords had marginalized everyone else and were now in charge, with the assistance of their Ethiopian allies. The two EU and US diplomats and I met for lunch in Nairobi. After exchanging pleasantries, I asked them what their thoughts were regarding this turn of events. I was stunned to hear them express their dismay that the warlords had come out on top, and that the conference was heading toward a government of warlords. My response was short: they were responsible for this outcome, and must take ownership of it. But the magnitude and full implications of warlords claiming to represent genealogical groups and tradition, and leading the march toward democracy, did not register on them.

My third experience of the relations between Somalis and aid agencies came when a leading development agency asked me to conduct a desk and field study on the drivers of conflict in Somalia. After convoluted negotiations that lasted for several weeks, we agreed on the practicalities of the field visits and where I would stay in the country. One of the sticking points was my refusal to stay at the UN compound inside the heavily guarded Mogadishu Airport, where even Somalis with permission to visit the premises are treated as foreigners or criminal suspects on their own soil, in a manner reminiscent of apartheid. The agency's major concern was my safety, but my priority was having easy access to the people I needed to interview for the study without necessarily compromising security. In the end, I signed a note releasing the agency from any liability if anything were to happen to me while I was in the country.

In Nairobi, I began to interview members of the UN staff for Somalia, other relevant NGOs, and the diplomats of countries involved in Somalia. The first thing I noticed was the language they shared (with the exception of UNICEF) in defining the nature of the conflict, in dated social anthropology ways. My attempts to reframe the issues with them went nowhere, and they were dismissive of alternative approaches to the problem.

A second bone of contention with the sponsor was the discussion of the "clan" as the core variable in their political analysis of the conflict.[7] The sponsor was flabbergasted that I disagreed with their understanding of Somali issues. Needless to say, I insisted on my approach, which considers conflicts among genealogical communities the consequence, not the cause, of the political problem (Samatar 1992).

Despite such disagreements, I produced my report and delivered it on schedule. One of the employees of the agency who read the report, told me later that no one else who had done work in Somalia for the agency had framed the problem as I did. My framing produced a set of policy proposals at odds with their current strategy. My host added that the conceptual frame of the report, and its substantive political analysis, had helped her gain a better understanding of political problems in her own country.

I was able to stand firm against the agency, and uphold my intellectual independence and integrity, because I could afford to. I did not need a job or an income from the agency, if it decided not to hire me. I narrate this story to show the huge pressure potential Somali consultants or employees of such agencies confront, given their dependency on the agencies. Because of their precarious livelihoods, Somali employees of these agencies and other international organizations are compelled to become intellectually malleable foot soldiers of the new order, while the population remains a voiceless horde clinging to dear life under the gaze of the merchants of misery.

My fourth encounter with the merchants of misery was a daylong conference organized by a select group of European ambassadors involved with Somalia, in Nairobi, in 2004. A colleague invited me to the event, where I noticed a strange seating arrangement. At the front and center of the podium were the European diplomats, flanked on one side by two of their experts. Behind them, and partially blocked from view, sat two Somalis. The audience sat in a couple of semi-circles.

The diplomats spoke first and then gave the floor to the two experts, both of whom were white, and who analyzed the conflict in Somalia and how the population might be reconciled. Once the "conceptual frame and the relevant facts" were presented, the two Somalis sitting in the back row were *invited* to show slides of communal meetings in Somalia. The slide show was an embellishment to give the event an aura of authenticity.

After the formal presentations were concluded, I asked two questions: I inquired first if the geography of the seating arrangement on the podium was by design or accident. I then queried the diplomats on whether they had been unable to find Somali experts to frame the conflict, and on why the two Somalis on their team had played such a perfunctory role. In their revealing response, they declared that "we are all working together to help Somalia." I met with the two Somalis after the event and learned that my comments and questions had apparently offended one, whereas the other argued with him and insisted that my remarks were supportive of them.

My fifth encounter was with the UN Secretary General's Special Representative for Somalia, in late January 2017. Somalia's parliament appointed an independent anticorruption commission to oversee the integrity of the 2017 presidential election, and I served as the chair of the commission. The envoy's assistant reached out to me as the commission prepared for the election. She told me that the envoy wanted to meet with the commission before the election. I asked her to provide the agenda for the proposed meeting so that I could ask the commissioners for approval. She replied that the purpose of the meeting was a courtesy call. I reported to the commissioners, and they agreed to meet with the envoy. The gathering took place a day later, and we gave the envoy the floor to initiate the conversation. To our collective bewilderment, he began his remarks by announcing that he was glad to honor our request to meet him. I immediately retorted that his deputy had requested the meeting. We adjourned the meeting after some brief perfunctory comments.

I include this encounter to demonstrate the dismissive and disrespectful attitude of some UN and other diplomats toward Somalis. The envoy was not prepared for the commission's refusal to proffer servile gratitude for being graced with his presence.

The sixth and final encounter took place between I and a Norwegian diplomat based in Nairobi, via email. An op-ed piece I wrote, titled "Carnage in Mogadishu," triggered the exchange. "Carnage in Mogadishu" was critical of the unconscionable destruction of Mogadishu by the Ethiopian occupying forces, and the ineptitude of the client Somali government to stop the savagery (Samatar, April 2007). Here is the verbatim email exchange:

Apr 1, 2007, Kristmoen Rina wrote:

Dear Professor Samatar,

I have not read your paper regarding Somali reconciliation yet, but will do so and revert back to you with comments. However, there are indications that you view the [Transitional Federal Government] as illegitimate. That is of course serious - as this is a government (could have been a better govt - but it is probably better than no govt) recognized by the UN Security Council. Somalia deserve peace and stability, and the somalis struggling inside Soamlia [Somalia] with their everyday life certainly deserve both respect and reflection from somalis in diaspora - who far too easy throw out destructive judgments, instead of trying to be constructive and take a positive part in somali politics. Before the planned reconciliation Congress it is of vital importance to get constructive views from persons like yourself, and I do hope that you are willing to play a positive role.

Wishing you a nice weekend!
With my best regards,
Rina Kristmoen
Norwegian Embassy
Tel: + 254 20 4251000
Mobile: +254 733 62 1978
>mail: rik@mfa.no
Below is my response to the diplomat:

-----Original Message-----
From: samat001@umn.edu [mailto:samat001@umn.edu]
Sent: Sunday, April 01, 2007, 8:00 PM
To: Kristmoen Rina
Cc: Dalen Kjell Harald; Jensen Runar
Subject: Re: Paper

Dear Ms. Rina Kristmoen:

Thank you for your plan to read my essay on reconciliation. It would have been appropriate to write your reaction to my position after reading the paper, but you have chosen to do otherwise and act on erroneous supposition. At any rate, let me respond directly to your reflex. It is quite strange that you can be so bold to tell me how to play a "constructive" role. There you go: as a diplomat from Norway (a country steeped in democracy and respect for citizens and human rights). I am astonished that you can tell an independent person what to think and how to behave without much regard. I have not callously come to the conclusion that the TFG and its leaders are illegitimate as I know the history of the entire process of its formation better than anyone else, including yourself. What ultimately make a government legitimate is the consent of its people and not the support of other outfits. The country of my birth is under Ethiopian occupation (illegitimate occupation by the same UN standards that you refer - I also know what responsible Norwegians did during the WWII). The UN Security Council has failed to tell Ethiopia to immediately withdraw from Somalia - due to the powers that be, and I had hoped that Norway would take a strong stand on this given its long and distinguished track record on these matters. I am astounded that you see my assessment of the TFG as a serious problem, but you do not see the indiscriminate massacres the Ethiopian troops are doing in Mogadishu as we speak. I certainly agree with you that a bad government might be better than none, but I am sorry to say that the TFG under Ethiopian occupation is worse that the bad government which you refer to. I can certainly support a process that is sufficiently open enough for the citizens to have a steadily increasing say about the fate of their country, but that was not the quality of the process which produced the TFG and which guides the so-called reconciliation which you are talking about (please read the paper before commenting).

You are absolutely right that Somalia deserves peace and stability and that all self-respecting Somalis in the Diaspora should serve the interest of peace in the old country. I want to tell you, for your information, that I have invested so much energy and time to support peace and reconciliation, but I do not need you to tell me to play a constructive role. Some modesty will go a long way rather than a patronizing attitude by novice diplomats to the Somali catastrophe. I am not surprised by your patronizing attitude

as I have seen it before by so many other Westerners. Unfortunately, that is one of the biggest obstacles to peace in the country.

If you want to have a constructive engagement with independent-minded Somalis who care about serious efforts towards peace and reconciliation, then you have a partner; but if not then stay the course. If you believe in the values that are enshrined in Norway's democratic system, then you would think twice about the TFG.

Sincerely,

Abdi I. Samatar
Professor & Director of Graduate Studies
Departments of Geography
University of Minnesota

Below is the Diplomat's brief response

Kristmoen Rina <rina.kristmoen@mfa.no>   Apr 11, 2007, 3:31 AM

to me, Dalen, Jensen

Preamble and Acknowledgments 15

Dear professor Samatar,

First of all: Thank you for taking the time to give me a long reply. Secondly: I had read your essay briefly - and have now read it thoroughly. Your thoughts on the way forward is indeed interesting, even though it is probably too late to avoid a big Congress (ref your idea about 30 people).

You probably know that the NGRC (National Governance and Reconciliation Committee) presently are in Nairobi for consultations. We will have several meetings with them.

I would indeed like to have you as an independent partner, and look forward to exchange views with you on the situation. It was not my intention to offend you, and I am very sorry if you feel my mail as an offense. I would again like to reiterate that every opportunity to bring peace and stability to Somalia should be sought, and the fact that diaspora can have a very constructive (or destructive) role should not be ignored.

With my best regards,
Rina Kristmoen
Norwegian Embassy
Tel: 4251000
Mobile: 0733 62 1978
mail: rik@mfa.no

***

That this junior Norwegian diplomat had the audacity to feel entitled to reprimand Somalis who had different ideas reflects the imbalance of power. Further, she never contacted me after this exchange.

Such power inequality between diplomats, donors, experts, and Somalis over the last three decades has had a numbing effect on the intellectual and political atmosphere in the country. Somalis' search for survival took precedence over ideas and national dignity. However, and in spite of their vulnerability, some Somalis maintain their mettle and resist this domination.

I remember one courageous peace activist telling me how several US and European scholars and experts who consulted for agencies milked him every year for information and analyses, and then reproduced that material in their reports or articles without crediting him with a co-authorship or declaring his significant contributions to the publication. He was livid when he told me of this. Subsequently, we agreed that he would take a leave from his job and join the University of Minnesota's graduate program in Public Affairs. Tragically, he will never be able to write his story. Unknown criminals murdered him two months later, in 2005.

The intellectual environment is not as bleak as the above tales paint it. In spaces both inside and outside the country, the resistance is still alive. For the past twenty-five years (from the late 1990s, onward), I have met young students and their teachers, all across the country, who are not dependent on the handouts of the donors, and who, in principle, reject their ways of seeing Somalia. Unfortunately, these women and men do not have access to the scholarly resources they need for translating their critiques and sentiments to scholarly thought.

Many universities have been established in the country since the late 1990s. However, most of them are not worthy of the name. A few of the pioneering institutions have met some of the educational needs of students, but their focus has been to provide students with "technical" skills for gainful employment. This technical orientation has left a gaping hole in the intellectual advancement of Somali youth because of the absence of critical social sciences, history, and humanities, which are central to the emergence and development of civic ideas and education, indispensable to the regeneration of the civic movement.

In addition, the dearth of libraries and seasoned scholars who can act as role models and mentors continues to undermine any effort to produce knowledge and challenge the established order. Beyond universities and libraries, the scarcity of public forums where new ideas can be cultivated and ventilated, and where ordinary citizens can access civic education, continues to undermine progressive social change.

A possible source of revival and resistance to the dominant worldview is young Somalis in the diaspora. Just as in Somalia, many of these students' studies are in disciplines that lead to employment in the professions. However, a minority of them have concentrated on earning advanced social science degrees, and a handful of these are doing their research on various aspects of Somali life. Some of them (e.g., Said, 2002; Ibrahim 2017, 2018) have begun to challenge Euro-American scholars who cling to their orthodoxy, and who profit from consultancies in Somalia.

I vividly remember the story of a Somali woman who was invited to a workshop organized by the Rift Valley Institute, a British consulting firm based in Kenya. The discussions in the gathering narrated the usual Somali "problems." However, the woman contested their discourse and raised challenging questions. Organizers summarily expelled her.

Similarly, another group of young Somalis challenged what they dubbed *cadaan* (Somali for *white*) studies. The establishment of the *Somaliland African Studies Journal*, whose entire editorial board consisted of non-Somalis, provoked this group's ire. A white member of that editorial board responded in an offensive and predictable manner. He reacted no better than establishment or orthodox scholars—those the late Edward Said described as refusing to question the reality of their illegitimate location in the power matrix (Said 1981).

As a social anthropologist in the twenty-first century, the board member should have known better the importance of the critics' concerns, but many European and US scholars of Somali society are tethered to the discourses of the 1950s. He should have taken stock of how issues of power and knowledge have been debated elsewhere in African and Middle Eastern studies, and should have known that silencing the "native" belonged to a bygone era.

I salute the defiant spirit of these young Somalis and encourage them to think strategically by setting up a scholarly and political agenda that has its own center of gravity, and is cognizant of developments around the world. Engaging with the merchants of misery is futile.

Over the course of my long journey and intellectual growth, I incurred huge debts to family, friends, teachers, colleagues, and communities where I did my field studies. The names noted below is an abbreviated list of the many I cannot name individually, nor summarize their considerable contributions. I am most grateful that I had unconditional support from all, and often at critical times.

Foremost among these is my late maternal cousin, Fadumo H. Asker, who opened her home to me while I labored in the Firth Brown Steel and Iron Complex in Scunthorpe, UK, so I could save money for my studies in the United States. Fatima was one of the kindest people, and helped me stayed focused on my objectives when the working conditions in the factory seemed satanic and too much to bear.

The dean of admissions at the University of Wisconsin–La Crosse, Gale Grimslid, went well-beyond the call of duty to assist me in getting to the university on time for fall registration. He was also kind enough to pick me up from the La Crosse Greyhound bus station after a long bus ride from New York.

My professors Fred Staner, Bruce Mouser, Joel Lazinger, Joe Heim, Jim Lafky, Lorraine Flaherty, Bob Wingate, and Larry Johnson made La Crosse intellectually more exciting than it would have been without their mentoring.

Other mentors at Iowa State University who helped me find my intellectual bearings were Professors Riyad Mahayni, Charles Hoch, and Lee Fletcher. They collectively provided intellectual guidance that got me out of the doldrums of undergraduate education.

The University of California, Berkeley, qualitatively altered the course of my professional life in ways I could not have imagined during the alienating days in Sculthorpe's satanic mills. Campus life was intellectually inspiring and politically stimulating, sometimes to the point of exhaustion. The mixture of activism and political and intellectual debates was as instructive as the formal graduate courses I took. I had my first encounter with these debates in the famous Sproul Plaza during my first week on campus. A group of students were debating US military involvement in Central America, and most specifically, in Nicaragua. These debates were laced with discussion about the nature of capitalism in the region, and the reproduction of poverty and domination. I was so impressed with the debates that I regularly visited the plaza every Friday afternoon for much of my time in Berkeley.

Courses and seminars taught by Professors Michael Watts, Richard Walker, Jack Potter, Ann Markusen, Alain de Janvry, and Carl Rosberg provided the intellectual foundation that enabled me to reimagine African development and Somali studies.

Dr. Micheal Haldeman and Ms. MaryAnn Halderman in Albany, California, provided wonderful friendship for many years.

Colleagues at the University of Iowa and the University of Minnesota, such as David Reynolds, Joel Barkan, Michael McNulty, Allen Isaacman, Phil Porter, John Adams, Richa Nagar, Bob and Susanna McMaster, Bud Duval, Adam Beldsoe, Madeleine Cahuas, Kurt Kipfmueller, Dan Griffin, Kathryn Grace, Glen Powell, Sara Braun, Tina Bekerleg, and the Interdisciplinary Center for Global Change Program, made for a vibrant intellectual community.

My associates at the University of Pretoria Department of Political Sciences, such as Rina, Jane, Roland, Chris, Heather, Sandy, Quraysha, Anthony, Robin, Rentia, Chris N, and Gerhard are the kindest of colleagues. Professor Maxi Schoeman who led the department for nearly twenty years is a most generous friends who has modeled what transformation means in the South African academy - Kudos, Maxi. Thank you all for creating an intellectually welcoming and stimulating environment, and for that, I am forever grateful.

My brother Ahmed Ismail Samatar (Haji B) has been both a mentor and a co-conspirator in this journey. Tusmo and Sama have been a blessing. I salute young Somalis, intellectuals, or just ordinary citizens, who refuse to succumb to the othering of their humanity, and who maintain their faith in the need for political and intellectual liberation.

My wonderful friend, Bashir, made my long stay in Mogadishu in 2021 as interesting as it could be, given the challenges of what used to be a beautiful city on the western shores of the Indian Ocean, and I am deeply thankful for his generosity and kindness. I wish Somalia had a thousand Bashirs.

Abdirashid (Concern) is one of the most spiritually generous Somalis I know, and provided civic companionship for the last year.

Ahmed Yusuf and Mohamed Aden always provided sound and wise counsel when I needed it. Abdirashid X offered similar sport, advice, and friendship. A most special thanks to Abdimalik Yusuf and Asad for their dedication to the Somali cause.

Other friends have backed this intellectual agenda in different ways for many years. Among these are Abdimalik Yusuf, Abdillahi Ahmed (Asad), Zuleikha Said, Mohamed Muse (Feedha Yare), Moos (Feedha weyne), Arraleh, Dr. Ibrahim, Dr. Suad, Ware, Abdulahi Hassan Ali and the rest of the Hiil Qaran team.

Colleagues at Mogadishu University and University of Kismayo have been civic pioneers and role models of what civic identity looks like in the most difficult of circumstances.

My gratitude to my wonderful friends, Abdirashid and Amina in Johannesburg, and particularly the three "R" daughters.

To wonderful Hashasha, whose faith, resilience, and ambition is absolutely inspiring.

To Kassahun Checole for his incredible generosity and for taking the time to read the entire manuscript and supporting its publication. I am grateful to Mary-Ann Short for copyediting the manuscript at an early stage.

To Abti Hogsade for being a pioneer and ice-braker.

To my sister Amina, who made enormous contributions to our family, particularly in the later years of our parents' lives, and we are abundantly and forever indebted to her for her immense sacrifices.

Finally, my late mother, Halimo Abdillahi Kahin, who modeled what it meant to be a loving mother, and a kind and courageous human being. Every day, I celebrate her steely determination to educate her fatherless children in the most challenging of circumstances.

And to my late father, Ismail Samatar Mohamed, without whose audacity and foresight the first elementary school in our village would not have been built, and for standing up to conservative elders and religious men who opposed its establishment. Ironically, that same school has been recently named after one of those religious men. It is almost certain that the stories in this book and many others would have never seen the light of day without Aabo's steely fortitude and unbelievable imagination.

Bibliography

Amin, Samir. "Accumulation and Development: a Theoretical Model," *Review of African Political Economy,* vol. 1, no. 1 (1974): pp. 9–26.

----------------. "Underdevelopment and Dependence in Black Africa: Origins and Contemporary Forms," *The Journal of Modern African Studies,* 10, no. 4 (1972): pp. 503–524.

----------------. *Unequal Development: An Essay on the Social Formations of Peripheral Capitalism.* New York: Monthly Review Press, 1978.

Bernstein, Henry. "African Peasantries: a Theoretical Framework," *The Journal of Peasant Studies,* vol. 6, no. 4 (1979): pp. 421–443.

Burton, Richard. *First Footsteps in East Africa.* London: Tylson & Edwards, 1894.

Goulet, Dennis. *The Cruel Choice: A New Concept in the Theory of Development.* New York: Antheneum, 1978.

Haley, Alex. *The Autobiography of Malcolm X.* New York: Ballantine Books, 1964.

Hancock, Graham. *Lords of Poverty: The Power, Prestige, and Corruption of the International Aid Business.* London: Mandarin, 1989.

Huddleston, Trever. "An Unbroken Friendship. Jordan, Z. Pallo, editor. *Oliver Tambo Remembered.* Johannesburg: Macmillan, 2016: pp. 334–337.

Iliffe, John. *A Modern History of Tanganyika.* Cambridge: Cambridge University Press, 1978.

Sh. Ibrahim, Ahmed. "Changing of the Guards: Politico-Religious Authority and Islamic Education in Mogadishu, Somalia," *Islamic Africa,* vol. 9 (2018): pp. 133–162.

-------------. *The Shari'a Courts of Mogadishu: Beyond African Islam and Islamic Law.* New York: PhD Dissertation, SUNY, 2017.

Kitching, Gavin. *Classes and Economic Change in Kenya: The Making of African Petite-Bourgeoisie.* New Haven: Yale University Press, 1980.

Lewis. I.M. *Pastoral Democracy: A Study of Pastoralism and Politics Among the Northern Somali of the Horn of Africa.* London: Oxford University Press, 1961.

--------------. *A Modern History of Somaliland: Nation and State in the Horn of Africa.* New York: Longmans, 1965.

Mamdani, Mahmood. *Politics and Class Formation in Uganda.* New York: Monthly Review Press, 1976.

The Holy Quran. New Delhi, Islamic Book Service, 2003: pp. 540–543.

Rodney, Walter. *How Europe Underdeveloped Africa.* Washington, DC: Howard University Press, 1981.

Said, Edward W. *Covering Islam: How the Media and the Experts Determine How We See the Rest of the World (fully revised edition).* Random House, 1981.

Said, Edward W. *Culture and Imperialism.* New York: Vintage, 1993.

Said, Zuleikh Salim. "State Decomposition and Clan Identities in Somalia," M. Phil Thesis, Oxford University, 2002.

Samatar, Abdi Ismail. *The State and Rural Transformation in Northern Somali, 1884–1986.* Madison: University of Wisconsin Press, 1989.

------------------------. "Structural Adjustment as Development Strategy? Bananas, Boom, and Poverty in Somalia," *Economic Geography,* 69, no. 1 (1993): pp. 25–43.

------------------------. Mogadishu's Carnage & the Death of the TFG & its Fraudulent ...

------------------------.www.hiiraan.com/print2_op/2007/apr/mogadishu_s...

----------. Debating Somali Identity in a British Tribunal: The Case of the BBC Somali Service," *Bildhaan: International Journal of Somali Studies*, vol. 10 (2010): pp. 36-88.

Samatar, A.I. and Samatar, A. "The State, Agrarian Change, and Crisis of Hegemony in Somalia," *Review of Africa Political Economy*, vol. 43 (1988): pp. 26–41.

Samatar, Ahmed Ismail. Editor. *The Somali Challenge: From Catastrophe to Renewal?* Boulder: L. Rienner Publishers, 1994.

Saul, John S. *The State and Revolution in Eastern Africa*. Portsmouth: Heinemann Educational Publishers, 1979.

Shivji, Issa G. *Class Struggles in Tanzania*. Portsmouth: Heinemann, 1976.

Swanson, Nicola. *The Development of Corporate Capitalism in Kenya, 1918–77*. Berkeley: University of California Press, 1980.

Watts, Michael. "The Etiology of Hunger: The Evolution of Famine in a Sudano-Sahelian Region," *Mass Emergencies,* vol. 4 (1979): pp. 95–104.

Endnotes

1 A few of us were not the beneficiaries of the German money and had little idea of what the expectations were.

2 In mid-late 1970s, expatriates totally dominated major social sciences literature on Somali society.

3 See Surat Dukhan's description of the human made calamities (The Holy Quran. English Translation with Original Arabic Text, 2003)

4 Edward Said best captured the essence of such relationship in the absence of formal colonialism. "In our time, direct colonialism has largely ended; imperialism…lingers where it has always been, in a kind of general cultural sphere as in specific political, ideological, economic, and social practices."

5 I remember doing some work with a British colleague from the University of New Castle, in 2005. We had to get security clearance from the UNDP office in Nairobi. We met the chief security officer and told him that we were planning to go to Mogadishu. He panicked

and adamantly told us that we could not proceed with our plan. He said Mogadishu was too dangerous, and he informed us that he had received reports in some parts of the country, near Baidoa, which indicated that the terrorists are on the move. I listened to his ranting, which lasted for over an hour. We ignored the warning, went to Mogadishu, where we spend five days, did all of our work, and came back to Nairobi safely. I went to see the UN security officer and told him that we are back from Mogadishu after doing our work for a week. He was speechless.

6   This claim demonstrated, from Lewis's vantage point, that Somalis should not dream of thinking differently from his agenda when it came to analyzing their society. His stance reminded me of what the apartheid architects of Bantu Education had in mind for the residents there. The heroic Churchman, Trever Huddleston, who fought the apartheid regime through his entire life, said the following about that system: "I was there in Sophiatown, when the Minister of Native Affairs, introducing Bantu Education Act in Parliament, said, 'We are telling the native he is being educated for certain forms of labour: there is green pastures in which he has not right to graze." "An Unbroken Friendship," Z. Pallo Jordan, editor. *Oliver Tambo Remembered*. (Johannesburg: Macmillan, 2016), pp. 334–337.

7   It was bizarre to watch some of these well-groomed actors as they strenuously tried to figure out what my genealogical identity was.

1
Somali Political Identity:
Confronting the Orthodoxy

I suppose we can all differ as to the exact point where good writing becomes overwhelmed by racial cliché. But overwhelmed or merely undermined [scholarship] is always badly served when an author's [scholarly] insight yields space to stereotype and malice. ***And it becomes doubly offensive when such a work is arrogantly proffered to you as your story.*** (Achebe 2000, p. 41. Bold is mine)

They cannot represent themselves; they must be represented. (Marx quoted in Said 1979, p. xv)

Somalia has become notorious for its failed politics, and the degradation of the life of the population. What is less known by the Africanist community is that two theoretical and political projects compete to explain the nature, the causes, and the consequences of Somalia's political catastrophe. These entail divergent readings of Somali political history, and the relationship between cultural or religious and political identity. Accordingly, they offer diametrically contrasting recipes for remaking Somalia.

The older of the two projects is anchored in British social anthropology. This discipline was the handmaiden of colonial rule because it Orientalized the natives in the colonies, and thus facilitated European domination and imperial reproduction (Asad 1973a, 1973b; Said 1979). Its advocates have focused on the dynamics of cultural-political differences between Somalis rather than their commonalities (Lewis 1961). Scholars and activists committed to this way of seeing the Somali world come in three variants: those faithful to the old orthodoxy, who continue to reinvent the past; those who argue that distinct colonial traditions account for the different political landscapes in northern and southern Somalia since 1991; and those who see ethnicized mini-states as the way to the future of a new, different Somalia.

The alternative attempt to understand the Somali world and the country's recent calamity is rooted in a political economy and social history whose genesis was inspired by the struggle for freedom from colonial rule, the search for justice, and the desire for civic belonging and a common future. Scholars writing in this vein (Samatar 1994, 1988; Kapteijns 2001; Besteman 1998, Cassanelli 1982) consider the rich cultural heritage of the Somali people as a complex and *contingent* factor in the making of Somalia's political development, rather than as an unmalleable historical albatross. Further, the differences in the colonial experiences and inherited administrative forms between the former British and Italian Somalilands are ones they deem not an unbreakable shackle on the agency of the people, but a challenge Somalis seek to overcome as they search for a common future. These scholars reckon Somalia's political catastrophe to result from not the violation of some deep-rooted primordial forces or different colonial traditions, but the interplay between two political forces with contrasting imagined Somali futures (Anderson 1983).

In this chapter, I demonstrate that the first school of thought presents the Somali calamity as if it is a consequence of the workings of the people's cultural tradition. In so doing, it advances solutions that reinforce political conflict and social discord in the country. In contrast, the alternative framework provides a narrative, anchored in Somali political history, that demonstrates that the political and humanitarian catastrophe resulted from not tradition, but politicized genealogy used as a Trojan horse by a significant segment of the political elite to loot public resources and perpetuate their tenure in office. The alternative approach thus distinguishes cultural identity from political identity, and offers a common civic agenda for rebuilding the social and political fabric of the country.

The first section of this chapter presents the key arguments of the dominant school in Somali studies. The second narrates the theoretical framework for the alterative explanation of the Somali disaster. The third lays out the road map for the rest of the volume.

Genealogy as Political Identity

It is now very common among expatriates interested or involved in Somali affairs, and some younger Somalis, to talk about the

Somali political disaster in ethnic terms. The intellectual roots of these ideas go back to precolonial explorers such as Richard Burton (Burton 1894) and colonial scholarship. However, the person most responsible for popularizing this framework was I.M. Lewis, the late British social anthropologist who established the foundation for the dominant ideas about culture and politics in Somali studies. Lewis was the leading scholar on Somalia for several decades, from the late 1950s until the early 1990s. I divide his numerous contributions into two categories. In the first, his contributions seemed to somewhat appreciate traditional Somali democracy and the vast cultural values that the population shared, by treating the Somali world outside the colonial and capitalist context. His second category totally reverted to Orientalizing the Somali as the prototypical "tribal" man—and failed to recognize the "tribal" woman at all.

Lewis's foundational scholarly contributions to the study of Somali history and politics were two volumes produced in the 1960s: *A Pastoral Democracy: a Study of Pastoralism and Politics Among the Northern Somali of the Horn of Africa* (1961), and *A Modern History of Somalia: Nation and State in the Horn of Africa* (1965). These two books are the gold standard for this approach of understanding Somali society. *A Pastoral Democracy* is a good description of what the author *imagined* to be Somalia's democratic political tradition. The central objects of his description of Somali tradition were nomadic pastoralism; the genealogical divisions among the Somali people; and the deliberative communal Shir, a consultative process of adult males. Such portrayal of pastoral life provided a narrative of the movement of the population and their stock, and the ways they managed communal affairs.[1] *Pastoral Democracy* contains a detailed description of the rural conditions in what were then parts of British Somaliland. Lewis did not speak the local language, however, and his detailed description of cultural-political and economic life of Somali pastoralism is based on what his Somali translators told him. Much can be learned from this narrative regarding the details of everyday life. Nevertheless, its core thesis is the description of the Somali and "his" cultural-political order: "I have concentrated upon the *divisions* in Somali society because it is only through them that the Somali *political structure* can be understood" (Lewis 1961,

p. 295. Italics are mine). In addition, he stressed a Somali's bellicose nature: "The northern Somali are essentially a *warlike* people who readily engage in battle" (Lewis 1961, p. 250. Italics are mine). The fundamental intellectual contribution of the book (to Western scholarship) was the identification of the genealogical structure of Somali cultural groups, alongside the description of the decentralized precolonial communal structure and relations. Lewis and his intellectual disciples consider these two qualities central to understanding Somali political identity, the character of the Somali person, and the politics in Somalia. From politics, terrorism, to piracy, the assumptions embedded in these two ideas have dominated analysis of the country, particularly since the late 1980s, as demonstrated in the rest of this section.

The timing of Lewis's thesis and his narrative are ironic for two reasons. One, he was completely oblivious to the transformative historical forces at play in the colonial empire at the time he was doing his fieldwork and writing the first book. In that very late hour of the colonial era, when the "winds of change" were felt everywhere in Africa, Lewis gave no significant reflection to the colonialism of the previous eighty years and its effects on pastoral democracy.

Two, Lewis was unable to appreciate how his positionality, and therefore inherent bias, as a British academic supported by the British Colonial Social Science Research Council influenced his study of the Somali people (Asad 1973, pp. 14–15).[2] Hence, Lewis's work ignored that he was writing about a population subjected to colonial domination for nearly eighty years and agitating for liberation from British rule. If Lewis had realized the colonial context of his subjects, he might have reworked his analysis and titled the book, *Pastoral Democracy* **Under Colonial Rule**." Such a reformulation would have examined how traditional pastoral democracy was no longer autonomous, and how a bigger power framed the latitude of Somali affairs. In other words, what he described as *pastoral democracy* was the remnant of an earlier political economy that had lost its center of gravity and social cohesion. What gave coherence to the precolonial pastoral tradition was Somali communal self-reliance, in which households were mutually dependent, given the distribution of the means of livelihood, livestock, pastoral and farming land, and water sources, and the absence of an external power, whose shadows constrained and reconfigured the ways of tradition. For instance, the fragmentation of grazing lands into separate colonies by Britain, Italy, and Ethiopia introduced a new risk to the pastoralists' livelihoods and made them subject to new authorities who demanded taxes and a colonial code of conduct (Farah, forthcoming). In addition, the administrative and trade centers that had been at the margins of pastoral life eventually became the colonizers' center of political and economic power, and overshadowed nomadic ways (Samatar 1989).

Pastoral Democracy failed to appreciate the political reality of colonial rule, and it was even less successful in comprehending the implications of significant restructuring and commercialization of the economy (Samatar 1992). The creation of a colonial state, and the commercialization of livestock, induced new forms of urban growth, and the establishment of powerful political and economic structures. Town and city residents, nestled in the interface between the outside world and rural Somalia, had more political influence than those living in the nomadic setting. These colonial developments during the previous eighty years severely compromised the autonomy of the pastoral tradition, and the destiny of the Somali people was no longer in the hands of nomadic populations practicing their pastoral democratic tradition. The towns and the colonial administrative apparatus in Somaliland provided the platform for Lewis to cast his anthropological gaze over the pastoral milieu. In these spaces, the seeds of postcolonial politics germinated, and the population mobilized for liberation, signaling the passing of an era. This process paved the way for a Somali world qualitatively different from the preceding household-based and small-community-anchored political and economic culture (Samatar 1989).

In retrospect, the late 1950s and early 1960s were a strategic period to unearth the dynamics of this transformation and its enduring repercussions for the Somali people. But that would have required a set of conceptual tools that Lewis's brand of social anthropology lacked. As a result, he produced a readable book, but one lacking the analytic rigor to open up ways of seeing this world new to him, and unable to take stock of the transformation of the previous eighty years. The value of the contribution of *Pastoral Democracy* was limited by the way it treated Somali history as an intransigent and fixed cultural and political fossil, and ignored global transformations of the nineteenth and twentieth centuries that had significant bearing on the fate of the Somali people (Lewis 1961, 1965).

Despite its shortcomings, Pastoral *Democracy* was written in accessible language for non-specialists, and thus attracted several types of readers. It became popular with British readers because it was not critical of British colonial rule of the Somali people, and did not contain analytic language discomfiting British readers. It was widely accepted by its limited number of Somali readers, whose pleasure that their country and culture attracted the attention of a British scholar overruled their discrimination. Because of the absence of alternative scholarly publications on Somalia, *Pastoral Democracy* became, and still is, the introductory text for expatriates interested in Somali affairs.

Lewis's other major contribution during this period was *A Modern History of Somalia: Nation and State in the Horn of Africa*. *A Modern History*'s primary objective is "to provide a sociologically and anthropologically informed history of the Somali people" (Lewis 1965, p. vii). The book describes the territorial effects of multiple colonialisms on the Somali and their culturally based nationalist project. It appears to be a sympathetic reading of the plight of the Somali people and the challenges of overcoming artificial colonial boundaries that dismembered their land and separated families and kin groups from one another. Among the topics the book covers are the imperial partition, Sayyid Mohamed Abdulle Hassan's struggle against colonialism, brief reunification of the Somalilands under British occupations in the 1940s, and the problems independent Somalia faced.

A Modern History was valuable because it provided the first panoramic view of the nation's political history. However, much like *A Pastoral Democracy*, it did not break new ground in understanding the dynamics of pre-independence and postcolonial Somali nationalist politics. Lewis noted that the integration of British and Italian Somalilands into the Somali Republic "was one of the few successful examples of African unification" (Lewis 1965, p. 195). Nonetheless, his analysis of the postcolonial political tussles never escaped the grip of his traditional anthropological lens, and thus provided no sociological theory to frame the text.

For example, his political analysis of the democratic period was anchored in an Orientalist framework in its claim that the distinction between competing political actors was ethnically based:

> *The composition of the new government formed after the elections led to a prolonged and bitter conflict within the **Darod** leadership of the S.Y.L., and this, inevitably, had wide repercussions.... At the cost of several cabinet reshuffles, Abd ar Razaq and his supporters were able to survive until the Presidential elections of June 1967. President Aden Abdulle Isman, who was eligible for re-election, was supported by Premier Abd ar Razaq, to whom he was **related by marriage**.* (Lewis, 1965, pp. 201–202. Bold is mine)

This description of the Somali Youth League (SYL) as a Darod Party illustrates that Lewis had little understanding of the character of the SYL, and even less of the nature of political differences between key leaders in the party. For him, the only significant political divergence between the leaders was their genealogical pedigree, hence the reference to Darod. But the facts indicate otherwise.

First, the claim undermines intellectual rigor in its use of rumors in the streets of Mogadishu at the time, which Lewis failed to check against the reality of politics. He had good access to political leaders of various persuasions, including the president and prime minister, and it would have been easy for him to inquire of them the causes of elite political differences. Further, the SYL's longest-serving leaders, Abdullah Issa and Aden Abdulle Osman, who led the party for much of the crucial 1950s, were not from the Darod genealogical group, and were from the same town. If genealogy had governed the political decisions of these leaders, they would have sustained their grip on the party, but that did not happen (see Chapter 2).

Second, if Lewis had examined the composition of the central committee of the party, he would have seen that Darods did not dominate it. Third, Lewis insinuates that Prime Minister Abdirazak Hussen ("Premier Abd ar Razaq") supported President Aden in the 1967 presidential contest because of their familial relationship through marriage. Contrary to Lewis's assertion, Hussen was not related to the president, and the two leaders had been political allies since the early 1950s, despite originating from different genealogical groups. In fact, Abdirazak was a distant cousin of Abdirashid Ali Sharmarke, the eventual winner, whom he did not support for the presidency. Finally, the political conflict that marred Hussen's first government was not tribally based, because members of parliament from Abdirazak's own northeast region were among the most strident opposition (Lewis 2008).[3] What distinguished the government from the opposition was the opposition's political opportunism rather than tribal, or political, or ideological agendas (Samatar 2016, and Chapter 2 of this volume).

In summary, Lewis's two most important contributions to the study of Somali history and politics in those formative years were contradictory. On the one hand, he appeared to value the importance of traditional democracy, but he did not understand the economic foundations that made it possible. On the other hand, he essentialized Somali culture and turned it into a fossil. Because of the bluntness of his analytic tools, he was unable to see the power dynamics introduced by the colonial project, the nature of intra-elite political struggle, and that contest's influence on the political terrain in the country. Because of these omissions, the bedrock of his analysis of Somali politics remained a single variable—the clan, an immutable given in his view. For Lewis, all one needed to explain the most complex political problems in the country was the genealogical difference between the actors.

Lewis's second rendering of Somali affairs came after the collapse of the state in 1991. Drawing on the key element of his original work, his descriptions of Somali political and cultural history dropped any sympathetic interpretations. From here, onward, his scholarly and activist preoccupations were to push a divisive agenda that aimed to deepen the political significance of genealogical differences among the population, and that endorsed colonial division of the Somali people.

After the collapse of the Somali state, and fragmentation of the country into sectarian fiefdoms ruled by warlords, Lewis felt his imaginings about Somalis were vindicated. Although Lewis did not openly declare his support for the Somali National Movement (SNM), a sectarian political group operating out of Ethiopia in the

1980s, he did everything possible to endorse its political program. Like so many of the foreign supporters of the fragmentation of the country, he misinterpreted the history of some of the major events in northern Somalia since 1991. For instance, he claims that the SNM's decision to declare Somaliland "independence" in the town of Burao was firmly supported by the population of the region:

> *There was widespread hatred and distrust of the South (identified with Siyad's misrule) and a strong tide of public feeling favouring separatism. Bowing to this, the SNM leadership proclaimed [at a meeting] on May 18 that their region would **resume** its independence from the South.... This **pragmatic** decision reflected the desire of many people of Somaliland.* (Lewis 2008, p. 75. Bold is mine)

The facts of what happened in that meeting in Burao are quite different from Lewis's claims. There is no doubt that the vast majority of the Somali people abhorred the military regime, particularly during the last decade of its tenure. However, I observed that a very significant proportion of the northern population, not associated with the SNM, did not equate the regime with all southern Somalis, and therefore did not approve of the SNM's secessionist project. In fact, the SNM was so fearful of the public's reaction that it did not declare its intention to secede during its war with the regime. SNM leaders were categorical during this period, that secession was not part of their agenda.[4] At the meeting in Burao, the military wing of the SNM literally forced its agenda on the rest of the SNM and declared independence (Qalib, Elmi, Muhamad 2002). The upshot of the military wing using force in Burao has been the rejection of the Somaliland project by people in the east and west of the region, and a minority in the central area of Somaliland.

Lewis's ideological antagonism to Somali civic nationalism in the form of a united republic goes back to the early 1990s. One of his first major manifestos after Somalia collapsed was part of a consultancy report for the European Union (EU), "A Study of Political Decentralized Structures for Somalia: a Menu of Options" (Lewis 1995). Here, Lewis and other contributors to the report closely followed the clannist scripts to recommend that a loose confederate national administrative structure that mapped genealogical identities onto political boundaries was the most appropriate and sustainable way to resurrect a national government. Unfortunately, the report failed to examine how a dispensation anchored in tribal allegiance would produce a civic union of Somalis. Further, given the centrality of genealogy to political identity in their model, they were unable to provide a rationale that would prevent units from fragmenting into ever-smaller exclusive genealogical subunits.

While Lewis and his associates were lobbying the EU and others to endorse their political agenda, he started reimagining his earlier work and made every effort to cleanse from it any emphasis he placed on commonalities among Somalis. He began to stress differences among Somalis by essentializing both the genealogical groups and the individuals (Lewis 1993, 1994). Lewis's revisionist history started with the demonization of Somalia's pioneering nationalist warrior, Sayyid Mohamed Abdulle Hassan. Whereas in his early readings of Sayyid Mohamed, one could glean an element of neutrality, by the early 1990s, he was openly hostile to the struggle for independence. His sympathies were with the British colonial operations rather than the liberation struggle:

> *Nearly 80 years ago, a **brave servant** of the empire, called Richard Corfield, tried to **bring order** to the Somalis when they were in rebellion under a religious leader dubbed the Mad Mullah by the British. All Corfield got for his pains was a bullet in the head in battle and a place in the epic poetry of Somalia—a bloodthirsty hymn to victory that has lived on in a society steeped in antagonism to outsiders.* (Lewis 1992. Bold is mine)[5]

For the revisionist Lewis, Somalis were the demons and the colonial soldiers, who were trying to kill the freedom fighter and subjugate the population, earned the author's sympathy. Lewis's political transformation did not end with his empathy toward colonial rule, but went further to describe the Somali as an exceptional breed:

> *The first thing to underscore about the Somalis is that they are not as other men* (Lewis 1992). *Somalis receive their fundamental social and **political identity at birth** through membership of their father's clan.* (Lewis 2001. Bold is mine)

Although Lewis does not elaborate on the gist of these assertions, it is clear that he truly believed Somalis to be a peculiar type of human, in that their political behavior is predestined from birth. If genealogy were such a decisive factor, then how to explain contrasting shades of political opinions within the same genealogical groups, or even immediate families?[6] Continuing his revisionist project, he was even more categorical in his totalizing claims. He noted in a public lecture in London, in 2002, that certain clans have leadership qualities, but others lack them. Contrary to Lewis's incredible claim, some of Somalia's best leaders hail from those genealogical groups he describes as deficient. The new Lewis came full circle in 2004, when he repudiated what he had once described as "one of the few successful examples of African unification," and endorsed the sectarian secessionist Somaliland republic.[7]

The Disciples

Lewis's scholarly legacy did not end with his retirement and passing, but was carried forward by a younger generation of expatriate scholars, activists, journalist, and employees of development agencies. With the collapse of the Somali state, individuals and groups who worked for agencies and organizations, such as the War-Torn Societies Project (now defunct), United Nations Monitoring Group on Somalia and Eritrea, Life and Peace Institute, Catholic Institute for International Relations, and the BBC, began to take positions inspired by Lewis's writing. The most influential writings have come from Matt Bryden (1999), War-Torn Societies Project (2001, 2005), Hellander (1998), Heinrich (1997), Bradbury (2008), Gilke (1995), Harper (2012), and the International Crisis Group (2006). Academic writers who share the same predilections but are a bit more subtle in their advocacy include Menkhaus (2006), Hoehne (2001, 2009), and Makind (1991).

These writers follow Lewis in conflating cultural and political identity, and in assuming that a cultural variable—genealogy—singularly determines a Somali's political identity. Africanists may consider this reading of Somali society as a throwback to colonial-era narratives of African life, but in the Somali world, this kind of writing by others has become normal, particularly in the last three decades. These writers have been busy producing advocacy literature that minimizes the British colonial impact on northern Somalia, while claiming that northern Somali tradition survived colonialism. Such historical "facts," they posit, explain the different political outcomes in northern and southern Somalia since the mid-1990s.

One of the most sustained efforts in this regard is by Mark Bradbury. His most important thesis is contained in *Becoming Somaliland*. Here are the first words of the book's introduction:

> *On May 18, 1991, leaders of the Somali National Movement (SNM) and elders of northern Somali clans, meeting at the* **Grand Conference** *of the Northern peoples in the war-scarred town of Burco, bowed to public pressure and announced that the people of north-west Somalia were withdrawing from the union that had joined the colonial territories of Italian Somalia and the British Somaliland Protectorate in 1960.* (Bradbury 2008, p. 1. Bold is mine)

Beyond repeating Lewis's assertion, Bradbury makes three critical claims in his book that are central to Bradbury's argument. First, he declares that the northern Somali traditional system (meaning genealogical system) was not disrupted by British colonial rule. The preservation of this culture, he maintains, explains the stability of the North and the absence of violence in comparison with the South. Second, he asserts that a 1993 conference in Borama enabled clans in the North—because of their *close sociocultural relations, such as intermarriage*—to set the foundation for a stable Somaliland. Third, Bradbury pronounces the principle anchor of stability in "Somaliland" to be the amalgamation of the tribal system with government. Bradbury's explicit assumption is that southern Somalia lacked these features, and thus has been unable to restore peace and stability.[8]

A discerning reading of Somali history contradicts Bradbury's assertions. His first critical claim, that the impact of British colonialism was minimal on the North, originally came from Lewis (Lewis 1961, p. 28), but has been repeated by others. Here is how Bradbury's book reproduces it:

Chapter 1

> *It has been argued that due to the particular experience of British colonialism and the policy of light imperial rule—others have called it "benign neglect"—these informal rule-based systems have remained more entrenched and stronger among northern pastoralist communities than in southern Somalia. In addition, pastoralism retained a dominant role in the post-independence economy.* (Bradbury 2008, p. 246)

The point of this preservationist thesis is to provide a variable that will help mark the existence of major cultural distinctions between southern and northern Somalia, that might validate the claim. Here, the argument is that Italian colonial rule destroyed the authority of traditional clan elders in Italian Somaliland, but Britain maintained clan authority in their protectorate. The assertion, then, is that the conservation of such a tradition in northern Somalia enabled the people in the region to use precolonial mechanisms to avoid the violent and seemingly endless strife that has marred the South since the disintegration of national government in 1991. Bradbury and others aver that the South's endless conflict and political discord is because of the dearth of clan cultural anchor (clan leaders). Much like Lewis's original argument, this thesis contains serious factual errors and conceptual contradictions.

Factually, the northeast (Puntland) was part of Italian Somaliland, but the region has been more stable and peaceful than the south-central regions. If Italian rule and the destruction of tradition in the South had been a necessary and sufficient condition for the absence of peace and stability, then the northeast would have been as violent and unstable as south-central Somalia. In addition, the economy of the northeast was also predominantly based on pastoralism. Thus, if tradition is such a powerful causal force, it is difficult to comprehend why the eastern districts of the former British Somaliland, which have seen significant violence and political conflict, have not benefited from the preservation of tradition. Finally, pastoral regions in all of southern Somalia have traditions that are identical to those of pastoral regions in the North, but they have suffered a great deal over the last three decades, and the preservation thesis offers no account for the North-South divide.

The assertion that the British conserved "clan" authority is also belied by the historical evidence, as the British military governor authoritatively recognized in 1946:

A form of tribal administration would be particularly convenient in British Somaliland; but unfortunately there are no indigenous institutions here, nor are there any recognized leaders through whom authority can be exercised. The unit may be said to be the family—if not the individual.... If a tribal system ever existed in the Protectorate, which is not certain, it was destroyed by the Egyptians, who preferred direct control communicated through Aqils, who were government servants rather than tribal representatives, to indirect control exercised through native chiefs.... What the present government has been trying to do is to establish...some form of organized responsibility, within the existing tribal or sectional structures.... Parallel with this, we have started some native courts, and town committees, which are thought to be showing some promise, but they cannot be said to be tribal in their composition; while the laws and regulations which they administer are our laws and regulations—not indigenous ones.... Our type of administration requires trained and literate personnel.... Somalis, though at present illiterate, are extremely quick to learn, and when educated, show signs of being able to exercise authority; and it is perhaps safe to say that the most influential people in the country today are clerks and traders.... It is therefore thought that the natural leaders will be found as a product of our schools, rather than as selected or self-appointed members of our tribes. We shall therefore be well advised not to try to impose on the Somalis a bogus system of native authority, or delude ourselves that such a system can be artificially devised.
(Fischer 1946)

For over eighty years of British rule, the so-called chiefs, as employees of the state, had little autonomy, mostly only transmitting the instructions of colonial order, while the economic base of their communities was significantly transformed (Samatar 1989). Because of the subjugation of the chiefs to the state, whatever legitimate authority they had before colonization had long since vanished in both British and Italian colonies. In addition, over forty years of Somali administrations further corroded clan leaders' authority to the point that many of them became true vassals of the state, particularly during the military regime. Most elders became allies of the authorities during this period rather than defenders of their communities' interests. Given these changes, one cannot convincingly argue that it is the preserved fossil of precolonial genealogical authority that distinguishes northern and southern Somalia.

Bradbury's second critical assertion, that sociocultural relations, such as intermarriage, between the clans in the northwest facilitated the restoration of stability and governance to the region during the Borama conference in 1993, is dubious. I was in Borama during that conference, and observed most of the deliberations. I noticed that the residents of Borama were deeply worried about the presence of SNM militias and some of their commanders, who had previously ransacked the town. Evidently, the sociocultural relations that Bradbury imagined did not have any currency to quell these fears, neither had they worked earlier when the SNM plundered the town in 1991.

My observations during the conference were that the elders in the gathering were not the decisive force that led to the agreement. Instead, it was the leadership of one man, Mohamed Ibrahim Egal, and his political acumen that made the conference a success. Egal was the last democratically elected prime minister of the Somali Republic. This gave him stature no one else in the meeting had. He had political experience and personal relationships with some of the major figures in the meeting. Many non-SNM communities also recognized that he was not affiliated with the SNM, which gave them confidence that he might be the bridge to a new order. In addition, those non-SNM participants who were not keen on SNM's secessionist project thought that Egal's leadership, given his own political ambition (Yahya 2003),[9] might lead to a dispensation independent of SNM.

There is evidence to support this. I have in my possession an open letter Egal wrote to the military dictator shortly before the collapse of the Somali state, in which he clearly articulated his unionist stance, and he never endorsed the SNM publicly or privately.[10] In the end, Egal was able to mobilize enough of the opinion makers in the gathering to outwit Abdiraham Ahmed Ali and other SNM heavyweights, to become the new leader of Somaliland. Within a few months of the Borama meeting, Egal used his skills to degrade SNM's influence, and deployed his old political acumen and bribes to ride roughshod over everyone.

Further, although claiming the political significance of intermarriage, Bradbury fails to explain why intermarriage between different genealogical groups in the East did not lead to the same political reconciliation as in the West.

In his third critical claim, Bradbury alleges that the integration of the so-called tribal authorities-—*beel* (tribal) system—into government in Hargeisa created a more stable authority than a government elected by the population (Bradbury 2008, p. 99). Unfortunately, Bradbury does not sufficiently probe this system and how the elders who occupy the upper house of the regional parliament are selected. If he had, he would have found that there were no communal meetings to debate the legitimacy of these elders. Many of the elders are manufactured, as was told to me by one of my maternal cousins who became an elder. When I asked in 1999, how he became an elder, he said, "Egal helps us gain the post and pays us, and then we support him in return."

This is not to say that all elders are counterfeit constructs, but the process of becoming an elder politician has little to do with traditional ways. In the old Somali tradition, elders gained their authority from their wisdom, integrity, and intelligence. Having the government, and others with particular political agendas, paying elders undermines and subverts whatever autonomy elders have had historically, and exposes them to corruption and political machinations.[11] It is because of these circumstances that the *beel* system has had no success in advancing citizenship based on commonalities, or transforming government into an integrated institution rather than fragmented tribal fiefdoms.

Bradbury fails to grasp these fatal flaws of political tribalism, and the dysfunctionality of governments, based on tribal political formulas. The consequence of this tribalized political scheme is that citizens do not have equal access to services from government ministries, because different "clans" dominate different ministries. Such an arrangement does not benefit common citizens, and the system is highly susceptible to corruption and nepotism. The system resembles that of *Animal Farm* more than a democracy (Orwell 2019).

A clear example of the corrupting influence of political ethnicity is the administration's failure to institute a judicial order free from discrimination. Further, the system has been unable to resolve conflicts in the East and West. Last, the idea that a democratic political practice prevails in "Somaliland," as promoted by Bradbury and his cohort, is belied when authorities in Hargeisa ruthlessly suppress those who articulate views different from theirs, consistently blocking public debate about the status of the region. The arrests and imprisonments of poets, journalists, and youths who have raised questions about the secessionist project have received international attention.[12]

The only place in Africa where traditional authority and democratic governance have been working side by side for over a half-century is in the Republic of Botswana. Postcolonial Botswana leadership understood that political ethnicity and creation of common and equal citizenship were oxymoronic, and consequently, barred traditional authority from meddling in politics. Appropriately, the House of Chiefs in Botswana deals only with cultural and traditional communal issues. Leaving liberal democratic practice to parliament and government, and confining the chiefs to the cultural sphere, has prevented a divisive politicization of cultural identity. Although government pays the salaries of the chiefs, they remain autonomous in the dominion of culture, and political leaders have refrained from politicizing those cultural venues. Botswana thus provides a model of what works for those who want to preserve the traditional system in the cultural sphere while developing democratic governance (Samatar 1999).

Other contributors to the ideas of cultural differences between northern and southern Somalis, and the contrasting political values of local "clan" authority, purvey the same logic. Matt Bryden (1999), through the work of the War-Torn Societies Project and the International Crisis Group (2001, 2004, 2005), has stressed the validity of cultural and political differences between Somalis in the two regions, and the need for the international community to recognize Somaliland as an independent republic. More recently, Mary

Harper (2012) of the BBC, in a book titled *Getting Somalia Wrong*, reproduced nearly all of Lewis's arguments, but without the sophistication of Lewis's social anthropology. As if to demonstrate her amateur knowledge of Somalia and Somalis, and display her prejudices, she writes, "Somalia points outwards and upwards towards the Arab world.... Its shape resembles the horn of rhinoceros; it is sharp and aggressive" (p. 15).

Such a description of the Somali map shows Harper's lack of geographic imagination, and ignorance of the animal's behavior. First, the rhino is aggressive only when threatened. Second, if Harper had an open mind, she would have seen the Somali coast and its geographic location as a bridge connecting African and Asian cultures and civilizations, rather than seeing Somalia as looking away from Africa. Harper also revisits another theme that the new generation of European and US Lewisians have dealt with: Somalis' presumed aversion to a national government:

> *It is vital to understand the survival of the nomad "ethos" in Somalia because it helps explain the country's resistance to a centralized system of government. As Lewis explains, a hierarchical pattern of authority is foreign to pastoral Somali society, which, in its customary process of decision-making, is democratic almost to the point of anarchy.* (p. 24. See also, Menkhaus 2006, Hoehne 2009, Hagmann and Hoehne 2009, Bryden 1999, Bruton 2009)[13]

These claims, drawing on the work of Lewis, fossilize Somalis, ignoring that urban political elites destroyed the Somali state and hold it hostage. These superficial remarks, and other essentializing statements, are made throughout the text, which adds very little to a better understanding of Somalis and their land. In essence, she totally misunderstands the country and the people.

Finally, her master concept is the "clan". She goes much further than any of her contemporaries to deny the possibility of a civic bond among Somalis, while arguing that Ethiopians and Kenyans, who each have vastly diverse cultural traditions, religions, and languages, have civic commonalities (Harper 2012, p. 31).

A final rendering of this reading of Somali political history and dynamics comes from the United Nations Political Office for Somalia (UNPOS) and some US and European academics. UNPOS's clan map of Somalia (mid-1990s) was partially adopted from an old and inaccurate map in one of Lewis's books. UNPOS was assisted in re-introducing this, with the help of consultants, including Menkhaus.[14] For most Western embassies in Kenya that deal with Somalia, this map has been used as an intellectual-ideological compass for understanding the nature of Somali politics. Somalis who come through the embassy gates are asked which clan they belong to so that the authorities can determine their political orientation. I had my own experience with this mindset when the US envoy to Somalia in 2004, asked me my "clan."

Major Western countries and their African allies wield tremendous political power in the ventilation of the Somali problem, and this map provides a simplistic orientation for those eager to gain quick and superficial expertise about Somalia. For instance, some European and US "experts" on Somalia believe that re-establishment of a national government with significant authority is not wise, and could be counterproductive. They pull out the clan map as justification of this claim (Menkhaus 2006, Hoehne 2009, Hagmann and Hoehne 2009, Bryden 1999, Bruton 2009).

In a nutshell, common to the old social anthropology orthodoxy and its new permutations is the enduring centrality of the clan to understand identity and politics in Somalia. As one example, they claim that the critical role clans played in northern Somali politics since 1993, has induced a democratic form of government, while they also argue that the divisive nature of clan politics is what destroyed the old republic. Despite such contradictory assertions, the evidence from both the North and the South of the country shows that *political ethnicity* further deepens the balkanization of the Somali people, and has alienated them from one another. According to a 2010 survey by the National Democratic Institute, the vast majority of Somalis "are inclined to think of Somalis as one people, united by a single religion, language, culture, and physical appearance, with religion being the strongest tie. Therefore, clannism is considered an affront to the idea of Somali unity, and is identified as the most significant source of conflict within the country.... It breeds injustice.... Clan is considered a 'cancer' that afflicts Somali society." (CEADs vol. 2, p. 2012)

Despite knowing that evidence does not support them, advocates of this discourse have not attempted to resolve this riddle in their schema. Thus, both the old orthodoxy and its offspring turn southern Somalis into the Other, and fail to recognize the enormous commonalities that ordinary Somalis in the old republic have. Further, writers in this stream of thought seem oblivious to the real culprits behind the Somali catastrophe: those with sectarian agendas in the old republic who hailed from the South or North, and who continue to dominate both regions. The advocates are confounding the appearance of the problem, with its essence. Their analytic contradiction has led them to become advocates of fragmentary groups, and elevated their prejudices against the civic unity of the Somali people. Their exposé of Somali history misses the complex dynamics that have shaped Somali politics and the tendencies that cut across regions and groups, and to which I now turn.

Shared Cultural and Political Values as the Basis of Civic Bonds

It was fashionable in the 1960s, to portray Somalia as a *unique* democratic nation-state in Africa because of its perceived *cultural and social homogeneity*. The US Embassy in Mogadishu expressed the democratic character of Somali politics as well as anyone:

> *In the arena of African politics, Somalia has fared well. No coups, no civil wars, no internecine splits have marred its nine-year history. Its people—united by **language, culture, and religion**—form a national state which will probably remain intact for the foreseeable future. Elections for the presidency and parliament have demonstrated the system's ability to transfer power democratically. The country's ex-president and two former prime ministers are today all in parliament—not imprisoned, exiled, or dead.* (US Department of State, July 8, 1969. Bold is mine)

This description, based on cultural explanations, of Somali democracy tells only a small part of the story because it equates cultural homogeneity with political and social cohesion. Writers in this discussion assumed that all governments that were democratic in *form* would attend to the collective interest of the population.[15] Such interpretations of Somali politics supposed that the population's collective political interest was culturally determined. Unfortunately, this stream of thought, and the related political practice, perished with the rise of a military dictatorship just a few months after the embassy writer penned these words. Since then, the positive political contribution attributed to Somali cultural homogeneity has been turned on its head.

For the past three decades, the argument has been that Somalis' cultural differences in the form of genealogy have been more significant than their vast cultural commonalities. Advocates of this thesis fail to grasp that this claim is the other side of the same cultural coin, and therefore neither of these folk-based propositions are sufficiently robust in explaining Somalia's pioneering democracy or its current political catastrophe. By no means can this be interpreted as if cultural values do not matter, but the crux of the issue is in *the ways these cultural signifiers are relevant or irrelevant*, as Naim's work on Islam and the secular state has demonstrated for the role of religion in politics (Naim 2008.)

I think both the positive and the negative cultural rationalization of Somali political dynamics and political identity are seriously flawed and have limited explanatory value. I introduce, instead, the concept of shared cultural identity and political values as an alternative way of framing and understanding the roles culture and cultural identity play in Somali political dynamics. One can think of shared values as consisting of two separate but related bundles: traditional cultural commonalities, and more contemporary political values that are embedded in public institutions. Shared cultural values are a wad of attributes that Somalis have in common, and whose cohesive power to sustain communal bonds is *contingent* on the political *context* rather than on some primordial magic. Among such key values are language, oral poetry, religion, kinship, and pastoral and peasant livelihoods and urban communities (Samatar 1994).

The Somali language has been the fundamental thread that has held Somalis together over millennia, and has been the single most important cultural feature that distinguishes Somalis from other related African people in the Horn of Africa. Moreover, Somalis' oral poetry is a renowned, rich tradition that has been the principal forum of cultural archive and exchange.[16] The combination of a single language and a vibrant poetic culture has been the quintessential signifier of traditional Somali identity, predating colonization. Islam became an additional unifying factor, although Somalis share this faith with other communities in this region of Africa, such as Oromos and Afars. Although the advent of colonization introduced Christianity to a very small Somali minority, Somali cultural heritage retains its dominance as a unifying force across religions and political territories. Essentially, these three cultural factors have been the defining features of the Somali.

Pastoralism and peasant agriculture, which other communities in the Horn of Africa practice, provided the material basis for the culture. These values evolved over millennia and enabled the people to identify themselves as Somalis. Male genealogy, another element of the cultural repertoire of the Somali people, had the dialectical quality of *separating* them into families and *bringing* people together (including maternal ties) as kin groups (e.g., Tol and Xidid) (Samatar 1994). Thus, genealogical difference was a subset of the broader cultural identity of the Somali people. Despite their shared cultural values as Somalis, the ability of the population to think collectively as a political community (nation) was negated by the absence of centralized political authority, and the decentralized nature of livelihoods—a feature they shared with men in other societies on the African continent (Samatar 1989).

The imposition of colonialism, and the fragmentation of their lands into five separate colonial territories, ignited the first spark of national consciousness. Colonial rule had a dialectical effect on the Somali people. It simultaneously united and divided the population, but its core political effect was to segregate people into ethnic groups to facilitate colonial domination. Colonial authorities selectively extracted those elements of the society's tradition that were amenable to their manipulation. The deployment and creation of chiefs as an extension of colonial rule, and the use of genealogy to draw political boundaries between communities, are cases in point.[17] As the colonial state tried to pacify the people through the manipulation of tradition and the imposition of violence, it quickly turned free people into subjects, and thus transformed the cultural identity of the people into a political project of national concern. The seeds of national political identity, rather than localized belonging, were sown during this period. Such sentiments were directed against the colonial state, and as a result, the state became an object of disdain, as well as a potential instrument for national reinvention.

The liberation struggle was complex, having at least three facets whose purpose was to create a belief that the Somali people were a political unit. First, its objective was to undo the humiliation of colonialism and offer the population a Somali-centric agenda. Abdillahi Sultan Timacade's spiritually moving poem, *Kana sib Kana Saar*, captured the mood and substance of this agenda (Timacade 1960). Second, the liberation movement endeavored to undo the damage done by Italian and British colonialism by containing centrifugal forces within the population and generating political dynamics that accentuated their commonalities in order to reverse the politicization of genealogical differences. Somalia's leading liberation party was the Somali Youth League (SYL), which was founded in 1943. Members had to take the following oath in declaring their commitment to all Somalis and to the country:

> *I swear by Almighty God that I will not take any action against any Somali. In trouble, I promise to help the Somali. I will become the brother of all other members. I will not reveal the name of my tribe. In matters of marriage, I will not discriminate between the Somali tribes and the Midgan, Yibirh, Yaha, and Tomals.* (Public Records Office, FO371/63216)[18]

Third, offering Somalis a political center of gravity involved the deployment of cultural instruments—such as poetry, folklore, Islamic tradition, and music[19]—as a unifying chord. These were meant to cement their belief in common destiny and distinctiveness from other polities. Having a political center of gravity was aimed to neutralize colonially induced political and cultural fragmentation of the population, and to create a collective political logic for the country, using the new state (Muro, February 2004; Tubeec, song "Alla manata ayaanta"). SYL, as the leading liberation party, carried this banner.

The liberation and unification of two Somali territories in 1960 created a republic unlike most of the newly independent states in

Africa. Somalia had the exceptional advantage of having a population with deep and strong common cultural values on which the new state could imagine and build its national project. Although the new nation was unique in the ways I have described, not all members of the political class endorsed the essence of liberation, which sought justice and good governance as a foundation of the new political identity. Thus, postcolonial Somali politics had two major tendencies: one strove to use shared cultural values as a foundation for national political development, and the other was more concerned about exploiting minor cultural differences among the population for particularistic ends.

Whether the state became a vehicle to reinforce traditional commonalities and build *new* shared political and cultural values, or whether it was deployed to accentuate minor cultural differences in the community and deepen the political boundaries marked by the colonial regimes, defined Somalia's postcolonial political environment. Political development in the postcolonial context meant reforming institutions left behind by colonial rule and turning them into political organs, which effected a political belonging that went well-beyond the old culture. Producing accountability, justice, and equal treatment under the law, and fairly distributing the costs and benefits of independence and development, were central to the creation of common citizen-based identity that reinforced the attractiveness of the old culture. The alternative was to use state authority to segment the population into sectarian groups, and to deploy state power unjustly, in the process, destroying the possibility of common citizenship.

Reading Somali political identity and political history through a singular lens is tantamount to a continuation of the colonial era, and dovetails with the sectarian agenda. Unfortunately, the struggle against the colonial mindset and the sectarian mantra has been severely hampered by the political catastrophe in the country, as well as the ideology of the major international actors and their intellectual companions who peddle divisive politics. Thus, the crying need for an alternative Somali intellectual voice—a decolonized and liberated voice—across the broad intellectual landscape.

The Book

What are the implications of this way of framing Somali cultural and political identity for Somali life? Among the tenets of the shared-values scheme is the fundamental axiom that *cultural and political identities are socially constructed, and historically and geographically context dependent.* Moreover, these identities are dynamically complex and not preordained by either biology or history. This means that Somalis have agency to fashion their common future rather than being collectively condemned to a fossil-like identity.

Finally, the essence of socially constructed reality is that it is always dialectic and dynamic. My purpose in this short book is to use the shared-values approach and historical contextual analysis to provide an alternative way of framing and understanding Somali political and cultural issues: I use three subjects that have attracted sustained scrutiny in Somali studies since the early days of independence.

First, Orientalists have argued that Somali politics can be understood only through the lens of ethnicity. I offer a contrasting framework that provides a different explanation of the nature of postcolonial politics, and what went right and what went wrong with Somali democratic politics in the 1960s.

Second, similarly, Islam and its role in Somali life has been poorly framed, and ill-understood in the literature, particularly in the last three decades. I give a reading of Islam's role in Somali affairs that differs by being sensitive to the historical context of the country and the needs of the population.

Third, much of the literature on "Somali" piracy has been Orientalist in its approach, and as is usual for such analyses, could see only one dimension of the matter. In contrast, a radical political economy approach offers a more nuanced and less prejudicial understanding of piracy in the Indian Ocean.

Chapter 2 reframes the nature of Somali democracy during the first decade of independence. Chapter 3 reinterprets the role of Islam in Somali politics, and more broadly, in public life. Chapter 4 reimagines the piracy off the Somali coast. The conclusion summarizes the significance of the alternative approach to Somali studies and for the country's future.

Bibliography

Achebe, Chinua. *Home and Exile*. New York: Oxford University Press, 2000.

An-Naim, Abdullahi Ahmed. *Islam and the Secular State*. Harvard University Press, 2008.

Anderson, D.M. "Clan Identity and Islamic Identity in Somalia," *CEADS Papers*, vol. 2. Somalia, 2012.

Anderson, Benedict. *Imagined Communities: Reflections on the Origin and Spread of Nationalism*. London: Verso, 1983.

Asad, Talal. *Anthropology and the Colonial Encounter*. London: Ithaca Press, 1973.

--------------. "Two European Images of Non-European Rule," *Economy and Society*, vol. 2, no. 3 (1973):pp. 263–277.

Besteman, Catherine. "Primordialist Blinders: A Reply to I.M. Lewis," *Cultural Anthropology*, vol. 13, no. 1 (1998): pp. 109–120.

Bradbury, Mark. *Becoming Somaliland*. Oxford: James Currey, 2008.

Bruton, Bronwyn. "In the Quick Sands of Somalia: Where Doing Less Helps More," *Foreign Affairs*, Nov/Dec. 2009.

----------------------. Clan and Islamic Identity in Somalia." *CEADS Papers*, vol. 2: Somalia, March 2012. Center for Security, Armed Forces and Society. Kingston, Canada.

Burton, Richard. *First Footsteps in East Africa*, two volumes. London: Tylston & Edwards, 1894.

Bryden, Matt. "New Hope for Somalia? The Building Block Approach," *Review of African Political Economy*, vol. 26, no. 79 (1999): pp. 134–40.

Cassanelli, Lee V. *The Shaping of Somali Society: Reconstructing the History of a Pastoral People, 1600–1900*. University of Pennsylvania Press, 1982.

Elim, Haji Dahir; Muhumed, Haji Jama; and Qalib, J.M, Interviews, July 2002.

Fischer, G.T, Brigadier. Military Governor, Shiekh. Letter to Foreign Office, January 31, 1946. PRO, FO 1015/132.

Farah, N. Crabs in a Basket (Forthcoming).

Gilkes, Patrick. *Acceptance Not Recognition: the Republic of Somaliland, 1993–1995*. London: Save the Children's Fund, 1995).

Hagmann, Tobias and Hoehne, Markus. "Failures of the State Failure Debate: Evidence from the Somali Territories Journal of International Development, vol. 21 (2009): pp. 42–57.

Harper, Mary. *Getting Somalia Wrong: Faith, War, and Hope in a Shattered State*. London: Zedbooks, 2012.

Heinrich, Wolfgang. *Building the Peace: Experiences of Collaborative Peacebuilding in Somalia, 1993–1996*, Life & Peace Institute, vol. 3 (1997).

Hellander, Bernhard. "The Emperor's New Clothes Removed: a Critique of Bestman's 'Violent Politics and the Politics of Violence,'" *American Ethologist*, vol. 23, no. 3 (1998): pp. 498–491.

Hoehne, Markus. "Mimesis and Mimicry in Dynamics of State Formation and Identity in Northern Somalia," *Africa* vol. 79, no. 2 (2009): pp. 252–281.

———. "Political Representation in Somalia: Citizens, Clanism and Territoriality." *In Whose Peace is it Anyway?: Connecting Somali and International Peacemaking*. London: Conciliation Resources, 2001: pp. 34–37.

International Crisis Group. "Somaliland: Democratizations and its Discontents," ICG report no.66, July 28, 2004.

———. "Somaliland: Time for African Union Leadership," ICG Africa Report no. 110, May 23, 2006.

Lidwien, K. "The Disintegration of Somalia: a Historiographical Essay," *International Journal of Somali Studies*, Bildhaan (2001): pp. 11–52.

Levy cited in *CEADS*, vol. 2 (2012): Somalia.

Lewis, Ioan M. *Pastoral Democracy: a Study of Pastoralism and Politics Among the Northern Somali of the Horn of Africa*. London: Oxford University Press, 1961.

———. *A Modern History of Somalia: Nation and State in the Horn of Africa*. London: Longman, 1965.

———. *Understanding Somalia and Somaliland* (London: Hurst Publishers, 2008).

———(ed). *A Study of Political Decentralized Structures for Somalia: a Menu of Options*. Unpublished report commissioned by the EU, EC Somalia Unit, and UNDP Office for Somalia, from the London School of Economics and Political Science, 1995.

———. *Blood and Bone: The Call of Kinship in Somali Society*. Lawrence, NJ: Red Sea Press, 1994.

———. *Understanding Somalia: Guide to Culture, History and Social Institutions*. London: Haan Associates, 1993.

———. "In the Land of the Living Dead," *Sunday Times*, August 30, 1992.

———. Court Statement (London, 2001).

———. *People of the Horn of Africa (Somali, Afar, and Saho)*. London: Routledge: 1959.

Mamdani, Mahmood. *Citizen and Subjects: Contemporary Africa and the Legacy of Late Colonialism*. Princeton: Princeton University Press.

———. Mahmood. "Race and Ethnicity as Political Identities in the African Context." Nadia Tazi, editor. *Keywords: Identity*. New York: Other Press, 2004, pp. 1–24.

Makind, Samuel M "Politics and Clan Rivalry in Somalia," *Australian Journal of Political Science, vol.* 26, no. 1 (1991).

Menkhaus, Ken. "Governance Without Government: Spoilers, State Building, and the Politics of Coping." *International Security,* vol. 31, no. 3 (2006) pp. 74–106.

Muro, Mohamed. Interview, Brussels, February 2004.

Murphy, Martin. *Somalia: The New Barbary? Piracy and Islam in the Horn of Africa.* London: Hurst & Company, 2011.

Orwell, George. *Animal Farm and 1984.* Houghton Mifflin Harcourt, 2003.

Said, Edward. *Orientalism.* New York: Vintage, 1979.

Samatar, Abdi Ismail. *The State and Rural Transformation in Northern Somalia, 1884–1986.* Madison: University of Wisconsin Press, 1989.

------------------------. "Social Classes and Economic Restructuring in Pastoral Africa: Somali Notes," *African Studies Review* vol. 35, no. 1 (1992): pp. 101–127.

------------------------. *Africa's First Democratic: Somalia's Aden Abdulle Osman and Abdirazak H. Husen.* Bloomington: Indiana University Press, 2016.

------------------------.. *An African Miracle: State and Class Leadership and Colonial Legacy in Botswana.* Portsmouth: Heinemann, 1999.

Samatar, Ahmed I. "The Curse of Allah: Civic Disembowelment and the Collapse of the State in Somalia," *The Somali Challenge: From Catastrophe to Renewal.* Boulder: Lynne Reiner, 1994: pp. 95–146.

----------------------. *Socialist Somalia: Rhetoric and Reality.* Zed Books, 1988.

British National Archives. Public Records Office, FO 371/63216.

Timacade, Abdillahi Suldan. *Maandeeq.* 1969.

_____. *Kana Siib Kana Saar.* June 26, 1960.

Tubeec, Mohamed S. *Alla Manata Ayaanta.* Hargeisa: June 26, 1960.

------------------------. Wa Mahad Alle Madaxeen Banaan, Radio Hargeisa, 1960.

US Department of State, Research Memorandum, RAF-10, July 8, 1969.

War-Torn Societies Project. *Rebuilding Somalia: Issues and Possibilities for Puntland.* London: HAAN Associates, 2001.

------------------------. *Rebuilding Somaliland: Issues and Possibilities.* Lawrence, NJ: Red Sea Press, 2005.

Yahya, Abdulkadir. Interview, Mogadishu, 2003.

Endnotes

1 Although Lewis had permission and support from the colonial government of the British Protectorate, his description of Somali traditional life did not take account of the corrosive impacts British rule had on Somalis.

2 As Talal Asad noted in early 1973, this sort of anthropology was not meant to be consumed by the natives. "It is not a matter of dispute that social anthropology emerged as a distinctive discipline at the beginning of the colonial era, that it became a flourishing academic profession toward its close, or that, throughout this period, its efforts were devoted to a description and analysis carried out by Europeans, for a European audience of non-European societies, dominated by European power. And yet there is a strange reluctance on the part of most anthropologists to consider seriously the power structure within which their discipline has taken shape."

3 Another manifestation of Lewis's misunderstanding of Somali politics was his characterization of the first Somali president, Aden, as "Hawiye" politician, when in fact, Aden was elected to the presidency unopposed in 1960, after the former British and Italian colonies united to form the Somali Republic. (Lewis, *Understanding Somalia and Somaliland*, p. 33.)

4 I have an open letter in my file, written by Silaanyo immediately after the regime collapsed, in which he states the need for the formation of collective national leadership for all of Somalia.

5 Lewis contradicts his own early description of Somalia as friendly to outsiders: "...there can be few countries where the foreign researcher

is more welcome or given greater freedom to carry out his work without let or hindrance." (Lewis, I.M 1969).

6   Consider my brother, Ahmed Samatar, and I. We come from the same gene pool and grew up in the same home, but our political views are different. If genealogy really mattered, we would be each other's mirror image in politics, but we are not.

7   Lewis attended a meeting hosted by the Somaliland leader in London, in 2004, where he endorsed the project openly. See also, Lewis (January 18, 2001— "UN Paperclips for Somalia"), and Samatar's response in Hiraan Online (Feb 2, 2001).

8   The foundational assertion of the book misinterprets the facts. The first error is that the Burco meeting was not a Grand Conference of all the representatives of the people of the North. Rather, it was confined to a few involved with the SNM and others *they invited*. Secondly, he misses that the dominant forces in the meeting were the SNM's militias, who openly forced the gathering to declare independence without any discussion or debate. The third misunderstanding is that, given the insecurity in most parts of the region at the time, and the hostility between SNM and non-SNM communities, there was no collective public pressure clamoring for this outcome. Finally, the SNM did not openly articulate a secessionist agenda during the war with the military regime, and consequently, there was no chance for communities in the region to deal with the matter before the gathering in Burco. If Bradbury had been a serious scholar seeking the facts about what happened before, and at, the Burco Conference, his first task would have been to study Somali political history, and specifically, examine the problematic nature of the secessionist project. Taking the claims of the SNM and its supporters at face value, and as a point of departure for his work, made it impossible for him to think of any other understanding or explanation of Somali political problems and what went wrong in the Somali Republic. As a result, he became a political advocate for the recognition of "Somaliland" as an independent country, rather than a discerning thinker and writer.

9   It was known to some of the people that Egal had traveled to Mogadishu and met with Ali Mahdi in 1991. Egal tried to convince Mahdi about a new way of reworking the union and restoring the republic under their joint leadership. Mahdi was too myopic to appreciate Egal's talent and capacity.

10 Some of these individuals actually told the authors about Egal's na-

tional ambition. What they did not know then was that Egal went to Mogadishu and had dealings with Ali Mahdi to figure out a way for Egal to lead the government. The meeting between Egal and Mahdi took place in 1991. Abdulkadir Yahya, who was the chief of staff of Ali Mahdi, reported this to me in 2003.

11 See the commotions surrounding the selection of "traditional" elders in 2012, for the Somali political transition in Mogadishu. Money was the authority rather than traditional legitimacy.

12 A young female poet was imprisoned for three months in 2017, before she was sentenced to a three-year prison term for holding up Somalia's national flag in public. She was later released after much public uproar and international pressure.

13 This thesis homogenizes all types of governments Somalia has had since their independence, and ignores that most Somalis hunger for a national government that is democratic and that can serve the population's needs. Other writers in this vein, but take a different tack, are K. Menkhaus (2006), who argues for what he calls a "mediated state." This is not a new idea, but one which Lewis articulated nearly fifty years earlier (Lewis, *Pastoral Democracy*, pg. 1). Similarly, Hagmann and Hoehne (2009) challenge the notion of anarchy in Somalia by underscoring the existence of localized forms of authority. Unwittingly, they endorse the notion that Somalis are loathe to national governmental authority.

14 The information that Menkhaus associated with this map was provided by a former staff member of UNPOS who took part in the map's development, and who wanted to remain anonymous (Interview, Nairobi, December 2004).

15 The point is that there are governments that are democratic in form, but which are deeply corrupt. Such regimes do not serve the national interest. The 1967–69 Somali regime was such a democratic establishment.

16 Among the major poets are" Mohamed Abdille Hassan, Qamaam Bulhan, Abdillahi Suldaan Timade, Hassan Shiekh Mumin, Mohamed Ibrahim Hadrawi, Areys Issa, and Ali Elmi Ayare.

17 As Mamdani noted in seminal work on the subject, Africans who shared culture were segregated into tribes by colonial masters, while immigrants and European settlers who had different cultures were brought under "citizens" (Mamdani 1996).

18 The British Administration was not supportive of the Club's anti-tribal stance, as indicated by the following report by a senior officer: "It is noted that the promise not to reveal their tribes is causing a certain amount of worry to the Civil Affairs Officers in their capacity as Judicial Officers, as it is necessary in Court cases to record the tribe of the accused and of the witness. When asked for their tribes, members of the S.Y.C. now state simply that they are Somalis" (Public Records Office, FO 371/63216).

19 Abdillahi Qarshe's moving song for the Independence Day, "Waa Mahad Alle Madaxeen banaan," is an exemplar of the times.

2
Reframing Somali Politics:
The Democratic Era[1]

If I do what you are asking me [to take your bribes], then who will marry my daughter, *as I will be so disgraceful.*

—Omer Borey, member of YL Central Committee, 1967.

Independence and unification in 1960 engendered incredible euphoria, but the jubilation concealed looming troubles. Some political elites harbored a civic political project aimed at creating a governance system in which those in authority were democratically accountable to the population, and to building a nation where citizens were equal under the law. Others backed a sectarian political project to win state power through whatever means possible, and to use that authority to perpetuate their tenure and accumulate private wealth.

In the Lewisian interpretation of Somali political history, the fundamental difference between the two political camps was their genealogical identities, and not their governance and ideological orientations. This chapter provides the material evidence that the distinction between the camps had very little to do with genealogical identity, but much to do with the two groups' contrasting visions about the role and nature of government in the postcolonial nation. The two camps struggled for power throughout the democratic period, each dominating government in two distinct periods. The civics had the upper hand from independence in 1960 until the 1967 presidential election, and the sectarians dominated political affairs from 1967 to 1969.

The chapter consists of three sections. The first narrates the rise of the democratic camp and the efforts it made to consolidate an accountable system of government. I substantiate this claim with historical material relating to the constitutional plebiscite, the municipal and parliamentary elections of 1963 and 1964, the appointment of new government in 1964 and its reform efforts, and the historic and radical public service reform that the government pursued.

The second section describes the corrupt political maneuvers of the sectarian camp, and the steadfast effort of the president and his team to honor their oath of office and face the challengers while respecting the dignity of the office—despite this meaning the defeat of the civic wing of the political elite.

In the third section, the narrative turns to the modus operandi of the new sectarian regime and its effort to undo all the progressive accomplishments of the previous seven years, and transform the country into a single-party state.

The chapter concludes with a reflection on the importance of this narrative for reimagining Somali political history and the country's future.

The Democratic Experience

The origins of the postcolonial Somali democratic experience goes back to the formation of the leading liberation party in the country, the Somali Youth League (SYL). The league started as a social club in 1943. Despite its superficial social orientation, the club was driven by nationalist aspirations. The Somali Youth Club openly morphed into a political party in 1947, changing its name to the Somali Youth League (Samatar 2016). From the club's beginnings, and after its transformation into the SYL, the oath that members were required to take countered Italian and British colonial strategies of using genealogical affiliations to divide Somalis politically (British Archives, FO371/63216).[2] After renaming itself, the party's first major engagement was to advocate for the unification of four Somali territories held by the British. The politics of the Cold War militated against unification, and Italy reclaimed one of the five colonies, but this time as a United Nations trust territory.

Italian rule was restored on April 1, 1950. Knowing the SYL opposed it, the Italian administration attempted to break the back of the SYL and empower Italy's Somali clients, but was unsuccessful. During the transformative decade of the 1950s, the SYL manifested three characteristics that enabled it to guide the territory toward independence and unification with British Somaliland. First, it maintained its democratic character by running its affairs transparently, and by electing its leaders democratically (Samatar 2016, Chapter

4). Second, it upheld its nationalist principles against the onslaught of the Italian regime, which desperately tried to extend its tenure by deploying the classic colonial strategy of dividing the community into ethnic-political groups. Third, the SYL doggedly strove for the creation of a democratic union of British and Italian Somalilands.

The creation of a united and democratic Somali Republic became a reality when delegates from British and Italian Somalilands met in Mogadishu in 1959, and in early 1960, and signed an agreement to that effect (Contini 1969, p. 8). Shortly thereafter, a draft constitution prepared in Mogadishu was sent to Hargeisa, capital of British Somaliland, for modification, as deemed necessary. In the end, nothing was deleted and only two articles dealing with civil service administration were added. Once the national flag was hoisted in Hargeisa on June 26, 1960, senior politicians and civil servants in Hargeisa moved to the new national capital in Mogadishu. The union of the two territories took place on July 1, 1960, the same day the trust territory gained its freedom.

Setting Constitutional Foundations

The new provisional government turned its attention to integrating the two contrasting colonial civil service systems the republic inherited, and creating a coherent national policy. Three items dominated the first year of the republic. These were the plebiscite on the draft constitution, the election of a permanent president, and the appointment of a government after the provisional period ended. The dynamics generated by these three events transformed relations among the elite from being inspired by the euphoria of independence and unification, to being governed by political expediency, personal interest, and civic ethics. Of all these events, the most vital was conducting the constitutional plebiscite.

Educating the public about the draft constitution, and holding the plebiscite, were the first major duties of the new government. The campaign to mobilize the population created fertile ground for emerging political factions to begin contesting. Two senior government ministers who were unhappy with recent political developments took advantage of this opportunity to advance their interests. Mohamed Ibrahim Egal (leader of the North) and Sheikh Ali Jimale (a long-time member of the SYL) campaigned against the Constitution. They thought that defeating the charter would discredit the president and the prime minister as national leaders, and bring down the provisional government. They campaigned vigorously in their respective regions, and quietly but effectively articulated two ideas.

First, Egal and some of his northern associates (Arraleh 2003) told the public that southern domination of key positions in the national government meant that the North was not an equal partner in the union. Second, Jimale and his team peddled the sectarian idea that Prime Minister Abdirashid Ali Sharmarke's government was dominated by the Darod genealogical group, ignoring that the president, Aden Abdulle Osman, who appointed the prime minister, was a member of Jimale's kin group.

President Osman and the rest of the government were aware of this campaign and made every effort to counter it and educate the public about the contents of the Constitution. Given the low literacy rates of the population, the government extensively used the two national radio stations, Radio Hargeisa and Radio Mogadishu, to familiarize the public with the substance of the draft constitution. The government also sought the support of opinion makers in the regions to help the public understand the essence of the document (Osman, June 15, 1961). Key leaders of the government also worked hard to win support for the Constitution, and they made certain that the public understood that it did not belong to the government, but was a consensual national document that should be endorsed or rejected on its merits (Osman, June 21, 1961).

The referendum day, June 20, 1961, was peaceful. All predictions were that a substantial majority of voters would endorse the charter, but stiff opposition was expected in two regions (US Department of State, March 13, 1961). Six out of the eight regions endorsed the Constitution, and two rejected it.[3] The rejectionist areas were led by Jimale and Egal, the politicians campaigning against the Constitution. Jimale was unhappy that the provisional president had not appointed his friend, Abdillahi Issa, as prime minister in 1960. Similarly, Egal, the most eminent northern political leader, felt unappreciated despite being called to run the Ministry of Defense of the new republic. Unlike Jimale's region, Hiran, where the majority of the deputies went along with Jimale, Egal's northern region saw a significant number of northern deputies break ranks with Egal and campaign in favor of the Constitution. This explains why the Constitution was approved in one region of the North, with a significant proportion of the population in the entire northwest supporting it. From the plebiscite was born a new African republic, closing the curtain on the colonial political order (Somali Republic 1961).[4]

Those who had opposed the Constitution quickly shifted their attention to the presidential election. This group, nicknamed the Katanga Group, after a secessionist group in Congo Kinshasa (now the Democratic Republic of the Congo), had an opportunity to challenge the provisional president in his bid for a regular six-year term (Osman 1961, various entries). The campaign for the presidency started long before the constitutional referendum. The two candidates for the post were the incumbent, Osman, and the minister of health, Jimale. Adding to the drama, both Osman and Jimale hailed from Belet Weyne, and had been senior members of the ruling party. The candidates adopted contrasting campaign strategies. Jimale was unwilling to declare his candidacy until immediately before the constitutional plebiscite. However, his candidacy was an open secret in the capital. His presidential ambitions were fueled by his anger toward President Osman for selecting Sharmarke as prime minister, and he tried to mobilize those who felt the same, as well as other members of parliament (MPs) who desired ministerial posts. To win enough votes, Jimale and his group promised appointments to many of these people.

In contrast, Osman was assumed to be a candidate by the public and MPs. Many MPs who felt that he was the right man for the job, given his performance over the previous year, quietly endorsed him. Osman had a hands-off approach to the campaign, including not making promises to MPs in return for their votes (Osman, July 4, 1961).[5] There is no record that he actively wooed MPs to vote for him. Nevertheless, Prime Minister Sharmarke and some of the senior cabinet members worked on his behalf.

These divergent styles and agendas came to a head at the National Assembly on July 6, 1961. Parliament started its deliberations at 9:30 a.m., as scheduled. Three ballots were required unless one of the candidates won two-thirds of the votes in the first ballot. The results of the first ballot were announced at 10:15 a.m. Each candidate received sixty votes, and one vote was disqualified because it was not decipherable. In the second round, Sheikh Ali Jimale advanced by two votes. Once this was announced, many thought Jimale would win the last and final round (US Department of State, July 10, 1961). Osman's quiet sentiment, recorded in his diary entry on that day, reveals his self-effacing manner:

> *The results of the first balloting were announced: 60 for me, 60 for Sheikh Ali, 1 vote annulled. It is clear that those who were fighting for me have been made fun of by at least 16 deputies, who deceived them.*[6] *The second balloting was disappointing for me: 62 for Sheik Ali, 59 for me, but the third and last balloting had inverted the sides: 62 for me, 59 for Sheikh Ali! So I am reconfirmed President of the Republic for 6 years. God help me! I am sure that I have not only a quiet conscience, but also have all the good intentions for my country and for my people.* (Osman, July 6, 1961)

Osman's self-confidence that he could have a good life outside politics and the presidency gave him an outlook that was in sharp contrast to most of his peers. He trusted nearly all his contemporaries, even when they had deceived him or betrayed their oath. He had faith that people can reform themselves and learn from past mistakes (Osman, May 9, 1961).[7]

Holding a presidential election was a signal of maturity of some of the Somali elite, but it also marked the start of electoral politics driven less by the urgent needs of the country, and more by expediency.[8] The most visible manifestation of the politics of personal gain and public loss unfolded immediately after the election as a new government was formed. Although Jimale's quick congratulatory visit to Osman suggested a willingness to support the new administration, his camp began scheming how to extract concessions from Osman. First, a group of MPs allied with Jimale planned to put forward a parliamentary motion to annul the election (Sheikh Mukhtar, July 2005).[9] Eighteen MPs signed the petition challenging Osman's victory, but the president of parliament refused to accept their plea. When Osman heard about this, he noted that Jimale's group had the right to petition parliament, and that the Assembly president should give them their due:

> *I received the President of the Assembly. He asked what I think about the famous motion and if communication regarding it must be given to the National Assembly. I said I find it in bad faith, but sincerely I do not see how he can avoid asking the Assembly if it is to debate or not.* (Osman, July 16, 1961).

This issue dragged on for another month, until the assembly president requested the opinion of the Supreme Court. The court rendered its opinion on August 12th, that the incumbent had received the necessary majority in the third and final ballot, and therefore was justly elected president.

President Osman began the constitutionally mandated consultation with public leaders to nominate a new prime minister as Jimale's group lobbied to have a say as to who should be the party's nominee. The first person Osman consulted was the president of parliament, Jama Abdillahi Qalib. Qalib suggested that Sharmarke be nominated.[10] If genealogy mattered, this distant cousin of Egal would have acted otherwise (Osman, July 8, 1961).[11]

A self-appointed group, led by Abdullahi Issa and Mohamed Ibrahim Egal, decided to find a prime minister. They suggested Jimale for prime minister, and then argued that if the president was not willing to appoint Jimale, he should give their group a chance to pick someone else because they had the backing of nearly half the MPs. Osman rejected their suggestion, being mindful of setting a dangerous precedent in which the president was considered the representative of only those who voted for him rather than the entire country (Osman, July 13, 1961; US Department of State, May 1, 1961),[12] as the Constitution required (Somali Republic 1961, article 69).

Despite Jimale's group mounting a spirited campaign to win the premiership, most MPs, including a substantial number from the North, and other respected individuals the president consulted, advised the president to retain Sharmarke as the prime minister. Sharmarke received the letter of nomination from the president on July 11th, and accepted the honor. Sharmarke met with Jimale, who demanded that half the cabinet positions be given to his supporters before he would take part in the new government. The prime minister designate rejected Jimale's conditions. He thought that acquiescing would turn his government into a dysfunctional institution. While Sharmarke was pondering the makeup of the cabinet, Osman sensed the prime minister's unwillingness to confront the challenge. He recognized Sharmarke's difficult task of forming a government that could secure a confidence vote, given the opportunistic behavior of many MPs. Nonetheless, he was disappointed with Sharmarke for not vigorously using his platform to outmaneuver the few extremists in parliament. He used a Somali proverb to underscore his disappointment: *"Halkii cir laga sughayay ayaa ciiraano katimid."* (Where rain was expected, fog came instead.) (Osman, July 16, 1961).

An agonizingly long period of negotiations ensued, and the prime minister designate had to compromise by increasing the number of ministers and undersecretaries. These moves were meant to appease some of the MPs and get their support for the new government during the vote of confidence in parliament. This attempt almost backfired because many of the prime minister's supporters were enraged by the inclusion of people they considered opportunists. Further, the president was less concerned about the prime minister making concessions than he was about the increase in the cabinet size, which included a number of incompetent MPs (Osman, July 25, 1961). In addition to the expanded number of ministerial portfolios, several new undersecretary positions were created. Despite Osman's qualms and his own (ibid),[13] the prime minister finally selected fifteen ministers, who took the oath of office in the presence of the president.

These compromises failed to satisfy several ambitious MPs who wanted to be ministers but were excluded from the new lineup. To thwart them, parliament approved a bill to limit the size of the cabinet to fewer members than Sharmarke had selected. President Osman did not mind the reduction in the size of the cabinet, but he threatened to veto the bill unless it was made to conform to article 81 of the Constitution: an "ordinary law can limit the number of ministers and not the number of undersecretaries and ministers without portfolio" (Osman, August 14, 1961). Parliament revised the bill, the president signed it (Osman, August 15, 1961),[14] and Sharmarke went back to the drawing board. Three cabinet members—Abdi Hassan Booni, Osman Mohamed Ibrahim, and Omer Sheikh Hassan—offered to resign to make things easier for him. Further, the prime minister met with his undersecretaries, and after a thoughtful discussion, they all resigned and asked him to select any five of them and leave the others out. Sharmarke was able to reduce the size of the cabinet to satisfy the new law. At long last, parliament began debating the program of the government. Prime Minister Sharmarke defended his program and chided parliament for making it nearly impossible to establish a government. Ambassador Andrew Lynch of the United States reported:

> *[The prime minister said,] "There is an old saying... 'according to which the Government is a mirror of the parliament from which it is drawn.' Moreover, the Parliament should respect the wishes of the people who have elected it. Therefore, to reduce the number of Ministries it is first necessary to reduce the ambitions of the deputies. That can happen only if the office of Minister and Undersecretary are considered not as a personal prerogative, worse yet as a source of profit, but simply as an honor and responsibility. I hope that some such miracle may take place." [He added] that during his year as Prime Minister, no less than 106 deputies had asked for appointment to Government office.*
> (US Department of State, August 26, 1961)[15]

On August 23rd, parliament concluded its debate on the government's program, and Sharmarke's government, received an overwhelming vote of confidence (ibid.[16] In this political jousting, there was no sign that the prime minister or president had favored their genealogical groups.

Political issues came up and challenged the government over the next two years, but the ones that defined the challenges facing the country, from the president's vantage point, were electoral fraud and corruption. The municipal and parliament elections of 1963 and 1964 became a turning point in the tussle between the two political camps.

Municipal and Parliamentary Elections

Despite the population's enthusiasm for the unification of the two former colonies and the establishment of a democratic republic, all political parties, whether from the North or the South, lacked the organizational discipline or ideology that could sustain structured civic politics. Without political party anchors in a country whose population was largely illiterate, a majority of senior political men plotted to prolong their tenure and enrich themselves through corrupt schemes. MPs were strategically positioned to prolong their tenure because they elected the president, approved government policies, and endorsed cabinets. Disgruntled MPs could, and did, shake the confidence of the government to pursue its agenda after the referendum of 1961. This arrangement could have easily paralyzed the government were it not for the commitment of the president, and a significant number of MPs, to the constitutional order to give priority to the national interest over their personal fortunes.

This difference in priorities between the civic and sectarian forces came to the fore in the management of the municipal and parliamentary elections of 1963 and 1964. The last nationwide vote had been the constitutional plebiscite of 1961, which was widely seen as an accurate reflection of the people's will. In addition, the presidential election of 1961 was a cliffhanger, which demonstrated that the incumbent did not gerrymander the process. In spite of these democratic precedents, there was a great deal of concern that the municipal and parliamentary elections might not meet the same standards.

The 1963 municipal election was the first of its kind since the republic's formation. Constituent districts elected local councilors, who then chose mayors. Nationally, the Ministry of Interior appointed civil servants as regional governors and district commissioners. There were 58 districts and 1,114 voting stations. According to the electoral system, political parties were required to register with district authorities their intent to compete, and the authorities verified candidates' names and signatures with party voter lists. The opposition parties dreaded this step. Some commissioners were blatantly partisan, and used their authority to deny some parties the right to register. But some opposition parties had not followed the law to properly register. These tried to blame their problems on local authorities' incompetence. Whatever the reason for rejected applications, political parties could appeal to the Supreme Court after exhausting other channels.

President Osman was worried about the governing party using state resources, and its control of the state's administrative apparatus, to gain undue advantage in the municipal elections, and thus set the stage for its dominance in the forthcoming parliamentary vote. Consequently, he urged the prime minister and his colleagues to run an honest election. The president had encouraged the prime minister to ensure that representatives of the national police force be present inside polling stations to guard against fraud, but the government did not do this.[17] Although Prime Minister Sharmarke appreciated Osman's message and was committed to fair play, his government failed to put systems in place to ensure clean elections. Some local administrators, such as district commissioners and regional governors, ignored the president's warnings, the government's instructions, and the electoral laws, and turned a significant number of polling stations into scandalous embarrassments. This fiasco took place in large measure because of the absence of opposition party representatives at most polling stations. Although opposition parties were required to have observers in each station, their national reach was limited, leaving many stations unattended.

Voting day came on November 26, 1963, and polling took place in a largely peaceful environment. The five major opposition parties collectively had candidates in about half the districts, whereas the SYL had candidates in all but one of the fifty-eight districts, and even ran unopposed in eighteen districts (US Department of State, December 5, 1963).[18] The SYL won six of the eight regions and lost the capital, Mogadishu. Immediately after the results were announced, opposition parties lodged petitions with the president to register their misgivings about the results. In addition, there was an attempt on the life of the governor of the Northeast region, where the Somali National Congress (SNC) and the Somali Democratic Union (SDU) lost to the SYL. President Osman lamented the behavior of the dominant party and the opposition:

> *Many of the telegrams of protest from the last few days that I received give sufficient indication of the dissatisfaction [in various areas] of the parties outside of SYL, and thus demonstrate that the attempt to make things go smoothly, without doubt, did not succeed everywhere. The government is not at fault for this, but it is the custom of the majority of Somalis who possess power that they cannot give up their partisan spirit and easy abuse of power and misdeeds. It is also the fault of acts which are out of the orthodox and possibly illegal.* (Osman, November 30, 1963)

Evidence suggests that the municipal election results were not an accurate reflection of public sentiment, and this was considered a bad omen for parliamentary elections only a few months away (ibid).

The results made the president and his civic associates aware that unless more was done to ensure fair play in the forthcoming parliamentary election, the consequences could be violence and political instability. In the meantime, parliament held discussions on expanding its number of seats before the election, but the president resisted and told those behind the proposal that it could be entertained only after the election, and that any expansion should be based on actual population figures (ibid).[19] The parliament also drafted a new bill for the election and submitted it to the president for comment. Osman suggested dropping or changing some items. Among those he slated for deletion was one that called for a 24,000-shilling golden handshake for current MPs who failed to win re-election. A second item required that civil servants who wanted to run for parliament must first resign their post, which the president felt was unfair, given that the old rules permitted them to take a leave of absence during the campaign, and to resign afterward if they won (Osman, December 1 and 3, 1963). A third critical suggestion he made was to add an item to empower the police to guard polling stations and ballot boxes from start to finish. Further, the president noted that the bill should provide more protection for all parties during the course of the campaign and the election.

The bill was resubmitted to parliament. After much deliberation, parliament approved a final version that dropped the golden handshake but ignored most of the other suggestions by the president.

President Osman was furious and expressed his dismay as follows:

Chapter 2

> *The National Assembly sent me the approved text of the political electoral laws for the next referendum. I was displeased that [the item dealing with the police was left out] which means that many could cheat...and the police are prohibited from entering or having anything to do with the [polling station] if not specifically requested by the chair of the station. It is clear therefore, that my intention to have the polls watched by the police is legally unsustainable, given what is contained in article 34 number 2, and also that we need to find how to prevent this inconvenience. If not, these elections will result in lost efforts and won't end up being very calm! Of all the recommendations that I gave, only the ones relating to the admission of public officials to be candidates, without making them first resign their posts before, has been adopted.* (Osman, January 14, 1964)

Osman was disappointed with the electoral law, but maintained pressure to ensure a fair outcome (Osman, January 21 and 25, 1964).[20] He made numerous interventions to mediate between the parties and to encourage the government to follow the law. In one instance, he had to push the Hiraan branch of the SYL to be honorable, because some of its major figures tried to delist Abdillahi Issa from leading its candidate list (Osman, January 31, 1964). Despite all the efforts made to maintain peace and stability, violence flared up in the central region on March 29th. Before the police forcefully intervened, several people were killed in Dhusamareeb, but order was eventually restored (Osman, March 31, 1964).

The day before the polls opened, the president assured the population that despite attacks on the country by Ethiopia, the election would be a testimony to the maturity of the Somali people:

> *During the past two months [Osman] had striven, together with the Government, to give full guarantees to the political parties that the electoral law would be obeyed and that devices would be adopted to correct possible loop-holes and imperfections in the law itself. Therefore, the elector ought not to trouble himself to do more than go to one of the polling stations in his electoral district and vote, only once, for the party in which he has the most faith, and then to return peacefully to his daily occupation. He further declared that it depended on the electoral officials at all polling stations and electoral offices, (there are almost 5,000 of them) as*

to whether the election would be a big success or tragic farce and failure. He stated that neither the country nor the Government desired or had any interest in election irregularities of any type. He warned those that might attempt to commit fraud that they would not only damage themselves due to the consequent pangs of conscience and punishment under the law, but they would also damage the entire nation due to the bad precedent created. (US Department of State, April 3, 1964)

Election Day came on March 30th, and despite the war with Ethiopia, there were no major troubles regarding the vote. Government mobilized its resources to ensure that all went well. Public offices were closed, except in health and security, and a significant number of public employees were deployed in the polling stations. In addition, the police were very active in securing the stations and watching for fraud, and all the major political parties had their observers in most stations. There were 1,130 precincts, and the government deployed 45 responsible officials in each district to manage the process, which went smoothly. The US Embassy reported that this was a well-run election:

By general consensus, this election was the fairest ever held in Somalia. The government press understandably hailed the event as spotless proof of Somali democracy in action. More accurately, high government officials including General Abshir, Police Commandant, are generally satisfied that it was well run and fraud held down. (ibid.)

As the results trickled in, it became clear that this was the most competitive election in the country's history (US Department of State, May 21, 1964). The governing party, SYL, gained barely a majority of the seats in parliament. It was able to command that slim majority because of the ten districts where opposition parties did not compete. These districts netted the SYL twenty-one deputies. Elsewhere, the opposition ran a credible campaign, as the results show. Although the three major opposition parties garnered nearly 40 percent of the vote, their inability to form a coalition enabled the SYL to dominate the next parliamentary period. The primary reason for the fragmentation of the opposition was that each party leader itched to gain a national leadership post on his own terms, without compromising with other equally ambitious individuals.

President Osman registered his satisfaction with the outcome of the election:

> *The results are not so brilliant for the SYL and not everything went regularly like I had hoped, but I believe that the big scandal of inflation [of votes] that happened during the municipal election of last November did not happen this time, or at least were limited to [only a few places].* (Osman, March 31, 1964)

Despite the minor lapses underscored by the president, the election was a historic benchmark in the country's march toward democracy. It also illustrates that the principal fissures between elements of the political class were money and political appointments rather than genealogical identity.

Shifting Political Gears

Once the parliamentary election was concluded, attention immediately turned to the formation of the new government. The central political question was *whom* the president would nominate as prime minister. Most people presumed that the sitting prime minister who had overseen the successful parliamentary election in the midst of Ethiopian military aggression would be re-nominated. While this political storm was brewing, and after extended consultation with all major segments of civil society, President Osman made up his mind.

On June 6th, the president met with Abdirazak Haji Hussen and told him of his decision to nominate him.[21] Osman was contemplative on this day, and wrote the following after the announcement was made:

> *I am truly happy about Hussen and hope that he does not have any difficulties.... I exactly did what I had thought for a while and in spite of the decision of the Central Committee of SYL and its parliamentary group and other pressures. I pray to Allah with all my heart that Hussen is able to form a government and that then he works so I am not disappointed as I was with Sharmarke. Somalia needs a government that earns respect for its energy and*

respect for the laws and of the Constitution and for its honesty, and I think that Hussen has these qualities. (Osman, June 7, 1964)

The announcement was a political bombshell. Party politicians and opponents of Hussen went on the offensive to tarnish his image and derail his nomination in the parliamentary vote of confidence. Among those vehemently opposed to Hussen was Mohamed Ibrahim Egal, one of the leaders of the SNC, who told a senior diplomat at the US Embassy that:

> *Hussen is unpopular and has many enemies, including [Egal], and that the SNC would certainly vote against him at every opportunity that presented itself. Egal stated that the Italians also don't like Hussen because he is not corruptible and that he has many foes among provincial governors because of his arbitrary and high-handed way of forcing decisions and acting without any sense of compromise.... Egal stated that Hussen is rather tactless person and was not a good politician because he was very willful. This was in reply to my suggestion that Hussen would probably go slow in changing policies of Sharmarke especially the drift towards the Sino-Soviet bloc. Egal stated that Hussen would give no consideration for political tactfulness if he wanted to change the policy and he wouldn't do it slowly, and that once Hussen wants to do something, nothing deters him.* (US Department of State, June 9, 1964)

Africa Report best summed up the challenge posed by Hussen's nomination:

> *Hussen's character as a tough minded, fair and enlightened leader was noted by many. His friends say he is firm, but fair. His enemies say that he has the makings of a tyrant. Nobody disputes his courage, nor the drive to work 18 hours a day, to the detriment of his health, even after a serious operation at Walter Reed Hospital in Washington, DC.* (*Africa Report*, November 1964, p. 6)

But it was some of the old SYL guards who were most shocked by the nomination. Immediately after the announcement was made, the party's secretary general, Yasin Nur Hassan, convened a meeting of the party's parliamentary group to challenge the nomination. The discussion lasted until midnight and was exceptionally animated.

After another day of meetings, a committee was set up. At the end, the committee came to no conclusion, deciding to simply not oppose the president (Osman, June 11, 1964).

Once the party's position became clear, Hussen withdrew whatever reservation he had and moved quickly to think about government policy and the membership of his cabinet. Before going any further, however, he called on his departing chief, Sharmarke, to both seek advice and invite him to join the new government by choosing any portfolio. Sharmarke declined, and added that he could not see himself being sworn in by President Osman. Hussen's ambition was to both curb the size of the cabinet and select as many of the younger and more educated MPs to ministerial posts as possible. Although limiting cabinet size was difficult, partly because of intense political pressure, he was able to make headway on whom he selected. A disproportionate number of his selections happened to be from the North as a result of his commitment to look for potential high performers rather than a political calculation to privilege Northerners or particular genealogical groups (Africa Report, November 6, 1964, p. 6).[22]

Hussen shared his tentative list with the president on June 13th. Osman noted in his diary, "[the list] is not ideal, but I do not want to oppose it" (June 13, 1964). The one name that was missing from the list was Mohamed Abdi Nur Juuje, who the president thought should be considered. Hussen insisted on retaining Abdulkadir Mohamed Zoopo for his administrative skills, and thus disappointed Osman in not taking Juuje.

Here is the original list (Hussen, November 2001):

Name	Portfolio	Region
Ahmed Yusuf Dualeh	Foreign Minister	*(North)*
Abdulkadir Mohamed Zoope	Interior	(South)
Aden Issak	Defense	*(North)*
Ali Omer Scego	Grace and Justice	(South)
Yusuf Aden Bowkah	Information	*(North)*
Awil Haji Abdullahi	Finance	*(North)*

Kenadit Ahmed Yusuf	Education	(South)
Abdillahi Issa	Health & Labor	(South)
Mohamoud Issa Jama	Agriculture	*(North)*
Seck Abdullahi Mohamoud	Public Works & Communications	(South)
Osman Mohamed Adde	Industry & Commerce	(South)
Scek Mohamoud Mohamed Farah	State Minister for Somali Affair	(South)

The cabinet was sworn by the president on July 15th, before parliament gave its vote of confidence. Hussen selected his cabinet on the basis of skills and competence instead of regional and ethnic preferences. Most Somalis cheered the new PM for his audacity to shake up things, and were elated by the possibility of the new team translating the euphoria or independence into real national progress.

However, the sectarian political camp in parliament were angry and obdurate and began to fight back. Led by the SYL secretary general who tried to derail Hussen's nomination, they were joined by others, such as Ahmed Alloro. The latter inquired of the Supreme Court whether the president's appointment of Hussen was grounds for a legal challenge (Osman, June 20, 1964). After the Supreme Court rejected Alloro's scenario, he and his supporters collected signatures of twenty-five SYL members who opposed Hussen's appointment. Former prime minister Sharmarke was present at the meetings, but did not sign the petition (Osman, June 21, 1964).[23] By July 9th, the president was worried that Hussen and his cabinet might not get the necessary vote of confidence from parliament (Osman, July 8 and 9, 1964). The president's concern reflected fickle political winds in parliament. The leading party was in chaos and began sending contradictory signals to its MPs. For example, the CC of the SYL officially endorsed the new government, but on July 11th, the secretary general unilaterally "distributed a pamphlet to the deputies that was a sort of the order of the day that confirmed... that every deputy can act how they want towards the confidence vote in the government." Soon after this, Hussen realized that his government might not garner the necessary votes. The opposition within SYL was getting stronger, in addition to a majority of MPs in the two major opposition political parties. During the course of the debate it became apparent that MPs were least interested in the government's program, and focused on who was selected as a minister and who was left out. The president reflected on the political challenges facing the nation and the ill will of a significant members of parliamentarians:

> *I am told that our country is unfortunate with the irresponsible behavior of many of its men, who continue to see the problems of the country only in terms of their own interests and how it can further their interests. There has never been a government...that some of the representatives...did not try to avoid the consolidation [of their own power and interests] before the nomination, and then plot to give him [the prime minister] the vote of confidence. I dare say, though, that we've never had problems like today's with Abdullahi Issa in 1959, after the elections of March of that year, the declared opposition number[ed] 25 at the beginning, and were reduced to 13 because of the exaggerated response of these last people.... After the independence and the union...about half of the parliamentarians not divided by party made their intentions clear [against Sharmarke,] and the same thing happened when I asked Sharmarke to form a new government, after the Constitutional referendum of 1961. The same old trick[s], ever since 1959, are repeated today with Hussen, and therefore it is clear that they do not grow up! God save Somalis from the starving beasts in human form that are the supposed "representatives of the people."*
> (Osman, July 5, 1964)

Things came to a head as parliament came to a session to debate and vote on the government audit program. As the roll was called, opposition and government supporters stood even, at fifty-seven each. The last name to be called was Ali Mohamed Hirabe, a former minister and a member of the opposition. He said yes, but quickly retracted it and cast a negative vote. Government supporters tried to contest the retraction, but the prime minister designate intervened and spoke to the chamber:

> *My friend Ali was pro-Italian during the Trusteeship, then he joined SYL, became a Minister in the previous government, and then I removed him from that post. He has been a "yes-man" all his life, and his chance to say "no" today was betrayed by his "yes" habit. Since my government's fate depends on his vote, I*

want the President of the Chamber to count Ali's vote as negative, so he could be liberated today. (US Department of State, July 14, 1964) [24]

The public in the gallery roared with laughter, and even opposition members joined in. All Sharmarke's ministers, except two who were members of the new cabinet, cast a vote of no confidence. Many others decided to oppose the government because they felt slighted that their competitors had been appointed.

The implications of the vote of no confidence in the Hussen government were multiple. First, MPs of the two main opposition parties followed their leadership and their party's collective decision not to support the new order. This meant that there was some semblance of discipline in the two parties (ibid).[25] Second, other than the government, the ruling party was the greatest loser in this vote. The party was split between the old guard and Hussen's camp, and it appeared that the party had lost whatever political cohesion it had. Third, conventional analysis of Somalia generally sees the North-South divide as the major political watershed. This vote once more demonstrated how wrong this was. Nearly half the northern MPs voted against the government, which had just granted their region a disproportionate number of cabinet seats and some of the most important portfolios. Tribal affiliation also had no relation to the outcome. The majority of Hussen's genealogical group in the SYL had voted against his government (ibid).

Hussen's failure to win a confidence vote in parliament created a new dilemma for the president and the ruling party. A significant minority of the MPs in the SYL (thirty-four against and fifty-one for) had voted against its own government, and the opposition parties were looking to become part of a coalition government. These opponents were emboldened and thought that Hussen was fatally wounded politically. The failure generated new tension in the party and its central committee, which had intense debates that culminated in dismissal of the SYL secretary general on July 17th. In addition, the president saw the vote as a major setback for him and the country, but moved ahead on two fronts. First, he immediately accepted Hussen's resignation and tried to encourage the two sides of the party to bridge their differences. Second, he restarted the mandatory consultation process to gather wisdom from others for a new government, although he was certain that Hussen was the best and the only option forward (Osman, July 14, 1964).[26] Many of those he consulted told him to renominate Hussen, whereas a few others still adamantly opposed Hussen. One thing was certain, however: none of those opposed to Hussen suggested Sharmarke's name as an alternative. Among those the president consulted was Egal, who suggested that Osman nominate a non-SYL MP for the premiership—meaning, Egal himself.

After many consultations, the president finally felt confirmed in his wish to reappoint Hussen (Osman, August 22, 1964).[27] He urged Hussen not to significantly alter the composition of the first cabinet despite the SYL opposition to that cabinet remaining strong (ibid). Osman worried that the ferocity of opposition inside the SYL might shake Hussen's confidence (Osman, August 11, 1964), but once the renomination was made public, the center of gravity shifted back to the party and reappointment of the cabinet. A series of meetings chaired by the acting secretary general of the party made progress in healing the rift in the SYL. Hussen's challenge to the party was that these internal divisions might force him to form a coalition government, which would not be good for the SYL. While the party work was going on, Hussen also marginally readjusted his cabinet composition to diffuse political pressure and garner support for the vote without altering his government's agenda and strategy. Most memorably, Mohamoud Issa Jama, the minister designate for agriculture, in the failed attempt, offered to vacate his post so that more Southerners could be accommodated. He thought that might mollify many southern MPs who were upset by Northerners being given disproportionately more cabinet seats in Hussen's government than the previous one. In addition, the new cabinet consisted of fourteen ministers and seven deputy ministers.

As Hussen's forces gathered momentum, elements of the old SYL guard, and some of the opposition who retained their animus toward the new order, were concerned that the president might dissolve parliament and call for new elections if Hussen's second government did not gain a parliamentary vote of confidence. These worries were reported to Osman by the new president of parliament,

Ahmed Sheikh Mohamed Absiyeh, but Osman dismissed this as the fearful imagining of opportunist elements (Osman, August 27, 1964).[28]

Nearly two and a half months after the first government was voted down by parliament, the day of reckoning came on September 27th. Parliament began its debate three days earlier, and the most ardent critics were a few diehards in the SYL and the SNC. Haji Musa Boqor and Ahmed Allora took the lead and were followed by the SNC's Mohamed Ibrahim Egal and Jimale. Both groups pointed to the illegality of the cabinet, given that its size exceeded the constitutional limit of twelve ministers. But ten lawyers unanimously agreed that having the two state ministers without portfolios did not breach the constitutional limits. The number of ministers without portfolios, and deputy ministers, had no upper limit in the Constitution. The prime minister presented a summary of what was essentially the government's unaltered program (US Department of State, September 28, 1964).

In a change of fortune, ninety-one parliamentarians voted in favor of the government, and twenty-three opposed it.[29] According to the US Embassy, the crucial factor that produced this victory was the discipline exercised by the SYL's central committee (Osman, September 28, 1964; US Department of State, September 28, 1964).[30] Further, if the Orientalist assumptions had held sway, the confidence vote and cabinet selection would have been different.

Competent and Ethical Government

The deck was now cleared for a new effort to recharge the country's democratic institutions. Hussen knew that without effective and ethical public service institutions the chances for economic development were almost nil, and he invested all his energy into establishing them. Three issues central to the agenda can be distilled from the list of priorities. First, professionalizing the public service system was fundamental to all the government's reform efforts. Second, corruption at the highest levels was an obstacle to democratic governance and national unity. Finally, both the president and the new prime minister were devoted to the systematic reproduction of Somalia's democratic form of government through free and fair elections.

A short while after he accepted the appointment for the premiership and nominated his first cabinet, Hussen began to publicly articulate his government's commitment to a collective civic orientation and an efficient system of administration. He coined the apt phrase, for which he and his government came to be known, *Karti iyo hufnaan* (Competence and ethics). *Somali News*, the national daily newspaper, reported an address he gave to his cabinet on June 15th, articulating what distinguished the new government from old ways of doing the people's work:

> *The Cabinet of which you are part has indeed a special significance. It is, so to speak, the beginning of a new mandate. You have been called to take upon yourselves such heavy responsibilities through a selection based on strict considerations of quality, an essential element for a Government administratively and technically efficient.... It is obvious that some considerations have been set aside that are not consistent with the supreme interest of the nation, and never were. You all well know how widespread among the people the credence that many rise to power not in order to duly perform a high deserving function by serving the interests of the community, but in order to put their personal interests and those of certain groups before the interests of the nation. This belief has caused, as we know only too well, a recrudescence of the notorious plague of tribalism.... Having made this brief premise and stated that the new government is a responsible "working group" originating from a qualitative selection and not from a "balance" on regional or ethnic basis, it is our precise moral duty to tackle the complex problem with determination, in order to dismantle the above mentioned erroneous beliefs not only with words, but above all, with facts, a beginning for the strengthening of a national and civic conscience.* (*Somali News*, June 15, 1964)

These words stirred a great deal of wonder across the country. Although most people appreciated the sentiments expressed by the prime minister on the radio, they did not know exactly what to expect because this political agenda had no previous record in Somalia. For Hussen's opponents, such a declaration was tantamount to political war (US Department of State, August, 19, 1964).[31] The first material step to give substance to the agenda was the enactment of a decree that required all cabinet members to declare their assets and properties as required by the Constitution (Somali News, July 8, 1964, Somali Republic, 1961, p. 26).[32] The decree marked a sharp turn away from the old ways of conducting public business, and the president was delighted with this new departure. As a result of this and similar acts, Osman privately coined a nickname for the prime minister—*Dahirie* (Cleanser) (Osman, September 1, 1964).

A little over a month after his government was confirmed, the prime minister went to work on the government's budget for 1965. Somalia had run a budget deficit recently, and this year was no different. Hussen and his finance minister, Awil Haji Abdillahi, invested a lot of energy into reducing the deficit, and began a new process that would generate revenue and curtail expenditure, hoping to attain a balanced budget in the near future. Despite their efforts, it became clear that they could not balance the budget in the immediate future because of contractually binding financial decisions taken by the previous government, such as the economic agreements with the USSR. The budget was presented to parliament and debated in late December 1964. Hussen's political foes thought they could get rid of the government by defeating the bill, but a substantial majority of MPs voted in favor (seventy-five for, twenty-eight against), which indicated that the government was safe for now (Osman, December 27, 1964).

Immediately after the budget, the prime minister turned his attention to his top priority, reforming the state's administrative apparatus to make it more efficient. The groundwork for this had started in early 1962, when a UN-supported commission (The Establishment Commission) was set up to harmonize the inherited divergent bureaucratic systems of Italian and British Somalilands and reform it into an effective apparatus. The commission concluded its extended tenure, and its report was approved by the cabinet under Prime Minister Sharmarke. In the political pressure of the forthcoming election, the report was set aside in 1963. The commission's report proposed creating an orderly system in which every employee would have a personnel file. Administrative tables were developed for each ministry, and all staffing and promotions were to be based on qualifications and merit. Four grades (A, B, C, and D) were set up, and ranks within these positions were established (Hussen, January 2002).

For weeks, Hussen worked with the head of the commission, a Canadian national we know only as Mr. Hindle. As Hindle's tenure came to an end, he described for the US Embassy the commission's work and Hussen's seriousness about implementing its recommendations.

> *While Mr. Hindle gives unstinted praise to the Hussen government, on several occasions in the past he has remarked that Hussen may be ahead of his time; i.e., too progressive for Somalia's present state of political development.... Mr. Hindle stated that he has been working for long hours, at times until 4:00 AM, in private sessions with Hussen...on the reorganization of the Somali civil service. The task was difficult according to Hindle, because the civil service was more than doubled in the last two years of the UN Trusteeship Administration under Italy. Without further elucidation, Hindle claimed that this was done for political reasons. As a result the [government of the Somali Republic] has been saddled with the problem of an over-staffed civil service since independence.* (US Department of State, January 30, 1965)

After long hours spent studying the commission's report during the previous few months, Hussen announced his intent to implement the commission's recommendations. He told the commissioners that they need *not* be overly concerned with the political implications, because that was not their responsibility. He impressed on them that their sole concern should be how to create an effective public service. In this context, the prime minister recalled Mohamed Burraleh, an administrator of high repute, from his consular post in Moscow and appointed him as the new director general of personnel. Hussen met with his cabinet and threw down the gauntlet:

> *"Tonight, we gather to participate in decision-making which marks yet another important milestone in the development of the machinery of our civil service.... I am referring, of course, to the official approval of the re-organization of government and the re-establishment and integration of the entire civil service.... In a developing country like ours, it is essential that we make the*

> *maximum utilization of our human resources. We must ensure that duplication and unnecessary activities are eliminated. Our first step in this direction is the creation of a sound organizational structure which is the foundation upon which our public administration is to develop. The second step is the careful analysis of the organization structure to determine exactly how many positions are needed, what skills are required and where they should be located.... For the first time, we are able to determine our manpower requirements, both present and future. This will facilitate improved budgetary and financial control, and permit more accurate training and staff requirements for the future. The third and most important step is the selection and appointment of civil servants to give life to the organization, for it is the human resources who, in the final analysis, will determine the success or failure of this all important undertaking. I doubt very much if our civil service personnel have ever been subjected to the kind of screening which has just been completed in selecting officers for senior appointments.... Right man for the right job. I should mention at this point that the Somali Institute of Public Administration, which I mentioned briefly in my address last Wednesday, will shortly commence activities. A major priority will be training and development of our senior and intermediate staff."... [A few days later,] lecturing the assembled government, directors generals and high officials ...Hussen boldly stated anyone failing to pull his weight would be replaced.* (US Department of State, January 31 and February 6, 1965)

He was equally unrelenting and forthright when speaking to his party in February, as the US Embassy reported: "The government does not dare nor will it dare tolerate any breach of the law. If this sounded like a threat, said Hussen, it was so meant for the dishonest" (US Department of State, February 13, 1965).[33]

The cabinet met, and the die was cast. Here is how the US Embassy summed up the mood at the time:

> *On the night of January 27–28, now known among some top local Western educated officials as the St. Bartholomew's massacre, the Council of Ministers met for 19 straight hours, and with each minister having a chance to speak for the Director General of his ministry, went over the dossiers and made the decisions.... The government's action was a bombshell. It was clearly evident from Embassy's sounding of officials and public opinion that*

more was involved than severe administrative measures. This was a political action aimed at re-casting the modus operandi of the state. The old way of doing business was sloppy, or handing out favors to family and tribe, or seeking monetary gain in return for routine operations. And the men who were in charge of the government's business were known to have held high office, many since independence, too often without the qualifications for the job, too many because of tribal affiliations and despite evidence that they were living beyond their salaries. This latter point is important. Corruption led to general cynicism among the public and vitiated the stated aims of this and previous governments that the welfare of the people came uppermost. Most Somalis knew that the welfare of the officials came first. True, Hussen, from the time of his first appointment last June, has been talking about honest and efficient government. Apparently, no one was really convinced that he would or could make a general house cleaning.... The immediate man-in-the-street's reaction was therefore one of surprised delight. The prime minister had done what he promised; he had thrown the rascals out. The reaction among the discarded upper civil servants and their tribal and business connections need hardly be described. (ibid.)

At the end of the meeting it became clear that about 450 senior- and middle-level jobs in the civil service were targeted. Reform started at the very top, and the director generals of ministries were the first to feel the heat. Seven of the sixteen directors general were dropped from service, notably Nicolino Mohamed of Foreign Affairs, Hassan Gudal of Education, and Jama Ganni of Information.

By the third week of January, Hussen made two public speeches preparing the population and those in government services for the radical reform that was in the offing (Somali News, January 22, 1965; Hussen, December 2001). The cabinet had already agreed to push through the reform process. At the end of January, the prime minister reported to the cabinet and the nation that a serious shakeup of the government administration was unfolding. Some leading figures thought that the prime minister was courageous and absolutely on target to act swiftly (US Department of State, March 29, 1965; US Department of State, February 13, 1965).[34]

When the commission had unveiled its work, with the accent on the quality and quantity of civil servants needed for an effective Somali government, it stressed that numerous state employees, particularly in senior positions, had neither the experience nor the qualifications necessary for their posts. The commission recommended that these employees should be given two years, with salary, to requalify through training. Those who failed to capitalize on the opportunity ought to be discharged. The cabinet accepted the report, and Hussen gave orders for its strict and swift implementation. When the final tally of the dismissed, particularly at director general level, was made public it was a professional and political earthquake. Hussen's campaign also eliminated over a thousand temporary daily employees who had been added to the government rolls over the previous decade. Some of these people, including Hussen's brother, had no other source of income, and their dismissal was particularly painful for the prime minister. The vast majority of all those released from public employment were from the South.

The timing of the announcement was not accidental; parliament was not in session, and this gave the government until late April before legislators could challenge it. Senior people made redundant petitioned the president pleading their case. In their petition the discharged officers claimed that their democratic rights as well as due process had been violated by the government (US Department of State, May 10, 1965).

President Osman received the petitioners on May 3, 1965. Unfortunately for them, Osman had already signed the decree that authorized their dismissal. He told them that he could not help them, but urged those among them who felt wronged to seek justice in the courts (ibid).[35]

Parliament was the last authority that could reverse the government's intention to make redundant those civil servants deemed unfit to serve. Individual petitioners lobbied their representatives. They submitted the same petition to parliament and then mobilized their network to pressure MPs into action. But the government was well-prepared to fend off this challenge. Hussen organized his government's presentations in parliament in such a way that the most popular bills, in a list of twenty-three agenda items, were taken up first, and the contentious items were left to the last. Among the popular bills were those that allowed the government to support the family of deceased General Daud Hersi, and earmarked funding for pensions for the veterans of the Ethiopia-Somalia conflict of 1964. It appears that the prime minister's strategy was to exhaust the opposition with other details and some popular bills before they got to his administrative reform. Despite being outmaneuvered, the opposition was prepared when the dreaded items came up for discussion. Opposition within the SYL led the charge against the reform program and accused the government of thoughtless radicalism and cruelty. Among the fiercest critics were the former prime minister Sharmarke and his ally Ahmed Allora. Despite all the accusations leveled against the prime minister by the opposition, none claimed that Hussen and his government engaged in tribal politics in cleaning up the civil service. Reporting on the final debates, the US Embassy summed up the deliberation:

> *Each took several hours "to unburden themselves." However, Hussen patiently answered each point and scathingly called attention to the failings of the "deputy who formerly occupied the place I am now holding," i.e. Sharmarke. The votes on the civil service bills were respectively, 64–44, 72–38, 72–36, and 73–33, although the later vote on the Organization of the Government (with the extra Ministry of Communication and Transport)...was a closer, 58–46, and Hussen was over the Hump.* (US Department of State, May 24, 1965)

The passage of the civil service reform bills was not an easy task and marked a major milestone in the effort to institutionalize professionalism in government work, but it was not a finished product. Nevertheless, it signaled that a leadership with a different vision for the country was at work. Haji Bashir Ismail, vice president of parliament, summed up Hussen's qualities:

> *Hussen is a tough man; many deputies believe he has been excessive in his zeal for reform, though not quarreling with his objectives. Many dismissed civil servants have been calumnied by insinuation of (unproven though likely) graft and disloyalty. Nevertheless, the Assembly respects and praises Hussen's courage. He is the first prime Minister to have had any.* (ibid.)

Having set a new standard for the quality of those in public service, and taking the first steps in shifting the terms of engagement, Hussen and his team began to focus on the more arduous and mundane work of enforcing the laws and inducing a culture of accountability in state affairs. Hussen's government turned its attention to creating a culture of confidence in public service by going after three types of transgressions: eliminating tardiness and establishing a work culture based on duty and efficiency; fighting corruption at all levels, from junior public servants to top ministers, and keeping it on the public's radar; and eliminating political interference by honoring professional division of labor between civil servants and political leaders.

The prime minister set a daunting example of the new standards of professional behavior. Hussen was known, during his ministerial days, as a tough administrator who was exceptionally punctual, worked very long hours (Osman, February 2, 1966),[36] and pushed for efficient response to legitimate public demands. He brought this tradition to the whole government, and the word went out that Hussen meant what he preached. Public offices became vigilant in maintaining ethical standards. In addition to respecting working hours, the new order demanded that government transport be used as intended, only during working hours and in emergencies. The police were authorized to stop and inspect any government vehicle operating during nonworking hours to see if it had a permit to be on the road. As a result of this initiative, government vehicles in the major towns of the country disappeared from the streets after work hours, and this had an immediate effect on public opinion that the new regime was a breed apart from the old one.

Fighting corruption was much tougher than taking vehicles off the streets, but the government faced the challenge with zeal. The auditing service of the government was put on new footing and began to coordinate with the police's Criminal Investigation Department. One of the first joint investigations by the auditor and the investigative agency took place in Hargeisa. Over the previous year, the police noticed two government employees who seemed to have a lot more money than they were paid, and who took weekend excursions to Aden (now in Yemen). Mogadishu dispatched an auditor to Hargeisa to look into the affairs of the two men. According to the US Embassy report:

> The auditor requested the books of the Regional Accountant, Mohamed Haji Ahmed, and the Senior Auditor, Ali Mohamed Warsame. Within a few days, rumors concerning misappropriation of funds by these two men...which sprang primarily from their several marriages since appointment to control Northern Region funds and their weekend jaunts to Aden were confirmed. Mohamed was arrested and Ali suspended from duty during the investigation. Ibrahim Ali Liban, Comptroller of Customs at Berbera, who is slated to become the Accountant General at Mogadishu, has been designated to take charge of the investigation. (US Department of State, March 6, 1965; November 16, 1965)

There was no easing on this front, and similar investigations of corrupt practices in the civil service took place elsewhere in the country until the government's tenure came to an end.[37]

The government challenged public employees who were suspected of misappropriating public resources and misusing their offices, and the prime minister expected his colleagues in the political establishment to demonstrate ethical behavior and practice as well. He closely watched his cabinet members' public engagements. Senior police investigators and the audit service looked into claims that cabinet ministers and personnel were involved in corrupt practices, and they provided their results to the prime minister. After careful consideration of the report, Hussen authorized the police to pursue the matter vigorously and conduct a more intrusive investigation. In due course, the investigators submitted reports on three senior ministers and one deputy minster: Awil Haji Abdillahi (his Christian name was Anthony James) of finance, Ismail Duale Warsame of agriculture, and his deputy minister, Islao Mohamed, and Osman Mohamed Adde of industry and commerce. The national audit discovered that the minister of finance illegally used 300,000 shillings from the Postal Bank in Burao, for his election campaign in 1963–1964. The minister was made aware of the finding and told he had one of two options: be fired by the prime minister, or resign and retain some modicum of dignity. The minister resigned (Osman, January 1, 1966). President Osman urged Prime Minister Hussen to let the three others also resign. Hussen told Osman that he wanted to fire them and "not give them the satisfaction." The president urged the prime minister "to invite them to...[submit their resignation], and advise them that they [should] put themselves at the disposition of the judicial authorities" (ibid).[38] The prime minister made his move and called them separately into his office. The first to come was Osman Mohamed Adde, minister of commerce. Hussen had known Adde since the 1950s, when Adde was inspector of prisons and Hussen was a political prisoner in Mogadishu. The claim against Adde was that he was blocking the usual importation of tea so that his client, who was involved in manipulating tea importation by using the state's Trading Agency, could exploit the artificial shortage. Hussen confronted the minister with the evidence, but Adde denied any wrongdoing. The prime minister fired him with immediate effect. Note that Hussen and Adde were distant cousins, and that Adde's client was Hussen's first cousin.

Hussen's attention then turned to the minister of agriculture and his deputy. Ismail Duale knew why the prime minister requested his presence and arrived pleading for clemency based on the decades of acquaintance between him and Hussen. In his humorous and biting response, the prime minister told Duale that people in Hargeisa had already dubbed him *Dhul Cun* (Land Eater) during his governorship in that region, because of his corrupt land practices. Now, as minister of agriculture, the public labeled him *Dhir Cun* (Forest Eater), because of kickbacks he received from exports of banned forest products such as charcoal. In jest, the prime minister told Duale that the dismissal was a preemptive act, before Duale became *Dad Cun* (People Eater) (Hussen, November 2001).

The announcement of these dismissals was political thunder like nothing previous in the country's short history. *Dalka*, the independent monthly that had been a constant thorn in the side of the government, was stunned by these groundbreaking developments.

The important political development...has been the dismissal of the Minister of Industry and Commerce, the Minister of Agriculture and the Under-Secretary of Agriculture.... The dismissals were due to charges of corruption. This is an epoch-making development. No longer will the appointment to a ministerial post mean a license to rob.... Another important political fact is that the dismissal of a minister because he has been charged with corrupt practices is a development we could not possibly have expected from any of our prime ministers. The present Prime Minister has his faults—certainly many of them. But it would be neither fair nor honourable to deny him the support and praise he deserves for re-establishing the principle that even ministers cannot afford to be caught in compromising situations, involving the misuse of public funds or power of office. A third important aspect— perhaps the most important—is that the Attorney General's office has applied to the National Assembly for authorization to institute criminal proceedings against the two ministers and the Under-Secretary. Such a request must be moved in the assembly by a fifth of its members and must be approved by a two-thirds majority in a secret ballot. The requests for the authorization to prosecute in respect of at least ex-Minister of Industry and Commerce is believed to have been submitted to the President of the National Assembly some months ago. The one in respect of the Minister of Agriculture was apparently submitted at about the time of or after his dismissal.... The general belief in informed circles is that the requests for authorization were kept from examination in the last session by the President of the National Assembly. (Dhuhul 1966, p. 10)

Establishment of the Public Service Commission was another central effort in the government's attempts to institutionalize division of labor and powers, and to protect public servants from inappropriate meddling by political leaders.

An imprint of the regime was respect for the independence of the Public Service Commission, which was given the task of reviewing all promotions and demotions. Two instances highlight the professional protection the commission afforded civil servants, even when they had transgressed, and the regime's readiness to abide by the commission's rulings. The first case was that of Yusuf Dirir from Burao. *Dalka*, the independent monthly magazine, was popular among educated Somalis. It had a monthly article that was critical of the regime, and whose author seemed to have access to classified state information. An investigation found that Yusuf Dirir, an economics graduate from a British university, and a consular in the Somali embassy in Addis Ababa, Ethiopia, was using the diplomatic bag to transmit the articles to his friends in the Ministry of Foreign Affairs, who passed them to the editor of *Dalka*. The minister of foreign affairs intercepted and opened an envelope without a warrant and discovered an article destined for *Dalka*, with Dirir's signature. Dirir was summoned to Mogadishu. He stridently argued that the minister had no right to open his private letter, although he himself had no justification for the wrongful use of the diplomatic pouch. The minister accused him of illegal use of a state service and the publishing of confidential information. The case was submitted to the Public Service Commission with a demand that Dirir be dismissed. After careful deliberation, the commission reprimanded Dirir rather than discharging him. Disappointed, the government, nonetheless, complied.

Hussen's government and policies turned the Somali Constitution and its democratic principles into reality in the political life of the country more than had happened in any other country in Africa at the time. The division of labor between the executive branch and the legislature, between the political authority and the civil service, and the independence of the judiciary were remarkable achievements by any standards. Somalia's challenge was how to sustain and advance these wonderful democratic structures and political practices.

The Triumph of Sectarian Politics

We have the duty to educate our people, and with this, our representatives who are part of this population, and it's certainly not the best thing to act illegally under the impulse of passion: according to me, it's all about not accepting bribes of the representatives, always staying the course according to our convictions, and letting the government fall until the representatives have convinced themselves that they cannot win with immorality. It is this steadfastness in the constitution and the legal business, which will straighten out things, and steadfastness can only be obtained by those who are not afraid to lose their position. (Osman, August 7, 1964)

Hussen's reformist strategy frightened many self-serving politicians inside and outside parliament. Those sectarian elements in parliament set their sights on the forthcoming presidential election in 1967, as an opportunity to undo the reform by capturing state power. The first postcolonial Somali prime minister became their candidate to challenge President Osman. Sharmarke fired the first shot of the presidential campaign almost a year early. In contrast, Osman was not worried about his future, and would welcome whatever parliament decided, as he told a local reporter as late as November of 1966, who asked him if he would seek re-election (US Department of State, November 29, 1966).

Sharmarke left no stone unturned in raising campaign funds and wooing MPs to his side. He toured the Communist Eastern Bloc countries in November. Shortly after his return, he began meeting with MPs and told supporters that he had received much support from the Eastern Bloc (US Department of State, November 11, 1966).[39] Meanwhile, Sharmarke began to build a team among MPs. A key figure among these was Egal, who was promised the premiership in advance and in exchange for his support. The logic behind the Sharmarke–Egal team was that they could woo both the East and the West to support the campaign. Sharmarke and others were already working with their Eastern Bloc contacts and the Italian Communist Party, and Egal was dispatched to seek the support of his Western friends in early spring. He approached a US diplomat for assistance:

Mohamed Haji Ibrahim telephoned the morning of April 17, 1966, to request if we might talk. Egal arrived at my home about 6:15 p.m., was enroute to a dinner at the Syrian Embassy. Egal asked if I'd relayed our earlier conversation to the Ambassador. I replied I had, and the Ambassador had commented that it is not proper for the United States to intervene in the internal affairs of another country. President Osman is a fine man, and it would be inappropriate to contribute to his defeat. If Egal became Prime Minister after the elections, the United States would seek to cooperate with his government. Finally, if Egal did become PM, he would be assured America would not work behind his back for his subsequent removal from office. Egal said he respected this attribute and believed it fair. (US Department of State, April 22, 1967).[40]

Diplomatic rhetoric aside, at least one US agency, the Central Intelligence Agency (CIA), is alleged to have provided support for the Egal–Sharmarke team (Lermarchand 1979, p. 16), in accordance with the well-known fact that the United States regularly intervened in the internal affairs of countries whose policies it found disagreeable. Despite Osman's well-known reticence to seek another term, and his unflinching opposition to asking others to support him, groups of MPs and other notables regularly visited Osman during the first six months of 1967 to offer their support in the campaign. Among the people who approached Osman several times and offered him monetary support was one of the wealthiest merchants from northern Somalia, Haji Ahmed Haji Abdillahi, known as Hashiish. Osman noted in his diary: "Received the big northern merchant Haji Ahmed Haji Abdillahi Hashiish. He asked me to accept starting now re-election, declaring himself disposed to sending as much money as possible to see me re-elected" (Osman, January 4, 1967). Hashiish continued to implore Osman to accept his assistance, and visited him three more times with offers of financial support. The final offer came on May 1st (Osman, May 25, 1967).

Sensing Osman's diffidence, many MPs and other supporters prompted Hussen to exhort Osman to seek re-election, but the prime minister responded that he could not impose such a wish on the president (Hussen, April 2002). Lobbying Osman to run went on for several months, before the SYL annual congress met at the end of May 1967, and decided whom to support for the presidency (Osman, May 31, 1967).[41] The prime minister, who was also the secretary general of the party, nominated Osman. With seventy-seven members present at the nomination meeting, the final vote was forty-four in favor of Osman, thirty for Sharmarke, and three abstentions.

Still, Osman did not change his strategy, and consistently told those who came to endorse him to act on their conscience (US Department of State, May 27, 1967).[42] It fell to Hussen and his cabinet to mobilize support in parliament. Many MPs were oblivious to the issues at stake in the presidential election, and were simply driven by their appetite for money or a cabinet post. In the end, their vote became a commodity, plain and simple, to be sold to the highest bidder, and without the sanctity of a commercial-legal contract. Sharmarke's campaign deployed significant cash inducements, offers of ministerial and other positions, and protection from prosecution for the four MPs discussed earlier, who resigned or were fired in Hussen's rooting out of high-level corruption. The former finance minister, Awil Haji Abdillahi, was one of those promised refuge from justice by Sharmarke. However, he sent emissaries to Hussen to declare his support for the president, in return for retaining his parliamentary immunity. Rather than entertain the former minister's plea, Hussen was confident enough of Osman's chances in the campaign that he decided to ask parliament to judge the four MPs (Osman, April 2, 1967; US Department of State, May 8, 1967). The president of the assembly did not take up the matter, and without a guarantee of no prosecution from Hussen, the four MPs consequently found refugee from justice, which ensured that all of them would vote for the Sharmarke–Egal team.

Hussen and his team knew that they were seriously disadvantaged financially and otherwise, and they thus faced a serious moral dilemma. They could abandon their commitment to the civic ethos they had fought so hard to establish, and play the money game. Or they could hold firm—and face almost certain defeat and risk losing the democratic project. In the end, Hussen decided to offer some cash inducements to MPs likely to vote for Osman but tempted by the other camp (Osman, June 20, 1967).[43] These incentives were not a match for the slush fund of the Sharmarke–Egal team.

A further liability for the Hussen regime was the impossibility of accommodating particularistic political demands by MPs. A characteristic of intra-parliamentary politics was that members who came from the same regions or electoral districts competed for the same ministerial posts and other scarce resources. Each tried to outmaneuver the other, and failing that, each attempted to deny the other any post. The only acceptable scenario was if both MPs gained similar appointments or none (a zero-sum affair). Once one became a minister, the other joined the opposition. For instance, Hussen thought highly of the administrative capabilities of his Interior minister, Zoope. Juuje, from the same Upper Juba region as Zoope, had to be accommodated as minister without portfolio, and then as minister of agriculture to keep the Upper Juba deputies on the regime's side.

In the end, the entire Upper Juba delegation, with the exception of two members, asserted that they would support Osman's presidency if Hussen promised them that Zoope would not be a minister in Hussen's future cabinet. Juuje and the majority of his delegation had secretly agreed with Egal to vote for Sharmarke. A member of the of the Upper Juba delegation, Gaytano, informed Hussen that Juuje had tried to convince him to support Sharmarke.

As the fateful day approached, streams of delegates from parliament, and from the regions, saw Osman, offering him their support. The president thanked them, but kept his aloof stance, not certain about the integrity of some of the visitors. Hussen and his team were hopeful, but Osman was more realistic and calculated that he was unlikely to win because he was not willing to play by corrupt means (Osman, March 6, 1967).

That this corrupt lobbying persisted, revealed two character flaws of a significant number of MPs. First, although a slim majority of MPs recognized that the president was not a partisan leader—most aptly demonstrated when Egal sought Osman's advice about his political future—most of them, nevertheless, could not fathom the president's unflinching attachment to the national interest, and his unwillingness to engage in horse trading that would compromise his deeply held convictions. Second, most of them could not grasp Osman's political courage and his willingness to fight MPs to protect public interest, even when this could cost him votes in the forthcoming presidential election. Such audacity was on display just six months before the election, when parliament began to discuss a bill that would allow MPs who lost their election to collect 24,000 shillings. Osman wrote in his diary:

> *In the National Assembly, they are discussing a law initiated in Parliament... which is aimed at obtaining a liquidation of 24,000 shillings for each of them who is not re-elected in case of new election. I do not yet know if the enormity is limited to the liquidation, or if there are also other "instances" in the law, but I remember that initially the "enlightened" Hon. Giudicino had formed the sketch of the law with completely different pretenses from that of the liquidation: pensions, an increase in the daily allowance for foreign and interior missions, tokens of presence, indemnities for lodging, these were the currents running through*

the project! There is no doubt that those "worthy representatives of the people" will approve the liquidation, but what will I do? There are those who delude themselves that I will not have the courage to ask for a re-discussion and deliberation, because of the upcoming presidential election, but they are making a big mistake if they think about me that way. (Osman, January 3, 1967)

Advocates of the bill pushed it through, but the president was able to block it from becoming law. This was the second time he had returned such a law to parliament during his tenure.

The appointed hour for electing the president came on June 10th at 10:00 a.m. MPs took their seats, and the gallery of the chamber was fully backed with citizens. Sharmarke took his seat as an MP and was entitled to vote for himself, whereas Osman remained in the presidential villa and was ineligible to vote, but followed the proceedings via the live program over Radio Mogadishu. At 10:10, parliament appointed three vote counters—Ali Alio Barre, Salad Abdi Mohamud, and Mohamud Issa Jama—and five observers from the five parliamentary parties (Osman, June 10, 1967). Neither candidate won a two-thirds majority in the first vote, and it took nearly two hours to go through three ballots. In the first round of voting, Sharmarke received sixty-three votes and Osman fifty-seven; three ballots were illegible and annulled. It seems that the differences between the two candidates of six votes were easily accounted for by the four former ministers who backed Sharmarke in return for escaping justice, and two of Hussen's ministers who betrayed their own government (US Department of State, March 4, 1968; Osman, June 10, 1967). In contrast to these six, those who voted for Osman had refused to be bought, and apparently held the prime minister and the president in high regard. When the Speaker of parliament announced Sharmarke's victory, a deputy from Eyl (Sharmarke's home district) held up his pencil and declared with trepidation, "*Fidmoy kow*" (First trouble).

Osman's reaction to the loss was one of relief:

The government that was my supporter was tricked by people that made it believe to be on my side, but as far as I'm concerned, I consider the results as a blessing for me, that lets me return to be free without having to bow down to anyone! (Osman, June 10, 1967)

Sharmarke came to the presidential villa, and Osman congratulated him and promised to support him (ibid).[44]

Osman magnanimously offered to vacate the post early so that the new president would have the honor of presiding over the July 1st independence commemorations. He informed Sharmarke and the Speaker of parliament about his intentions, and on June 30th, he resigned. The new head of state was sworn in immediately.

Retrogressive Reform

The new regime was confident that Osman would not return to active politics despite his concerns about the direction the state was going, but they worried about Hussen, whose record of democratic reform and public service was recognized as trailblazing. This section narrates the effort made by the new authority to strip Hussen of his political base in the SYL, reform state institutions in such a way that they could consolidate power, and change electoral law so as to prevent their challengers from the civil service from entering politics.

The new leaders tried to clip Hussen's political wings with a concerted attempt to remove him from the SYL leadership. Their first step was to allow opportunist MPs, from other parties, who wanted a ministerial appointment to join the party. Hussen and members of the central committee bowed to the change after some initial resistance. The new leaders then tried to prevent Hussen from retaining the secretary general of the party because they felt that their political game plan would be unsafe with the former prime minister at the helm of the party. The top three government leaders initiated a campaign of innuendo against him and tried to buy votes of central committee members. They hoped that enough committee members would take the bait to allow them to call for a meeting of the committee to depose Hussen. Fortunately for Hussen, most members of the committee were not corrupted during the presidential campaign, because the majority of them were not MPs.

Among the first to report the conspiracy to Hussen was a committee member named Abdi, who was supposedly known for his opportunism. Abdi had been approached by the leaders, but rejected their plea and told them that their best chance of getting rid of Hussen was to let matters take their own course. But they were too impatient to wait. They approached several others, who also rejected their request. Finally, they came to an old man by the name of Omar Borey and pleaded with him to help them dislodge Hussen. But Egal and the team had struck a rock of integrity. The old man retorted, "If I do what you are asking me, then who will marry my daughter, as I will be so disgraced."

When this strategy failed, the government team turned to another trick. They decided to accuse Hussen of misappropriating public money, to the tune of 2 million shillings. Their claim was that he was corrupt despite his anticorruption drive during his tenure as prime minister. When the accusation was leaked, some MPs who had originally betrayed the Osman-Hussen team in the presidential campaign, such as Haji Bashir Ismail, Sheikh Mukhtar Mohamed (the president of parliament), Ibrahim Oonlayeh, and the wealthy businessman Yusuf Egal, openly challenged the accusation. They told the instigators that no one would believe their assertions and pursuing the scheme would immediately destabilize the regime and the country. To prevent it, they organized a meeting with Egal, Yasin Nur Hassan, and Hussen (Hussen 2001).[45] Hussen knew from a senior source at the Somali Central Bank that substantial government cash had already been evacuated to Egal's personal account (Hussein 2003).[46] The meeting went nowhere, and Hussen asked the mediators to let the accuser take the matter to court, because that would reveal who was behind the scheme. Finally, the mediators told Hussen that the regime coveted control of the SYL and wanted him to resign as secretary general. Hussen responded that the government would have to win party control through the established legitimate means.

After scheming and meddling for two months, Egal and associates were unable to push Hussen out of the SYL, and Hussen was very satisfied with the defense the central committee had given him. Hussen recognized that under the new regime, the SYL was doomed, and thereafter, unilaterally decided to resign from both the central committee and the party. For a short while, Hussen became an independent MP. He eventually formed a new political party, the Democratic Action Party (DAP), as the 1969 parliamentary election approached.[47] Several of Hussen's former ministers were key members (US Department of State, October 23, 1968).[48]

Within a short period, DAP became the most vibrant political affair in the capital. The regime was so terrified by the new party's influence that it tried to curtail the party's events, and there was discussion in senior circles that Hussen's speeches were insidious and a danger to peace (US Department of State, August 13, 1969). Recognizing that they could not arrest Hussen or close down the party's premises, the regime concentrated on using its executive power and majority in parliament to rewrite the electoral law to suffocate any political opposition in the forthcoming parliamentary election. Rewriting electoral law took center stage in parliament (US Department of State, June 5, 1968).

There were a few troubling changes in the proposed electoral law, but two propositions were particularly disturbing. First, the so-called quotient—a new formula for distributing seats—would penalize small parties. Second, the change in the rule governing civil servants who desired to run for office was dramatic. Under the new rule civil servants who wanted to run for parliament were forced to resign from their position rather than take the usual leave of absence, as had been the case in the past. The regime intended with this rule to frighten talented civil servants unhappy with the destruction of the merit-based system, into thinking twice before challenging prevailing political order.

The only challenge to the new law came from the national police and its commander, General Mohamed Abshir (US Department of State, February 12, 1969).[49] Abshir consulted with his US and Italian legal advisors about the constitutionality of the new law. The experts concluded that the legislation was in contravention of the Constitution (Abshir, September 2005). Abshir subsequently brought all his senior officers from the regions to a conference in Mogadishu, and asked them to examine the new legislation and present their advice (Qalib, June 2006).[50] After an intense examination of the law, the officers unanimously agreed that the law was not in agreement with the Constitution. General Abshir concluded that, because the police force is a national institution, it must not side with any regime or political party. Enforcing this unconstitutional law would be tantamount to the police favoring the regime in a political contest. Abshir instructed his officers to take the report of the experts to their regions and not to enforce governors' instructions pertaining to this law (US Department of State, February 21, 1969).[51]

When this decision became public, the regime went mad. The police were the purview of the Ministry of Interior, and the minister, Yasin Nur Hassan, appointed a more amenable commander (Abshir, September 14, 2005). Colonel Jama Gorshel, the new commander, reversed Abshir's edict, faithfully supported the government, and began to focus on the activities of DAP. On the orders of the minister of Interior, the police closed the DAP offices twice, April through July, and then in August (US Department of State, April 9, 1969; August 13, 1969).

Soon after these events Sharmarke, Egal, and Hassan began to reshuffle civil servants and strategically positioned their supporters as governors, district commissioners, and other local authorities.

The Egal group also has control over the government apparatus in its hands, and the recent wholesale switching of regional governors and district commissioners provides a fairly clear indication that this influence will be used in the election. To the extent that this is done by unethical or illegal means, there is likely to be serious trouble. In 1964, as the election campaigns began in earnest, the then president, Aden Abdullah Osman, publicly and privately worked to good effect, to ensure honest elections. One can only hope that a similar pattern will emerge in 1969. (US Department of State, August 28, 1968; October 23, 1968)[52]

These local authorities had a vital role to play in the election because they controlled government machinery in their localities. For instance, district commissioners, as agents of the Ministry of Interior, received pre-election registration forms from party candidates and verified party voter lists and signatures. The authorities created obstacles for those parties and independent candidates not aligned with the regime when they tried to register. In setting up this system, Egal dealt with political matters in the northern region, and

Sharmarke and Hassan managed southern affairs (US Department of State, January 15, 1969). For example, Egal asked Hassan to transfer one Hassan Woqooyi to Burao as governor to fend off challengers there in the forthcoming election, while Egal appointed Abdirahman Sheikh Ali, who was a judge in the court of appeals in Burao, as president of the Supreme Court.

> *Without any advance intimation, the Presidency of the Supreme Court was taken over on May 29 by a Somali, Abdirahman Sheikh Ali, replacing an Italian expatriate…who has held the post since March 1965.… While a satisfying gesture, the appointment as Chief Justice of a relatively young man with only seven years' experience, all of them in Somalia, is not likely to lead to any early improvement in the…administration of the justice system in Somalia.* (US Department of State, June 5, 1968)

Replacing the Italian president of the Supreme Court and his seasoned Somali deputy was meant to reform the court to a regime-friendly institution.

In the ensuing scramble for parliament, the government's strategy was to nullify the registration forms of as many candidates of the opposition as possible, particularly those who had voted for Osman in the presidential election (US Department of State, January 1969). Hussen and his party did not have the resources to field candidates across the entire country, and decided to concentrate on a few locations, such as Mogadishu, Garowe, Galkayo, Bula Burde, Belet Weyn, Baidoa, Dusamareeb, and Bur Hakaba, and a few other associates ran as independents in places like Burao. Meanwhile, the government's strategy to disqualify as many of these candidates as possible at the registration stage went into high gear. What happened to Zoope, the former Interior minister, and his campaign was one of the clearest cases of political manipulation of the system. Zoope presented more than the required number of voter names and signatures to the district commissioner in Bur Hakaba, but his list was tossed out. He appealed to the Supreme Court, only to face the court's new president. The court ruled against him. Because of this, the president of the court was popularly dubbed *Bur Liqe* (Devourer of the Mountain, referring to Zoope's hometown of Bur Hakaba (Zoope, December 1999; US Department of State, July 8, 1969).

> *In a decision which may well be an unfortunate bench mark in Somali judicial history, the Supreme Court on February 23, rejected the appeals filed by the DAP, SNC, [Hizbia Dastur Mustagbal Somali], and SDU when these parties were unable to register their lists of candidates for the March election in Bur Hakaba. The Court made only one announcement, saying that the Bur Hakaba appeals, as well as the appeals of SNC in Zeila, and appeals concerning intra-SYL disputes in Adale and Garoe, were denied on "technical ground."... The rejection of the Bur Hakaba lists, and in particular the DAP list of...Zoope...is the most significant, and from all indications, a blatant injustice which the [government of the Somali Republic] may live to regret. It is likely that President Sharmarke himself is the principal villain in this piece in that he apparently gave instructions to one and all concerned that the DAP list was to be blocked.* (US Department of State, February 26, 1969)

In the meantime, Hussen was busy trying to file the party's lists in Garowe, Galkayo, and Mogadishu. He went to register the party in two other locations. The 1969 election was the toughest for the opposition in the country's short history, and the machinery of the state was fully deployed to return the ruling regime to power. In contrast, Hussen and his party ran a shoestring operation. In addition to occasionally sending thugs to harass or intimidate Hussen, the regime turned its attention to the selection of the civil servants who staffed the polling stations. Most of the sixty-four political parties were allowed to have their observers in the polling stations, although the civil servants managed the stations.

Election Day came on March 26, 1969. Violence marred a number of areas, although the majority of polling stations in the country did not see any trouble. It has been estimated that nearly forty people lost their lives during the voting. After polling stations closed, the ballots were to be counted in the presence of all observers. In Garowe, the DAP representative was taken away by the police and jailed, and ballots were counted without any representative from DAP. The regional judge confirmed that the DAP won, but the central election office in Mogadishu gave the two parliamentary seats to the SYL. In Galkayo, Election Day ended peacefully, but the regime was eager to steal the two seats. Earlier in the day, a special police plane had delivered Hassan's aide to oversee the count. At the end of the day, all boxes containing ballots were taken to the district headquarters. The administrator claimed it was too late in the day to count the votes, and ordered that the ballot boxes be locked in storage until the morning. When the public became aware of this decision, a large contingent of Hussen's followers came to the headquarters and told the authorities that they would keep watch during the night. When the counting was done the following day, the DAP came first, and the SYL second. In Mogadishu, the DAP took a slim majority in the municipality.

Immediately after the tally of the election results was released, a storm of petitions flooded the Supreme Court, claiming fraud for SYL seats. Similarly, the DAP launched appeals to the court for the seats in Garowe. Unfortunately for the petitioners, the government had anticipated this and had stacked the Supreme Court. The president of the court, Bur Liqe, dismissed all the petitions, leaving the opposition without any options.

> *On June 30, the eve of Independence Day celebration, the Supreme Court quietly let it be known that it was collectively rejecting all of the thirty odd appeals filed with the Court after the Central Electoral Board certified the results of the parliamentary election on April 9.* (US Department of State, July 16, 1969)

Even before the dust settled and the new parliament was seated, nearly all the independent and non-SYL winners immediately switched allegiance and joined the ruling party. In addition, the most critical opposition party, the DAP, lost two of its new MPs to the rat race in the faint hope of gaining personal rewards from the regime. Sharmarke reappointed Egal to form a government. The size of the new government was much larger than the previous ones. Egal and his team could not bear to imagine the possibility of a significant opposition in parliament. They dispatched Jimale to persuade all SNC MPs to switch sides, hoping to convince Hussen to support the government and make unanimous and by acclamation the vote of confidence. But Hussen had strong reservations about the government's program and cabinet portfolios that had ballooned to thirty posts (US Department of State, June 4, 1969). When it came to the confidence vote, the government received overwhelming support, and Hussen was the lone opposition (Hussen 2002). But Egal's success had a vulnerable underbelly, as US diplomats recognized:

> *To stay in power, he has compromised himself by sanctioning rigged elections and imposing political controls on the Supreme Court, Police, and press. While these measures may have tightened the Prime Minister's control over inert bureaucracy, they also have made enemies. Egal must now tackle an imposing backlog of political and economic matters swept aside during the campaign and its aftermath. There is not, according to the local IMF [International Monetary Fund] representative, "a single financial law in the Somali Republic that has not been flagrantly disregarded in the last six months."* (US Department of State, July 8, 1969)

Hussen's strategy, as the lone opposition, was to focus on keeping the public's attention on the ways the regime was trying to turn the country into a single-party dictatorship (US Department of State, May 7, 1969).[53] The Supreme Court was already compromised, and the police had been brought under the regime's control. Now the regime could focus its energy on rearranging parliament to its liking (US Department of State, July 8, 1969).[54] Sharmarke, Egal, and Hassan knew that they could not buy all MPs all the time, and that enough disgruntled MPs could derail their well-laid plans, so they endeavored to change the constitution to turn parliament into a pliant institution. The government began a peculiar engagement in which it asked parliamentarians to consider changing article 58 of the Constitution, which gave MPs immunity from prosecution (Somali Republic 1961, pp. 18–19).

The leadership wanted to limit this immunity to actions performed only on the premises of the parliament. It sought to bribe enough MPs to agree to this proposition so the necessary two-thirds votes could be garnered to effect the change to the Constitution. Hussen focused his criticism on this agenda, and used his party and parliament platform to alert MPs and the population about what was at stake. He informed those in parliament who would listen to him that the regime's strategy with this constitutional change would be political suicide for MPs because they would not be safe from government arrest and intimidation outside the parliament building.

Hussen underscored the gradual and real erosion of civil service autonomy, citing civil servants who had been dumped by the regime without receiving due process from the Public Service Commission. Despite the huge majority the government had in parliament, it appeared that it was worried about Hussen's influence, and monitored his house and his movements, as one senior policeman reported to the former prime minister (Hussen, May 2002).

By mid-autumn, the regime appeared confident that it had consolidated its power, and was least worried about the military. Soon after the election, Egal toured military facilities in and around Mogadishu, and rumors began to fly that the three senior leaders of government were planning to change some of the most senior military leaders. It is in this context that there were discussions among the leaders of sending General Mohamed Siyad Barre to the Soviet Union for training (Abiib, October 1996).[55]

Meanwhile, President Sharmarke embarked on a journey to visit areas of political tension in the country. On a fateful afternoon in the town of Las Anood, one of the president's police bodyguards fatally shot him in cold blood, and the policeman was taken to Mogadishu General Prison.[56] The president of parliament immediately became the acting president in the absence of Prime Minister Egal, who cut short a visit to the United States to return to take charge of the affairs of the state. Once the president was laid to rest, Egal and Hassan took the reins of government and started planning for the election of a new president. They decided someone from Sharmarke's extended family ought to replace him, and began discussions with Haji Musa Boqor. Egal and Hassan insisted on this candidate, but did not have the votes needed to win. They resorted to their standard campaign tool kit of buying votes.

As the appointed day neared for parliament to elect the president of the republic, Egal and Hassan divided between themselves 1.5 million shillings they had collected from the Somali Central Bank. Egal took 1 million, and Hassan, 500,000 shillings. They invited individual MPs to come to their homes and collect their loot. As the MPs came in droves, Hussen and a companion watched the sordid affair from inside a private car parked across the road from Egal's

Lido beach house. After seeing enough of this business, Hussen and his friend went their separate ways to get some sleep.

Just a few hours before morning prayers, the military, led by General Barre, took control of the country. The coup makers annulled the Constitution and banned political parties. They declared that their most important mission was to bring corrupt and tribal politics to an end and rebuild the political and economic fabric of the country. For this, they received rousing support from the population.

Conclusion

Framing an issue is the first step in defining social and political problems. The school of thought in Somali studies that the anthropologist I.M. Lewis established, considers genealogical affiliation as the key framework for understanding political dynamics in the country. This chapter provides clear historical evidence that political struggles among the Somali elite in the democratic era were driven not by genealogical identities, but by competing political interests.[57] Members of the political elite were divided into two main camps: those who saw public power and the state as a vehicle for private gain, and those who considered the role of the state as an instrument to advance the national interest.[58] These groups dominated political affairs of the country during the period covered by this chapter.

Three historical events narrated in the chapter provide the evidence that genealogy did not dictate the actions of the political class. First, the discord among the different camps during the constitutional plebiscite was clearly not based on genealogy. Instead, two key leaders who were frustrated by their inability to get top ministerial posts for themselves or their partners used the referendum to get even with the president and his team. Jimale and Egal used their influence to mobilize their followers to vote against the Constitution. Jimale opposed the president, even though they hailed from the same genealogical group and both were elected to parliament from the same region of Hiran. Egal joined forces with Jimale not because they were from the same kin group, but because Jimale harbored the same political ambition of bringing down the government.

Second, the strong opposition that attempted to derail President Osman and Prime Minister Hussen's reform agenda in 1964, did not have a common tribal pedigree. Some of the diehard opposition members hailed from Hussen's genealogical group, and others came from the far corners of the country. What they all had in common was fear that the Hussen-led government would adhere to its civic principles and anticorruption agenda. The same was true for those in parliament who opposed the civil service reform.

Finally, the presidential election of 1967 provided the clearest evidence that lust for power and opportunism, and not cultural identity, created the gulf between the two camps. If genealogical identity had been the signifier of the majority of Sharmarke's supporters, then it is hard to explain why most MPs who supported him hailed from other genealogical groups. It was an open secret that Sharmarke's team distributed substantial amounts of money to a majority of MPs, and promised others senior positions in government if they elected him. The advocates of the tribal thesis have been unable to unearth meaningful evidence to sustain their overall argument. Corrupt money and lust for power trumped cultural affinity in politics during the democratic era.

These three historical instances confirm that ethnic political identity was not the decisive factor that determined political behavior and strategy of actors. Instead, it was lust for power and the resources that came with it that shaped the strategies and decisions of sectarian elements of the political elite during the democratic era. Given the fragility of the elite's economic base, many saw the state as a source of power and wealth. Those stuck in this mindset used whatever wedge that would enable them to mobilize supporters. That they sometimes appealed to genealogical ties to win votes did not necessarily mean that genealogy defined the population's political identity any more so than cash payments or promises of jobs.

Bibliography

Abib, Hashi. Interview, Ottawa, October 1996.

Abshir, Mohamed. Interview, Minneapolis, September 2005.

----------------------. Interview, Minneapolis, September 14, 2005.

Arraleh. Ali S. Interview, Nairobi, March 2003.

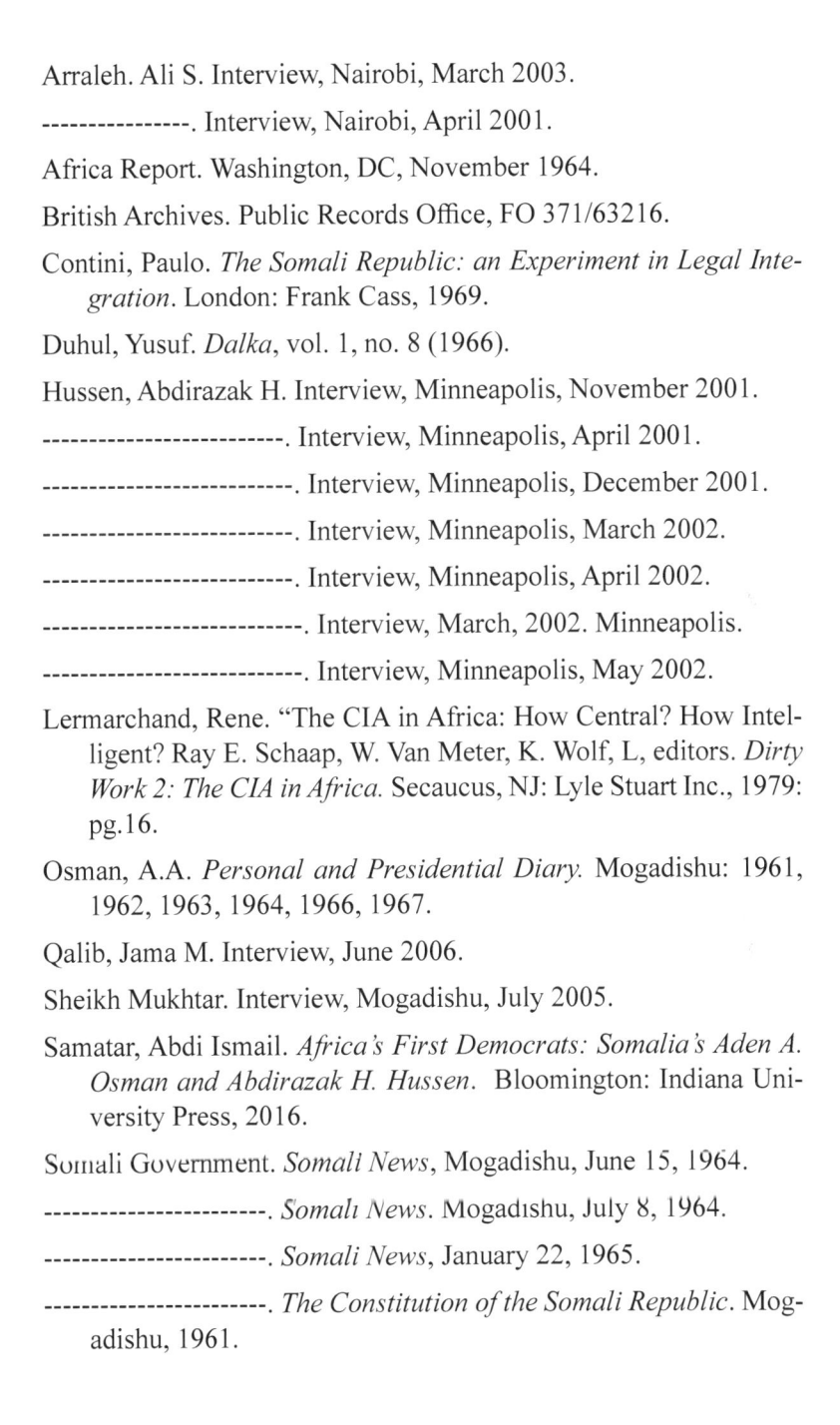

----------------. Interview, Nairobi, April 2001.

Africa Report. Washington, DC, November 1964.

British Archives. Public Records Office, FO 371/63216.

Contini, Paulo. *The Somali Republic: an Experiment in Legal Integration*. London: Frank Cass, 1969.

Duhul, Yusuf. *Dalka*, vol. 1, no. 8 (1966).

Hussen, Abdirazak H. Interview, Minneapolis, November 2001.

--------------------------. Interview, Minneapolis, April 2001.

---------------------------. Interview, Minneapolis, December 2001.

---------------------------. Interview, Minneapolis, March 2002.

---------------------------. Interview, Minneapolis, April 2002.

---------------------------. Interview, March, 2002. Minneapolis.

---------------------------. Interview, Minneapolis, May 2002.

Lermarchand, Rene. "The CIA in Africa: How Central? How Intelligent? Ray E. Schaap, W. Van Meter, K. Wolf, L, editors. *Dirty Work 2: The CIA in Africa*. Secaucus, NJ: Lyle Stuart Inc., 1979: pg.16.

Osman, A.A. *Personal and Presidential Diary*. Mogadishu: 1961, 1962, 1963, 1964, 1966, 1967.

Qalib, Jama M. Interview, June 2006.

Sheikh Mukhtar. Interview, Mogadishu, July 2005.

Samatar, Abdi Ismail. *Africa's First Democrats: Somalia's Aden A. Osman and Abdirazak H. Hussen*. Bloomington: Indiana University Press, 2016.

Somali Government. *Somali News*, Mogadishu, June 15, 1964.

------------------------. *Somali News*. Mogadishu, July 8, 1964.

------------------------. *Somali News*, January 22, 1965.

------------------------. *The Constitution of the Somali Republic*. Mogadishu, 1961.

United States Department of State. Foreign Service Dispatch 183, March 13, 1961.

----------. Foreign Service Dispatch 5, July 10, 1961.

----------. Foreign Service Dispatch 221, May 1, 1961.

----------. Foreign Service Dispatch, August 26, 1961.

----------. Airgram A-513, April 3, 1964.

----------. Airgram A-267, December 5, 1963.

----------. Airgram, May 21, 1964.

----------. Airgram A-365, June 9, 1964.

----------. Airgram A-198, September 28, 1964.

----------. Airgram A-198, September 28, 1964.

----------. Airgram A-365, June 9, 1964.

----------. Incoming Telegram, control no. 12455, July 14, 1964.

----------. Airgram A-112, August 19, 1964.

----------. Airgram A-427, January 30, 1965.

----------. Airgram A-32, January 31, 1965.

----------. Airgram A-439, February 6, 1965

----------. Airgram A-464, February 13, 1965.

----------. Airgram A-464, February 13, 1965.

------------------------------------. Airgram A-555, March 29, 1965.
------------------------------------. Airgram A-464, February 13, 1965.
------------------------------------. Airgram A-623, May 10, 1965.
------------------------------------..Airgram A-627, May 10, 1965.
------------------------------------. Airgram A-656, May 24, 1965.
------------------------------------. Airgram A-519, March 6, 1965.
------------------------------------. Airgram A-186, November 16, 1965.
------------------------------------. Incoming Telegram 26063, November 29, 1966.
------------------------------------. Airgram A-174, November 11, 1966.
------------------------------------. Airgram A-379, April 22, 1967.
------------------------------------. Airgram A-437, May 27, 1967.
------------------------------------. Airgram A-423, May 8, 1967.
------------------------------------. Airgram, A-267, March 4, 1968.
------------------------------------. Airgram A-423 October 23, 1968.
------------------------------------. Airgram A-117, August 13, 1969.
------------------------------------. Airgram A-339, June 5, 1968.
------------------------------------. Airgram A-27, February 12, 1969.
------------------------------------. Memorandum of Conversation with Abdulkadir Mohamed Aden "Zoope," February 21, 1969.
------------------------------------. Airgram A-55, April 9, 1969.
------------------------------------. Airgram A-177, August 13, 1969.
------------------------------------. Airgram A-396, August 28, 1968.
------------------------------------. Airgram A-420, October 23, 1968.
------------------------------------. Airgram A-11, January 15, 1969.
------------------------------------. Airgram A-339, June 5, 1968.

--. Airgram A-15, January 1969.
--. Research Memorandum, July 8, 1969.
--. Airgram A-32, February 26, 1969.
--. Airgram A-108, July 16, 1969.
--. Airgram A-85, June 4, 1969.
--. Research Memorandum, July 8, 1969.
--. Research Memorandum, RAF, July 8, 1969
--. Airgram A-72, May 7, 1969.
--. Research Memorandum, July 8, 1969.
Abdulkdir M. Interview, Djibouti, December 1999.

Endnotes

1 The material for this chapter is culled from Chapters 4 and 5 in my book titled *Africa's First Democrats*. Permission for republishing is given by Indiana University Press.

2 The British administration was not supportive of the Club's anti-tribal stance, as indicated by the following report by a senior officer: "It is noted that the promise not to reveal their tribes is causing a certain amount of worry to the Civil Affairs Officers in their capacity as Judicial Officers, as it is necessary in Court cases to record the tribe of the accused and of the witness. When asked for their tribes, members of the S.Y.C. now state simply that they are Somalis" (Public Records Office, FO 371/63216).

3 I am grateful to Said Shire for providing the original source. Referendum Costituzionle, 1961

4 It was in this referendum that the Somali people endorsed the Union Act embedded in the Constitution, which read, "The state of Somaliland and the state of Somalia do hereby unite and shall *forever* remain

united in a new, independent, democratic, unitary republic, the name of which shall be the Somali Republic." (My italics)

5   Osman's non-vindictiveness in political matters is best captured by remarks he made to his opponent, Jimale, a few days before the presidential election Osman.

6   This indicates that Osman's group thought they had more votes than actually transpired. Apparently, some deputies who promised to support Osman had no intention of doing so. This would be a feature of Somali parliamentary politics for decades to come.

7   Osman revealed his inner strength by telling the then minister of Interior, on May 9, 1961, several weeks before the election, that trust is key to success in life: "We spoke at length about the subjects of trust and mistrust. I let him read quotations from a book where it is said that in life, those who are equipped with trust have more chances of success than those who do not have trust. In these excerpts, Gandhi and his philosophy of Satyagraha are quoted. A believer in Satyagraha does not fear to trust his adversary, even if he cheated him 20 times. Being the essence of this faith is an unwavering trust in the human nature...I copied this quotation with intent to send them also to Sheikh Ali Jumale, but then I only showed him and let him read." (Diary, May 9, 1961)

8   Many local observers point out the incongruence between the popular endorsement of the Constitution and the parliamentary vote over the presidency as evidence that the public and the politicians did not share the same ethos.

9   Sheikh Mukhtar was a key member of parliament from the Upper Juba region, and would later became president of parliament.

10 This is an important fact for those concerned with Somali political history, since Qalib was a Northerner who was in a position to influence the process. He did not suggest his distant relative, Egal, as a possible MP.

11 Osman's diary, July 8, 1961.

12 Osman was so astounded by the irresponsibility of so many politicians that he compared the enterprise to a brothel, as everything was for sale and nothing was sacrosanct. He cherished the words of wisdom cabled a few days earlier by Naser Nahar, from Hargeisa: "Honesty is the best policy" (Osman's diary, July 13, 1961). Osman's political character was described in the following manner: "He is unique in

Somali politics as being the only man who has been able to a certain extent to rise above politics and maintain the respect of the people as a whole as the 'elder statesman' of the Somali Republic. Although by no means sacrosanct, he has managed to escape most of the criticism leveled against the Government by the opposition, and thus claim to be a non-partisan figure." (United States Department of State, May 1, 1961)

13 The president recorded his misgivings about the new cabinet in his diary: "Sharmarke let me swallow bitter pills with the increase of the ministries and with the inclusion in the government of certain individuals…while he left out valid deputies. I do not know for fear of what! I am sorry this thing is not a credit for him and it is disappointing."

14 The president's frustration with the opportunistic game of a significant number of MPs is best illustrated in an exchange he had with one of the key opposition leaders, Mohamed Ibrahim Egal. Egal asked the president to "avoid rushing through the premiership and the ministers. I told him not to worry, because I will avoid the occurrence of changes in the composition of the government. At worst, I will convene all 120 deputies in one room and ask them to name one candidate to the premiership without letting them get out until we accomplish our task and will them to dismantle the blocs." Osman's diary, August 15, 1961.

15 Ambassador Lynch noted that the prime minister's statement confirmed that he was "bowing to deputies who charged him with appointing Ministers and Undersecretaries for political reasons…"

16 The US Embassy notes that such a sizable majority was the product of most MPs fearing that if they did not support the government, the president might dissolve parliament (Ibid). There is no evidence in the president's diary to substantiate this claim.

17 The Somali police force, led by the able General Mohamed Abshir Muse, was regarded as efficient, non-partisan, and highly professional.

18 Since the opposition parties did not contest in these district, SYL won all the seats without voting taking place.

19 Osman suggested that if there was going to be any redistribution of parliamentary seats, then some should go to the North.

20 While the president was critical of the shortcomings of the govern-

ment and parliament, he also felt deeply proud of the system of governance in the country. Here is how he compared Somalia to other East African states: "Our Somalia seems to be an oasis of peace and rock steady stability. We owe this to the democratic regime, and I'd say, to the tribal equilibrium that does not allow one single ethnic group to dominate the country" (Osman's diary, January 21, 1964). Regarding the rebellions in Kenya, Uganda, and Tanzania, he writes that "these grave happenings in all four of the East African territories… makes the maturity of Somalis and the goodness of the parliamentary system, with all its weaknesses, shine" (Osman's diary, January 25, 1964).

21 It is quite clear from the consultation process that the president engaged in, that his only preoccupation about the appointment was to get the most competent and honest person for the job and the country. It was apparent to him that he would alienate many parliamentarians who were more interested in business as usual.

22 "[The] first cabinet caused consternation among the old guard, and excitement among young intellectuals. By Somali standards, it is highly unorthodox because the members were chosen without giving due weight to tribal and geographic balance. There was an effort to stress ability and education as criteria for holding office. Five members were from the north as against two northerners in the outgoing Sharmarke cabinet." (Africa Report, November 1964, p. 6)

23 The president was mindful of the purpose of these pressures, but he remained resolute. He acknowledged in his diary that many did not appreciate his stance: "It is strange that [few people know me well]… after so many years in public life, no body, I say no body, as far as it seems, believes that I would have the courage to ignore the decision of the majority party, leaving Sharmarke on the sidelines and entrusting Hussen to form a new government. Truly, I cannot understand what the people believed was being risked, acting according to the beliefs of my conscience, and why one does not remember that Sharmarke himself was chosen even though the majority of the deputies of the time were in favor…of Abdullahi Issa. (Osman, June 21, 1964)

24 Hussen confirmed the quote by the US Embassy (Hussen, April 2001). Also here is how the American Embassy reported the event: "Voting close throughout tense hour roll-call, enlivened by 15-minute uproar over whether Ali Mohamed Hirave's yes-no vote was yes or no. Hussen calmed hubbub by recommending "no" vote be allowed a minister who he said was conditioned by being yes man in previous

government."

25 According to the American Embassy, "only one non-SYL deputy broke party discipline, namely SNC, and voted for the government. Others in this party who did not support the party line abstained. Among these was Abdullahi Jirreh Duale, who personally informed the Embassy that he considered SNC's decision to vote against Hussen a mistake." (US Department of State, July 14, 1964)

26 The president noted in his diary "... I could have sent back the government to the parliament for a revote after the preparations of a 'motivated motion' as written in article 82, no. 2 of the Constitution that says, 'The National Assembly shows its confidence or no confidence by means of a motivated motion and approves by a simple majority with a clear vote.' But I thought that this motion wouldn't have changed anything. (Osman's diary, July 14, 1964)

27 On August 22, Osman was visited by a prominent Northern businessman who apparently supported his principled political stance. "The second visitor…was Haji Jirde Hussen—rich businessman and someone I have known since a long time ago (1943), from the time I did business from Belet Weyn to the North—he wanted to come to congratulate me on my courageous decision and my firm hand in the last political elections to today. I thanked him and told him that my behavior is not dictated for effect. I did not have to wrestle with my conscience and therefore I was not worn out." (Osman's diary, August 22, 1964)

28 Here is how Osman expressed his sentiments " …Ahmed Sh. Mohamed Absiyeh…told me about the usual unhappy representatives who are not sure about their future and fearing that I could dissolve the parliament and publicly announce new elections, once we are passed the period of one year from the proclamation of the results of the last election, so they are trying to amend Article 53 of the Constitution, in which the President cannot dissolve the Assembly during the first two years of the elections and during the last two years of the mandate of the same President of the Republic. These same representatives, besides, have already started to gather signatures from them members of the Assembly to present their motion… In the first case, depending on the unselfish worries of certain unworthy so-called representatives of the people, they should know that it is not a joke to dissolve the parliament, especially when in sixty days of dissolving it, new elections will have to be announced, and I truly do not know why I have to make those men suffer, and what or whose fault it is if they

know what they have done of fear of being 'fired'." (Osman, August 27, 1964)

29 A number of the diehards, such as Sharmarke, left the country a few days earlier, possibly recognizing that they could not stop the momentum in favor of Hussen.

30 Sharmarke, the former premier, did not come out openly to oppose the new regime, and he went on a trip to Europe during the final vote, but he worked behind the scenes to convey his displeasure. Yusuf Egal, Sharmarke's ally, invited the two men to dinner to help patch their friendship. Hussen offered Sharmarke, once again, whatever cabinet post he desired. But the former PM was in no mood for niceties. Instead, he expressed his anger over some of the contents of Hussen's first public speech on Radio Mogadishu, in which he associated, Sharmarke claimed, the former regime with corrupt and clannish ways. Hussen contested this and asserted that his written and oral speech specifically promised to attempt to curb corruption. A second meeting was arranged between the two, but made no progress in bridging the gulf. From then on, Sharmarke was firmly in the opposition. He rarely attended parliamentary sessions. He spent his days on Lido Beach, reading Italian novels and making rare appearances in parliament to cast a crucial vote. At Lido, he was visited by disgruntled MPs. (Hussen 2001)

31 To insure that his reform was something new, and that the democratic process would be respected, the new government changed the rules of the national radio to allow opposition parties to use the service. Here is how the American Embassy reported the new milestone: "The new policy of allowing anti-government statements to be published in the government press and broadcast over government radio was initiated by the Prime Minister and his Minister of Information Bowkah. Heretofore, political developments in the capital were largely obfuscated and often well garbled by the time they reached the countryside via the grapevine. Within the capital, uncertainty and the necessity to pass the news by word of mouth contributed to the incessant chatter in the coffee houses. All Embassy sources have been pleasantly shocked by this new departure in the treatment of domestic political news which reached the whole country simultaneously and viva voce. The refreshing frankness is apparent from the texts of all the statements and interviews which are enclosed as published in the August 14 Somali News." (US Department of State. August 19, 1964)

32 According to the article, "A Minister or Under-Secretary, during his

period in office, may not exercise any other public functions, except the electoral vote and the functions of deputy in the National Assembly, nor may he engage in professional, commercial, industrial, or financial activities. He may not directly or indirectly lease or acquire property belonging to the State or to public bodies except for premises to be used as his personal residence. He may not, furthermore, alienate or lease his own property to the State or to public bodies, or participate in a personal capacity in State enterprises or in enterprises controlled by the State, Somali Republic. (*The Constitution of the Somali Republic*, p. 26, Somali News, Mogadishu, July 8, 1964).

33 Here is how the American Embassy summed up Hussen's leadership: "The reform does not appear to have favored or spared any tribal segment of the population. The North may have gained a few positions owing to the better qualifications of its men. The army and other state organs may be next in line for reform. Hussen has demonstrated a high order of leadership in his effort to create a strong administrative framework for Somalia, and he has a good chance to succeed in fending off eventual opposition moves in the Assembly." (US Department of State, Airgram A-464, February 13, 1965)

34 There is plenty of evidence of a substantial number of Somali Government officials, MPs, senior party figures, and senior civil servants reporting to the US Embassy. For Instance, senior officers from the Foreign Ministry reported to the Embassy (American Embassy Transmittal Slip to the State Department, August 15, 1964). Here, a young officer briefs Embassy staff about dealings in the parliament regarding the vote of confidence. The young Somali man "apologized for not having visited me at home or especially in the Embassy for some time since, as he said, government employees are on notice not to call on foreign embassies unless it is strictly on business and that his 'sensitive work' has made him especially careful..." More seriously, and according to an American Embassy report "Acting Police Commandant Korshel informed the Embassy that he believed Ethiopian attempt to recover arms distributed by ex-Prime Minister Sharmarke government to nomads was one of the root cause of clashes in Ogaden, which were not concentrated in the border zones...." (US Department of State, March 29, 1965)

35 Unfortunately, the president's diary for 1965 is missing.

36 President Osman was deeply concerned about the health impact of the long hours Hussen worked: "Abdirazak Haji Hussen—Prime Minister—is in bed again with the flu. This evening, around after 9:00

p.m., I went to visit him at home, seeing that on the phone they did not say that he could get out. This man asks of his body more than it can give…" (Osman's diary, February 2, 1966)

37 There was no let on the fight, and numerous cases were brought to court in 1965. In one case, again in Hargeisa, the government lost its witness, who fled to Ethiopia. Here is how the case was reported: "Abdulkadir Abdi Dualeh, Assistant District Commissioner at Gebile in 1964, teacher at the Hargeisa Trades School, and sometime businessman, who was potential a key witness in the Government's case against former Hargeisa Governor Said Abdillahi Warsama, Deputy Governor Abdi Osman Nur, and several senior officials for alleged embezzlement of So.Shs. 1.5 million, escaped to Ethiopia November 15, 1965. Abdulkadir was arrested two months ago, charged with the maladministration of So.Shs. 100,000 relief funds provided by the Government for the needy after the 1964 Somali-Ethiopian border clash and released on So.Shs. 100,000 bail which was provided by leading businessmen Ahmed Haji Abdillahi 'Hashish' and Ali Warsama Wais, agent for Paul Reis in Hargeisa. Abdulkadir's hearing was scheduled for Monday November 15. He requested in court that day that he be permitted to retain an attorney. The Lower Court Somali Judge at Hargeisa commented that Abdullahi had had two months to retain legal counsel, but agreed to postpone the hearing until next day, November 16. Abdulkadir failed to appear in court November 16 and his car was found by police later in the day at Salaleh, a village due south of Hargeisa near the Ethiopian border…. Honest local administration in Somalia will lose if these senior officials from Hargeisa are not tried and convicted." (US Department of State, November 16, 1965)

38 On the following day, President Osman wrote the following about his PM: "Abdirazak H. Hussen is not so generous in pardoning those that he believes have done something wrong or have been an enemy…." (Osman, January 2, 1966). "Yesterday, I had asked him for the hundredth time to let it be—taking back the veto—about the question of the 'Rothman' cigarettes that he had blocked the introduction of in Somalia because he believes they are South African, but now seems to have blocked them only because of Haji Musa Boqor's interests. And so Hussen does not want to hear about it…" (Osman's diary, January 3, 1966)

39 According to the exchange rate of the time, 100,000 Shilling were equivalent to about $15,000.

40 In this conversation, Egal told the American of his plans as PM: "Egal commented that he established a campaign office within the past week, with Nicolino Mohamed in charge. Abdirashid Ali Sharmarke, Yassin Nur Hassan, and he checked in once a day and compared notes on where they stood. If elections were held today (April 16) Sharmarke would receive 80 votes.... In response to my query, Egal said Yasin Nur Hassan would be Minister of Interior, Abdullahi Issa, Minister of defense, and between him [and Sharmarke] would retain Foreign Affairs....Egal said...some years ago he had visited Addis Ababa, though this was not known to many of his closest friends, and also had established a sound friendship with the former IEG Ambassador in Somalia. His hope for a positive settlement of the Ogden problem would be the creation of a self-governing area in the Ogaden which would report to and be under the authority of IFG Ministry of Interior. He would also seek a complete elimination of customs duties, visa requirements, and other obstacles to intimate relations with Ethiopia. He hoped Somali students could attend Ethiopian schools, Somalia and Ethiopia would work together on economic development projects, and there would be free unhindered travel and communication between the two countries. Egal believed his contacts in Ethiopia are good enough that the IEG and HIM would work with him to settle the Ogaden problem. "We wonder if Egal's visit to Ethiopia coincides with the report given to President Osman stating that a check was given to Egal by Ethiopia? In addition, the appointment of Nicolino confirms that the Sharmarke–Egal team had successfully recruited most of those civilian servants dismissed through Hussen's reform program as well as protecting those ministers dismissed for corruption." Unfortunately, Egal was oblivious to the fact that Ethiopia was providing little, if any, education for Somali-Ethiopians.

41 At this stage, Osman appears to have assumed that he would be nominated and that he would run. He notes in the diary, as the SYL Congress entered its last day: "Once I am accepted to compete, I like to 'not bite the dust,' but I certainly won't be desperate, as I believe my adversary will be if he loses the race!" (Osman's dairy, May 31, 1967)

42 The two candidates were separately interviewed by *La Tribune*.

43 Zoope, the Minister of Interior, was a key player in maintaining some of the MPs, and on one occasion, he made the mistake of offering money to one of Osman's loyal supporter. Osman found out about this after the election: "The other day, Zoope had told me that Abdi Bille had refused to take 10 or 15 thousand Shillings that he wanted

to give him for the election! They should raise a monument to Abdi Bille!" (Osman's dairy, June 20, 1967)

44   Osman remembered Sharmarke's unbecoming behavior after he was not reappointed as PM in 1964, when the latter attempted to disrupt the transition, and automatically became an opposition member.

45   Hussen knew about a check that was cashed in Egal's name in Aden (South Yemen) in 1963, which General Daud reported. In addition, it was already known that Egal took over 300,000 shillings from the Central Bank shortly after he became PM. Ali Said Arraleh, the long serving Director General, told me that one of Egal's weaknesses was his use of public money as private cash. (Arraleh, Nairobi, 2001)

46   This information has been confirmed by Ali Said Arraleh. (Interview, Nairobi, 2003)

47   They rented the entire building, which enabled them to lease parts of it to businesses, and the revenue from this allowed them to pay the rent for the building and a fraction of the running costs of the party.

48   "Only eight of the 101 SYL deputies are known to have resigned to join forces in the DAP…" (US Department of State, Airgram A-423, October 23, 1968.)

49   Another part of the regime's strategy meant bringing the national police under the immediate and direct authority of the Minister of Interior: "The culmination of several actions limiting the autonomy of the police commandant included the hurried enactment by the GSR of a decree law on February 8, effectively transferring from the Commandant to the Minister of Interior the power to assign, transfer, and presumably promote all lower official." (US Department of State, Airgram *A-27*, February 12, 1969)

50   Jama Mohamed Qalib, June 2006. Qalib was the commander of the police in Hargeisa.

51   Abdulkadir Mohamed Aden, Zoope told the American Embassy that he knew of no attempt by Abshir or the police intervening to support a partisan political project (US Department of State, Memorandum of Conversation with Abdulkadir Mohamed Aden "Zoope," Mogadishu, February 21, 1969). The Governor was the leading authority in the region, and therefore represented the central government in directing government affairs in his areas.

52   The second report refers to Sharmarke loading the civil service with his friends and relatives.

53 By May 1969, a little over a month after the election, SYL commanded 121 out of the 124 seats in parliament. (ibid)

54 Here is the way in which an analyst of the US Department of State described the post-election, and how the regime was deeply damaged by corruption: "To stay in power, [Egal] has compromised himself by sanctioning rigged elections and imposing political controls on the Supreme Court, police, and press.... If he persists in forging a single party state— only one deputy is now outside the majority Somali Youth League (SYL)—the opposition, up-to-now accommodated within the system, could also turn away from democratic means." (ibid)

55 Hashi Abib was the Cabinet Secretary during Egal's tenure and retained that post for a period after the military coup.

56 The policeman was tortured by the authorities to find out who else was behind the assassination. But he remained adamant that he acted alone as a result of the communities' grievances regarding the "stealing of a parliamentary seat by SYL in the northeast of the country." The killer was brought to the National Security Court after the military coup, and he exposed his genitals to court to show the severity of his torture. He remained adamant that he acted alone and was sentenced to death.

57 There was an interesting example in the more recent history of politics in Somali region called Puntland. Despite the fact that most uninformed observers consider tribalism to be the grammar of Somali politics, Dr. Ali Issa, was the one candidate for the regional presidency who refused to buy MPs votes. Some thought that he assumed that at least his genealogical relatives in the regional parliament will vote for him. Not shockingly, all the thirteen members of his genealogical group voted for the candidates who paid them cash for their votes.

58 A handful number of the political elite were marooned in tribalistic ideology and sided with either of the first two camps, depending on how they interpreted the issue at hand.

3
Reframing Islam's Role in Somali Life

Nearly four decades ago, in the prophetic study, *Covering Islam*, the late Edward Said predicted the coming wars in the Islamic world:

> *If the history of knowledge about Islam in the West has been too closely tied to conquest and domination, the time has come for these ties to be severed completely.... For otherwise, we will not only face protracted tension and perhaps even war, but we will offer the Muslim world, its various societies and states, the prospect of many wars, unimaginable suffering, and disastrous upheavals, not the least of which would be the victory of an "Islam" fully ready to play the role prepared for it by reaction, orthodoxy, and desperation.* (Said 1981, p. 173)

The cataclysmic wars in Afghanistan, Somalia, Iraq, Syria, Libya, Sudan, and Yemen over the last two or three decades have consumed and displaced millions of lives and have no end in sight. Said's incredible ability to foretell that future was due to his discernment into the relationship between power and knowledge production. More recently, scholarship on the subject has reconfirmed Said's insights. Mahmood Mamdani's (2004) book *Good Muslim, Bad Muslim,* demonstrates how the wishes of the United States to dominate the Muslim world enabled certain kinds of scholars to produce "knowledge" about Islam that reinforced the colonial and postcolonial Western, and more particularly American, agenda. Mamdani's thesis is that Western scholars writing about Islam, and political actors engaged with the Muslim world, have categorized Muslims into two types. Muslims considered "good," are those who are amenable to the Western political agenda. And "bad" Muslims are those who have an independent political worldview.

Western scholars who study Muslim societies are not entirely of the same mold, as Said noted. Orthodox scholars are those affiliated with colonization and the West's desire to sustain its hegemony over postcolonial societies, and whose studies inform and are informed by Western strategic interests. These scholars occupy positions of prominence in the academy and think tanks because of their affinity with Western governments and institutions (Said 1981, p. 157). In contrast, antithetical scholars, though diverse in their approaches, produce knowledge about Islam in opposition to the orthodox scholars and their powerful backers.

Following Said's and Mamdani's theses, I posit that most Western scholars of Somali society, and particularly of Islam in Somalia, are of the orthodox type (e.g., Lewis 1994, Bradbury 2008, Harper 2011, 2019). A good example of this approach is a former US diplomat who asserted the following to explain the role of Islam in East Africa:

> *For historical and contemporary reasons, Africa is fertile soil for fringe elements of Islam to take hold.... Africa is an area of the world where **American interests** are most vulnerable and where there is one of the best opportunities to defend and propagate the values that are the underpinnings for democracy and the free market. The threat to U.S. interests in Africa is real.* (Stith 2010, pp. 57, 59. Bold is mine)

What is clear from the former diplomat's essay is that "American interests" are singularly central to defining the relationship between Africa and Islam. This argument provides little possibility to imagine the plausibility of mutual and equal interest between the United States and Muslim Africa. He presumes that the US agenda was worthy of following by others, even though the United States has been on the wrong side of history over Africa and the Islamic world for a very long time. The diplomat can be forgiven for his intellectual blinders, attributable to his training as a former employee of the Department of State. However, he is not alone in this worldview. In a similar fashion, a US academic uses 9/11 as the point of departure to frame his analysis of political Islam in Somalia:

> *In the aftermath of the **September 11 terrorist attacks** in New York and Washington, DC, Islamic politics and movements around the world are coming under greater scrutiny than ever. The Horn of Africa is of particular importance on this score as a region where **radical Islamist** movements have been increasingly active over the past decade. While the endemic conflicts on the*

Horn are attributable to a wide range of causes, **radical Islamic movements are intimately involved in some of the region's turmoil.** (Menkhaus 2002, p. 1. Bold is mine)

This analytic optic is driven by the concerns of the United States. For Menkhaus (2002), Le Sage (2001), and like-minded analysts, Islam is seen in terms of conflicts, terrorists, and opportunists. Rarely do these authors examine Islam and its role from the vantage point of Somalis or Africans. These writers miss the multiple roles Islam played, and plays, in shaping Muslim societies in different historical, social, and political circumstances. Further, such an instrumentalist approach is often blind to Muslim values and interests, and to the complex relationship between this faith and civic and political life in countries like Somalia (Ibrahim 2017).

This chapter takes a different view and asserts that a better understanding of the roles of Islam can be achieved through contextual geographic and political analysis (Ahmed 2011, Mustapha 2018, Abdullahi 2015, Soguk, 2011).

We can identify five broad periods in Somalia's recent history: the late precolonial period (late nineteenth century), the colonial period (late nineteenth century to mid-twentieth century), independence and a short-lived democratic decade (1960–1969), the long military dictatorship (1969–1991), and the equally long era of state collapse (1991–present). Two key theoretical axioms culled from the historical and contextual experiences of Somalis guide this discussion of Islam and Somali society. First, I posit that Islam played specific roles when peace and just authority prevailed in the nation. Second, Islam's role in Somali affairs went through a significant transformation when the nation was under political duress and when invaded from outside. The importance of context in understanding Islam's role in society is based on Islam being both an individual concern regarding the relationship between the believer and the creator, and a collective enterprise and institution. These two sides of the faith are deeply intertwined, and an observer cannot have a sound appreciation of one facet without paying attention to the other, as well as the context.

I contend that those Western analysts of political Islam and the political agenda that they reflect fail to comprehend the intertwined political and religious dynamics of Somali society and Somali concerns and motivations. This chapter consists of five sections. The first section schematically sketches the role Islam and the ulema played in the precolonial land of the Somalis. Second, part two describes how, after colonial forces invaded and occupied Somali territory, Islam became a major resource for Somali resistance to imperial domination, particularly in the British, Ethiopian, and Italian colonies. The third contends that, after British and Italian Somalilands became independent and formed the unitary Somali Republic, Islam played a unifying, if secondary, role in the political life of the nation during the democratic era. Part four demonstrates that the long and brutal military regime not only suppressed all political dissent, but also attempted to tame the ulema to serve as its mouthpiece. Some of the ulema were concerned about the authoritarian nature of military rule and the direction the country was heading. A few openly challenged the regime, others went underground and quietly resisted the tyranny, and others became employees and spokespersons of the regime. The fifth section discusses how the role of Islam changed when the state was destroyed by the warring sectarian militias. Muslim activists championed one of two political courses of action: segments of the Islamic community supported the indigent population caught in the humanitarian maelstrom through charity work, and a second group invested energy and resources in restoring political order by leading the resistance against warlords and terrorist warriors. Local, regional, and international actors significantly influenced both strategies. The chapter concludes with scenarios that are at odds with current dominant studies and political agendas.

Islam in Precolonial Somalia

This view of secular state neither depoliticizes Islam nor relegates it to the private domain. My proposal is opposed to domineering visions of a universal history and future in which the "enlightened West" is leading all humanity to the secularization of the world, in which the secularity of the state is the logical outcome. In the conception of secularism I am proposing, the influence of religion in the public domain is open to negotiation and contingent upon the free exercise of the human agency of all citizens, believers and unbelievers alike. (An-Naim 2008, p. 268)

For the most part, precolonial Somali society lacked an overarching modern state, and nearly all communities had an informal and localized political order dominated by male elders (Samatar 1989, 1994). The communal-based political system complemented the decentralized subsistence economy in which households controlled the means of existence. Pastoralists owned their livestock and had unimpeded access to wells and grazing resources. Where there was a need to constrain access to common property resources, the council of elders acted as the authority to do so, even without a physical force to ensure compliance. Instead, they brought their moral authority to bear on those few who contravened the council's decision. Individuals and households rarely breached the elders' diktats because, beyond the moral imperative, all recognized that their survival significantly depended on communal collaboration. Similarly, subsistence farmers owned the land they farmed, herded smaller flocks whose numbers were proportionate to the land's resources, and had equal access to communal grazing lands and water resources.

Another major feature of Somali life in precolonial times was the dominant role Islam played in the life of the population (Trimingham 1971). Nearly the entire population was Muslim, and men of the cloth were widely respected. Learned men of Islam were few, meaning that the majority of the population relied on an informal, rather than educated, understanding of the faith. Despite this, Somalis were firm believers. Somali clergy were divided into two groups depending on the depth of their knowledge of Islam and the reach of their geographic influence. Those who had some knowledge of the faith were called wadaads, and the more learned men held the more prestigious title of sheikh. Most settlements had a wadaad in their midst who was an instructor in the local Quranic madrassa, and who ministered to their communities during marriages, births and deaths, and at the annual religious festivities, such as the Mowliid (birth of the Prophet). Sheikhs were fewer in number, covered larger territories, and had followers from diverse communities. They trained the wadaads.

The ulema had several functions in precolonial Somali society. They were the repository of Islamic knowledge in the land, given the dearth of major centers of Islamic learning, other than the old cosmopolitan city of Harar. They taught Somali children to recite the Quran, and gave them some rudimentary knowledge about Islam and Islamic history. The ulema were transregional in their orientation, and consequently played an important Somali-wide role as identity signifiers (Cassanelli 1982, Ibrahim 2017). These unique qualities exempted them from getting involved in local conflicts among Somalis. Instead, the ulema were one of the *birre ma gaydo* (safe from the sword) group, and as such, led conflict mediation within and among communities. Given their Somali-wide reach and their centrality to Somali identity, the ulema mobilized the population during emergencies or crises. During prolonged droughts and times of need, they rallied the population to pool resources to support the neediest. Further, when external menace appeared on the horizon, the ulema took charge in leading Somalis to confront the enemy (Samatar 1982, Cassanelli 1982).

Such transformation of the ulema from peacemaker in the community, to leaders of the resistance movement, was a characteristic feature in many Muslim societies and mimicked the actions of the Prophet of Islam. This leadership evolved from Islam and the ulema cutting across the broadest shared values among Somalis, and superseding internal social and genealogical fissures. The earliest exemplar of this in precolonial times was Imam Ahmed Guray, who led the struggle against the expansionist Christian Ethiopia and its Portuguese allies in 1529–1543. Once the external menace disappeared, religious leaders went back to their routine lives.

Somali society's decentralized economic and political structure appears to have militated against the rise of theocracy. Historical evidence abounds that the ulema acted as consultants to traditional elders as the latter oversaw the affairs of the community (Cassanelli 1982). When alien colonial authority threatened, however, the ulema used their potent persuasive powers over communities for political ends.

Islam under Colonialism

With the opening of the Suez Canal in 1869, the Red Sea became a strategic waterway for Britain, which had its most important colony in the Indian subcontinent. Soon thereafter, Britain created a major military base in Aden (Yemen) to safeguard this strategic sea route. Britain established a foothold across the Gulf of Aden, in Somali territory, to secure meat supplies for its troops (Samatar 1989), and signed a "protectorate" agreement with some Somali communities along the Gulf of Aden coast and in the interior. Two other European powers and one African imperial power lusted for their share of the spoils in the region during the last quarter of the nineteenth century. From the west came the Ethiopian Empire, the Italians took over parts of the east along the Indian Ocean, and the French created a foothold on the extreme northwestern coast of Somali territory (Osman 2001, Hess 1966). Here is how a Somali poet saw these developments at the time:

> The British, the Ethiopians, and the Italians are squabbling.
> The country is snatched and divided by whosoever is stronger.
> The country is sold piece by piece without our knowledge.
> *And for me, all this is the Teeth of the Last Days!* (Samatar 1982, p. 92)

Somalis across the land were ill-prepared for these invasions in the absence of a unified political order and military establishment. In the localized settlements in Somali territory, the group with the widest reach was the ulema, and only they had the legitimacy to mobilize a Somali-wide response. The external menace facing Somalilands forced a transformation of the peaceful social role of the ulema. Britain's initial intervention was not aggressively intrusive. Nevertheless, demands it made on the local population, particularly in the main seaport of Berbera, attracted the attention of some religious leaders. By contrast, in communities in the western reaches of Somali territory, Ethiopia's marauding militias ransacked pastoral communities. Consequently, many members of these communities joined the incipient religious and nationalist leader Sayyid Mohamed Abdulle Hassan. Others appealed to the Sayyid to provide them protections against the Ethiopians. The Sayyid responded positively to their plea:

> In the name of God the Beneficent, the Merciful. My brothers, I come to you in the name of God, who is strong, all-wise, and ever-lasting. It is He who is with me and guides my steps. Infidel invaders have come to surround us. They have come to corrupt our ancient religion, to settle our land, to seize our herd, to burn our qaryas [villages], and make our children their children. The End Times are at hand. For what could this general corruption of the earth signify other than to warn us of the approach of the Last Days? The signs are here for him who would be instructed: the Muslim chafes under the tyranny of the unbelievers. Are there any among the Ogaadeen who have not felt the scourge of the Amhaar [Amhara]? Any who have not been despoiled by their odious raids? Not too long ago you heard how the Amhara fell on the Reer Amaadin...and carried off many of their camels in loot. If you follow me, with the help of God, I will deliver you from the Amhara. (Samatar 1982, p. 112)

While the Sayyid was mobilizing his people for liberation, Ethiopia and the British protectorate administration conspired to destroy the movement. But before they could act against him, the Sayyid, by 1900, had mobilized six thousand horsemen under his command. He immediately went after a large Ethiopian force in Jigjiga that was holding many livestock looted the previous season from pastoralists in the region. The Dervishes, as the Sayyid's troops were known, reclaimed the herds but suffered many losses (Samatar 1989, p. 38). Sayyid Mohamed and his troops then turned their attention to the British protectorate after the administration declared him a rebel and dubbed him the Mad Mullah.

The Sayyid was infuriated by the demands of the colonial officers in Berbera to abstain from calling for morning prayers, and alarmed by the Christianization of orphans. Sayyid Mohamed took the lead to rid the country of the colonial scourge (Samatar 1989). British occupation of Somali territory challenged Somalis' sense of self-worth, but there was no history of large-scale Somali mobilization against external threat in recent memory. The last experience of grand mobilization was four centuries earlier. Thus, it was extraordinarily difficult to mobilize the population for resistance. Other barriers to national mobilization and unified collective action were the scarcity of material and military resources, and nonexistent communications infrastructure.

Against the odds, the young Muslim leader rose to the challenge. He gained the attention of the Somali people through his appeal to Muslim dignity and Somali unity, and with his poetic prowess (Ciise 1976, Samatar 1982, Shiekh Abdi 1991). Sayyid Mohamed hitched his message of liberation to Somalis' strong attachment to their faith. Most Somalis rallied to his side, except for a few colonial lackeys, most of whom could not much hinder him.

Somali resistance against British rule lasted for twenty-one years, from 1898 to 1920. Despite the overwhelming military superiority of Britain, the Sayyid and his Dervish (Daraawiish) troops almost succeeded in driving the British out of Somali territory in 1910 (Great Britain 1910). The tenacity and resilience of the Daraawiish prevailed until hubris overtook the leadership, leading them to fight a conventional war, which they could not win.

In the end, the British resorted to warplanes, used for the first time in the colonies, to subjugate Somali freedom fighters. The Sayyid and his movement endured for more than two decades, despite overwhelming odds against them, because of their steadfast loyalty to the faith, and the population's common destiny. Disaster followed on the few occasions when the leadership deviated from these foundational principles.

Once the major Somali resistance was contained, British and Italian authorities in their respective colonies had the challenge of manufacturing consent from the population[1] (Lonsdale and Berman 1979). A common strategy for most colonial powers was to co-opt local centers of authority into their direct or indirect colonial administration. Both colonial masters attempted to enroll Islam and the ulema as subordinates to their administration. They were able to do so in many but not all instances. Under colonial domination, the ulema were split into two camps: one group accepted their lot and became a cog in the colonial wheel as *qadis* (judges) in sharia courts, which administered civil communal affairs, and the other group resisted colonial rule, either quietly or vigorously (Samatar 1989).

Co-opting members of the ulema into colonial apparatus quelled some of the antipathy toward colonial rule because the authorities deliberately heightened tribal identity as the principal *political* signifier in the native population. However, Sayyid Mohamed's resistance to colonial rule was not in vain, because he inspired the birth of the modern Somali nationalism movement. During this period of Islamic hibernation, anticolonial movements led by the Somali Youth League (SYL) and the Somali National League (SNL) emerged.[2] To challenge the colonial strategy of turning genealogical tradition into political identity, the major liberation parties did not use Islam as a counterforce, but instead deployed Somalis' common cultural heritage, of which Islam was a central pillar, as a counterweight. None of the thirteen founding members of the SYL, and none central to the formation of the SNL, were members of the ulema (Samatar 2016). The nationalist leaders were mindful that politicizing Islam could generate conflicts among the ulema. In addition, a politicized Islam would play into the hands of the colonial authorities by creating new divisions among the population. As a result, all major political parties, particularly the leading nationalist parties (SYL and SNL), infused their programs with Islamic values while keeping their political agenda civic in orientation.[3] They tapped Islamic sentiment to rally the public for independence, but never entertained a major political role for the clergy. Clearly secular and political, instead, the parties simply assumed the importance of the faith for Somalis' common destiny and used it when appropriate. Interestingly, very few members of the ulema sought to gain political posts, such as membership in a local administration, or even on district councils during the transition from colonial rule, including during the postcolonial democracy.

In the Italian Trusteeship, the SYL came to dominate the political landscape not long after its formation in 1943. Word of the SYL spread to all Somali territories, and *Somalinimo* (patriotic Somali spirit), which had lain dormant for a quarter-century, was resuscitated. Mogadishu became the hub of the nationalist movement. Italy had lost the region during World War II, but the United Nations returned the trusteeship authority to Italy in 1950 (Samatar 2016). The reinstalled Italian authorities did not wait for Somali resistance to emerge. They took a scorched-earth approach and terrorized the SYL and its followers, often using what nationalists viewed as pro-Italian Somali elements. SYL was outgunned and out-resourced, but maintained its resolve, and the population rallied around its message of national unity, common civic belonging, and freedom (UN Trusteeship Council 1952).

Italy's agenda of turning cultural genealogy into the principal Somali political identity got its first thrashing in 1954, when the nationalist SYL won an overwhelming victory in the municipal elections for the territorial assembly (UN Trusteeship Council 1956). What gave the Somali people confidence in the SYL's inclusive political program was the way that all were treated equally. The leadership exuded trust because of their tested commitment to the national cause. A most germane example of this spirit was the refusal of key leaders of the party to take up ministerial portfolios in 1956 (Hussen 2002). Nearly all the SYL members offered posts by the prime minister designate, Abdullahi Issa, declined their appointments, citing their lack of commensurate skills or experience to tackle the demands of such onerous responsibility. Faith in the SYL's principles, and fear of public shame, were the reasons for their honorable behavior.

Democracy and the Ulema

Political divisions between civic nationalist and sectarian political actors emerged in the North and the South during the dying days of British and Italian colonialism, but the civic nationalists remained dominant for almost a decade. After independence, Somalia's new leaders anchored the liberal national constitution on Islam, as articles 30 and 50 made clear. Article 30 declared, "The personal status of Moslems is governed by the general principles of the Islamic Sharia." Article 50 stated, "The doctrine of Islam is the main source of Laws of the State" (Somali Republic 1961)

Despite these foundational anchors, the state's political character was democratic, and senior political leaders were not concerned about political Islam (Samatar 2016). Witnessing the damage that the opportunistic use of political tribalism was doing to national and communal cohesion, the leadership recognized that the influence the ulema could command if they got involved in politics would be a powerful antidote to political fragmentation if fundamental principles of Islam formed the basis of the Constitution. Four conditions that prevailed in the country during those early years of independence worked against members of the ulema, as a bloc, becoming involved in political life. First, the ulema were not active politically, and therefore only a handful of them were elected to political office as members of political parties. The most senior sheikh in the first government was Sheikh Ali Jimale, who became the minister of Health and Labor. There is no evidence available that Jimale used his ministerial position as a platform for pushing a sectarian religious agenda. On the contrary, all the available evidence shows that his political approach was no different from that of his colleagues who lacked his religious credentials.[4] Second, the language of government was Italian and English, and most of the ulema were not conversant in either of these languages, which handicapped their involvement in formal politics. Third, the top political leaders were devout Muslims committed to an accountable and democratic system of government, and the ulema did not think they needed to get involved. Finally, the absence of political violence and intimidation made for an open political process that enabled people, including religious leaders, to freely express their criticism of government policies (Duhul 1997).

Still, in a few corners in the country, there were political rumblings. In particular, imams in two mosques in the capital occasionally used the Friday *khudba* (sermon) to criticize the government by misrepresenting its programs. President Aden Abdulle Osman incidentally became aware of them one Friday, when he went to pray in one of these mosques. As usual, and unlike other Muslim presidents, Osman drove his own car to the mosque, accompanied by only one security guard. He slipped into the back row, unrecognized by other worshipers. The vitriolic rhetoric of the imam's sermon so shocked him that he challenged the imam and gently corrected his misrepresentation. The imam, one of the Egyptian clergy residents in the country for extended periods to teach in one of Mogadishu's secondary schools supported by the Egyptian government, was dumbfounded and could not respond. President Osman quietly slipped out, as he had come, without any incident. Although Osman was concerned about Egyptian influence in this regard, the government did not embark on a security witch hunt.

There were no reports of Somali imams using the Friday sermons and the mosques as a platform to demonize the government. Somali imams brought their concerns to political leaders for discussion. In one instance, a major religious leader visited President Osman to request government support for his community's concern, and before he left the meeting, he asked the president if the government would consider banning Christian proselytizing in the country.[5] Rather than dismissing the request, Osman engaged the sheikh on his own terms, asking whether the cleric approved of Muslims proselytizing in non-Muslim countries. The sheikh did. The president then pointed out that if Somalia banned Christians from proselytizing, then non-Muslims would retaliate, and that would not be good for Islam. Osman told him that Somalis as Muslims must have the confidence to accept non-coercive proselytizing. After hearing this explanation, the sheikh was not offended by Osman's refusal, and left the president's office in peace (Osman, June 15, 1965). Such dialogue between the head of state and the public created an environment where the ulema did not feel that the government was repressive, or that their faith was in jeopardy.

The leaders of the first (1960–1964) and second (1964–1967) governments of the republic were aware of the influence that the ulema could command. They attempted to channel it toward reinforcing the population's commitment to the faith while watching against sectarian use of the faith for particularistic political ends. Somali leaders understood that using Islam to divide politically would be calamitous. For example, senior political leaders, for quite some time, entertained the possibility of using Latin as a script for the Somali language. Word spread in religious circles that the government's strategy was wrong, despite Latin's technical desirability and the population's preference for it (Hussen, March 21, 2006). Religious leaders argued that the use of Latin was tantamount to *ladiin*, Arabic for *faithlessness*. As an alternative, they proposed the Arabic script. Somali government leaders, seeking to avoid the explosive politics that the ulema's stance entailed, quietly put the project in the freezer. Keeping Islam as a foundational common denominator required that senior leaders play by the rules of the republic, and Osman and his team remained faithful to the Constitution. Unfortunately, those who followed the president and his team after their defeat in the 1967 presidential election strayed from those principles. Pervasive corruption, abuse of state organs, and rigged elections became the hallmark of the new regime. The International Monetary Fund (IMF) reported the magnitude of the corruption:

> *Egal must now tackle an imposing backlog of political and economic matters swept aside during the campaign and its aftermath. There is not, according to the local IMF representative, "a single financial law in the Somali Republic that has not been flagrantly disregarded in the last six months."* (US Department of State, July 1969)

Similarly, the US Embassy noted the magnitude of electoral rigging that took place during the 1969 parliamentary election:

> *In a decision which may well be an unfortunate bench mark in Somali judicial history, the Supreme Court on February 23, rejected the appeals filed by the DAP [Democratic Action Party], SNC [Somali National Congress], HDMS [Hizbia Dastur Mustagbal Somali], and SDU [Somali Democratic Union] when these parties were unable to register their lists of candidates for the March election in Bur Hakaba. The Court made only one announcement, saying that the Bur Hakaba appeals, as well as the appeals of SNC in Zeila, and appeals concerning intra-SYL disputes in Adale, and Garoe were denied on "technical ground."... The rejection of the Bur Hakaba lists, and in particular the DAP list of...Zoope... is the most significant and from all indications, a blatant injustice which the GSR [government of the Somali Republic] may live to regret. It is likely that President Sharmarke himself is the principal villain in this piece in that he apparently gave instructions to one and all concerned that the DAP list was to be blocked.* (US Department of State, February 26, 1969)

Further, most Somalis were at their wits' end with the regime, and the caustic poem that Somalia's most revered patriotic poet created for the season caught the mood:

> *Members of parliament when we assembled them in one place,*
> *Presidents and ministers when they were elected,*
> *Healthy minds and people we were facing the same direction,*
> *Then came those who confused us only to milk everything for their sole benefit, Never to lose an electoral seat whose only intention it was,*
> *In our rural areas they put a knife in every hand,*
> *Those hacks who bombarded us with fake wailings of sectarian solidarity,*
> *The poison they injected in us killed nobility of character,*
> *Lies and lies they festoon us with,*
> *Beware* (Timacade 1969).

Dictatorships of Mistrust and Re-emergence of Ulema Activism

Just when the population was on the verge of despair, the national army intervened and removed the regime from power with overwhelming endorsement from the population. The military's honeymoon lasted for several years, during which popular programs were undertaken, such as the adoption of the Latin script for the Somali language, a mass adult literacy campaign, the establishment of the national university, the effective management of the devastating drought of 1974–1975, and investments in infrastructure. Although the regime enjoyed popular legitimacy during this period, its governance paradigm was shifting quietly in troubling ways. True to its nature, the military regime slowly destroyed whatever was left of the public service establishment's professional autonomy. It put military officers at the head of every institution, and appointed loyalists to posts for which they were not qualified. Fear rather than respect replaced the relationship between military political appointees and the professional cadre. Then, by the mid-1970s, particularly after the Somali-Ethiopian war of 1977, recruitment and promotion in the military took a distinctly tribalist turn in ways never witnessed before in Somali public service, as the country's late vice president and minister of defense told me (M.A. Samatar 2004).

Political violence and intimidation, unknown during the heyday of Somali democracy, became the norm under the military.[6] The regime's "anti-corruption" propaganda was also relentless, and several senior government officials were sentenced to death for supposedly committing economic crimes against the state. Among the first victims of the military's tyranny was a group of ulema protesting a new law. The regime already had a bad reputation with the ulema, owing to its Marxist ideology (scientific socialism) and rhetoric, and then it passed a new family law in 1975. In sharp contrast to the democratic constitution, the military sidestepped sharia law and secularized family law. Announcement of the law on the national radio generated heated discussions about the religious character of the military leadership. The proclamation reinforced the misgivings many Somalis had about "godless communism." Thereafter, major imams began to preach in Mogadishu's mosques, defying the regime's authority to change such an elemental law. Conscious of the explosive potential of the challenge, the military rounded up ten imams and took them to a hastily arranged national security court that sentenced them to death. The sentence was carried out immediately. This heinous and criminal act violated the most cardinal feature of postcolonial Somali politics: open political debate without state coercion and violence.

Sectarian use of public power, and the murder of these religious leaders, quickly shattered the citizenry's faith that the regime had any remaining integrity. Having lost the popular mandate, the regime turned to every un-Islamic and undemocratic tool to prolong its hold on power, and mayhem prevailed for the ensuing fifteen years. The regime tribalized all the institutions, including the military (Samatar 2004, Abiib 1996), and set communities against one another, reinventing the colonial strategy of divide and rule. The politically fragmented opposition adopted the same strategy and mobilized communities along the same sectarian lines. The tussle between these forces quickly set the country on the inexorable path to civil war, which led to the total destruction of Hargeisa, the second-largest city in the country, and Burao. By using the national defense force against its own people, and massacring thousands of civilians, the regime shredded the cohesive fabric of the nation's shared values and alienated communities from one another (Africa Watch 1990). Civic-minded Somalis, whether secular or religious, lacked leaders and could not mobilize the population toward a different agenda. As the country's institutions progressively decayed, social fragmentation among the population deepened until the regime collapsed in January 1991.

The country quickly disintegrated as sectarian leaders and warlords turned their regions into semiprivate life-numbing fiefdoms. Economically, the country went into a tailspin. Political conflicts were tribalized and devolved into civil war. Communal strife claimed hundreds of thousands of lives, ruined the capital, and destroyed the country's public and private infrastructure. Hundreds of thousands of Somalis sought refuge in Kenya, Ethiopia, Yemen, Europe, North America, and beyond, while millions of others became internally displaced and subject to the whims of warlords and criminal gangs.

Warlords used food as a weapon against hapless people to manufacture Somalia's 1992–1993 famine. It was the worst famine in the country's history and consumed the lives of nearly a half-million people (Shanoun 1994, Lyons and Samatar 1995). The misery of the people, which was broadcast around the world, prompted President George H.W. Bush to send a large contingent of US military to the country to open the roads controlled by warlords and militia that were preventing food from getting to the starving population.

Dictatorial rule and an unproductive economy—and ultimately civil war—led hundreds of thousands of Somalis to pursue employment opportunities in the oil states of the Middle East, particularly Saudi Arabia and the United Arab Emirates. Others sought refuge in Kenya, Ethiopia, South Africa, Europe, and the United States. Somalis in the Middle East adopted an interpretation of Islamic practice more conservative than that in Somalia. Others studied in Saudi institutions of higher Islamic learning. Consequently, when some of these people returned to Somalia in the late 1970s and the 1980s, an ultraconservative political and religious shift in the country ensued, and the military dictatorship intensified its repression (for a similar case in Sudan, see Bernal 1994). One of the major but subtle ways reactionary Arab influences penetrated Somalia was through the building of mosques by charities and schools, and through the return of many conservative Somalis from those countries. The most visible demonstration of this influence is the radical change of Somali women's attire, from traditional and climatically suitable attire to a heavy plastic-like garb covering the entire body except for the face. This dress form particularly afflicts the vast majority of women who are poor and must labor under the tropical sun. Further, after the state collapsed, the Middle Eastern charities and organizations that aided the few schools that existed, or built new ones, introduced a deeply conservative Arab-based curriculum, often not even allowing the Somali language to be taught in those schools. Three decades of a deeply segregationist and untraditional culture have swallowed the country and oppressed women, even as dire economic circumstances have forced women to assume a vital and public role in sustaining their families.

During the early years of the first decade of the twenty-first century, a tense political environment prevailed in the country, particularly in Mogadishu. Exhausted by the tyranny of warlords and the decline in livelihoods and fortunes, the population sought refuge in Islam. These conditions coincided with an alliance between local warlords and the United States, which needed the warlords' services to capture "Islamic" terrorists who were accused of masterminding attacks on US embassies in Kenya and Tanzania in 1998. The stage was set for a confrontation between the United States' co-opted warlords on one side, and the religious leaders and the population on the other side.

The Rise, Fall, and Return of Political Islam

The desperate need for respite from warlord terror required some kind of civic order in the absence of a national government. This necessity led to the rise of community-based sharia courts in several neighborhoods in Mogadishu. The ulema managed these courts, which used sharia as the sole guide for dispensation of justice. Because of the population's deep attachment to Islam, the courts quickly gained legitimacy and financial support from business enterprises and neighborhood groups (Samatar 2006, Ibrahim 2017), and speedily became an alternative center of authority to the warlords' domination. Despite their contribution to peace, they were caught in the US hostility for everything Muslim shortly after the 9/11 terrorist attacks, and declaration of the War on Terror (Jeremy Scahill 2013). US intelligence services claimed that three terrorists, suspected in the bombing of US embassies in Kenya and Tanzania in 1996, were hiding in Mogadishu, and asserted that the sharia courts were sheltering them.[7] The CIA targeted the courts by hiring Mogadishu warlords called the Alliance for the Restoration of Peace and Counter-Terrorism. The denizens of Mogadishu found out about the US-warlord alliance and rallied behind the sharia courts. Shortly thereafter, in early 2006, the courts morphed into the Union of Islamic Courts (UICs).[8]

Several factors galvanized the public's support for the UICs and the people's uprising. Foremost was the fresh memory of the warlords' brutality over the previous sixteen years, and the resultant social and economic devastation of the city and the region. Then, the corrupt peace process managed by the Intergovernmental Authority on Development (IGAD), and supported by international donors, had imposed a divisive and fraudulent Transitional Federal Government (TFG) of warlords on the Somali people that alienated them.[9] Added to that, the international community failed to give the TFG the necessary support for it to function, which thoroughly undermined the TFG's credibility and the peace process. Further, the aid mafia, which operated from their comfortable base in Nairobi, the Kenyan capital, was deeply despised by the Somali people. Many believed that the aid organizations thought that their job security depended on the TFG remaining dysfunctional, and thus requiring tutelage from the "merchants of misery." Finally, Somalis perceived that the West, fed by false Ethiopian intelligence, was opposed to Islamic values and used terrorism as a pretext to sustain the dominance of their client warlords. This galvanized public support for the Courts (Samatar 2007).

The defeat of the Mogadishu-based warlords by the UICs catapulted it onto the national stage.[10] Threat from warlords had forced the UICs to move from securing neighborhoods to taking over the capital and the surrounding regions. The warlord-dominated TFG had not taken sides in the struggle between the warlords and the

UICs, but the latter had not, of course, supported the TFG.[11] The TFG made its preferences clear after the fall of the key town, Jowhar, in the Middle Shabelle region in early June 2006. Jowhar was the seat of warlord Mohamed Dheere, the chief ally of the prime minister and a major recipient of Ethiopian military support. Prime Minister Geedi accused the UICs of looting property belonging to the defeated warlords and some of the town residents, but independent observers contradicted most of those claims. Shortly thereafter, the president of the TFG demanded that the UICs hand over its weapons to his sectarian militias.[12] These accusations and dictates foreclosed any dialogue between the UIC and TFG. US and Western governments that had been reluctant to recognize the TFG before the emergence of the UIC panicked, to use the phrase of the former US assistant secretary of state for African affairs, Herman Cohen, and unconditionally supported the TFG to stymie the spread of the UICs to the rest of the country.[13]

Western political and financial support propped up the TFG's sectarian and dictatorial agenda. The TFG leadership now had enough money to bribe a majority of MPs to endorse the TFG's request for deployment of foreign troops in the country, although the Somali people have consistently opposed allowing foreign troops—particularly Ethiopian and Kenyan forces—into the country. UICs leaders reiterated its opposition to foreign troops in the country, particularly now that Mogadishu was liberated from the warlords. America and its Western allies, wary of anything that smacked of an independent Islamic movement, tried to intimidate the UICs into acceptance. The TFG's threat to deploy foreign troops had the unintended consequence of enhancing the popularity of the UIC and its claim to national leadership. When troops from Ethiopia—Somalia's sworn enemy—entered Somali territory and occupied several locations, including the president's residence in Baidoa, and the TFG accepted the occupation, the TFG lost all credibility in Somalis' eyes.

The warlords' defeat, and the TFG's increasingly apparent ineptitude, thrust the UICs into the national limelight. Members of the UICs themselves were a diverse group whose only common denominators were dispensing sharia-based justice in the neighborhoods and opposing foreign intervention. Most UICs members had neither the education nor the work experience to manage or administer national or regional affairs. Moreover, the defeat of the warlords was so quick and unexpected that the UICs had no time to reorganize and mobilize sympathetic others into a national coalition.

After securing the city and the region, the first real challenge that the UlCs faced was how to transform its loose association into a cohesive organization with a coherent social and political agenda that could galvanize the population. Their first attempt led to the formation of an advisory council, a *shura*, and an executive committee. The *shura* consisted of representatives of the groups that had contributed to the ouster of the warlords. It set broad policy ideas, and the executive committee implemented them. Although the UICs claimed that the shura and executive committee dealt only with matters internal to their association, in effect, they were the victors in the conflict, and the UICs agenda came to encompass the national authority (Samatar, July 2006).

The UICs cautiously made arrangements for governing the city and the region. Many citizens were troubled by the slow pace and by the little influence they had on the deliberations and decisions of the UICs, despite their support of the UICs during the critical phase of war against warlords.[14] But the concerned citizens themselves had neither a cohesive business community, nor an inclusive civil society organization with a coherent and serious civic agenda for the UICs to collaborate with. The dearth of broad-based community associations was in part due to the ever-present threat of warlord violence against them, but the restoration of peace and free movement of people in the city created opportunities for development of civic movement. The UICs mobilized neighborhoods to clean up refuse that had accumulated in Mogadishu during the previous seventeen years. This project brought together diverse individuals who nominally formed business groups, civil society organs, and the UICs, and laid a foundation for building trust, an essential ingredient for rebuilding community and public affairs.

The UICs and their associates won the battle against the warlords. However, challenges remained that dwarfed previous ones. Foremost among these were transforming a fragmented society into a national community with a shared agenda that could defend and rebuild the city, the region, and the country, and keeping at bay aggression from Ethiopia and its Somali clients, including most senior TFG leaders, and from Western powers who saw terrorism in anything Islamic. Reconstruction was not going to be easy, but the public's confidence in the Islamic faith was a major asset that should have been strategically deployed to facilitate this effort.

One of the first tasks in this regard was the transformation of the identity basis of the sharia courts. Originally, the sharia courts were established in neighborhoods or areas where particular genealogical groups were dominant, although all community members in the area were subject to the court's jurisdiction and its sharia law. Once the warlords were defeated, more genealogy-based courts were created in new areas to secure the peace. Now the challenge was how to transform the genealogy-based identity of the courts to neighborhood and faith-centered operations. The UICs did their best to link Islam to common citizenship in order to surmount the divisive exploitation of politicized genealogical identity. Overcoming the wicked political fragmentation was a long-term project, although some progress was made in that direction.

Transcending genealogical-political cleavages had to go hand-in-hand with sustained peace, a commitment to justice, and honest and transparent management of the people's business while they defended themselves against sectarian Somali politicians and their foreign supporters. This required an autonomous organization to find and manage Somalis skilled in city administration, public management, and development. Establishing such an organization would have been the clearest manifestation of the UICs' intention to establish an inclusive and accountable national order. However, UICs leaders were suspicious of skilled people who were not visibly religious, and some diaspora Somalis worried that joining the UICs administration would cause the West to label them as terrorist sympathizers. Unfortunately, the international community did not let the new Somali authority work through these obstacles and deepen the peace. Ethiopia received the nod to invade the country.

Ethiopia and its international backers justified the invasion on two grounds: to protect the recently established and internationally recognized TFG against what appeared to be an imminent attack by Somali Muslim militia, and to secure the Ethiopian border. The irony was that neither Ethiopia nor its allies came to the population's rescue when warlords had terrorized them during the previous decade. Instead, Ethiopia and its allies had armed the merchants of violence then, and continued to harbor defeated warlords, contrary to the promise of the IGAD.

Ethiopia's military invasion began with a dispatch of several thousand troops to occupy Baidoa, the TFG's temporary seat. The UICs realized that Baidoa's occupation was Ethiopia's bridgehead for a wider agenda, not to counter an Islamic threat, but to destroy the UICs and undermine the possibility of a united and independent Somalia. Consequently, the UICs sent a large number of ill-equipped and poorly trained troops to encircle the city and force the Ethiopian troops to withdraw. Instead, Ethiopia destroyed the UICs militias around Baidoa, and then launched a full offensive that captured Mogadishu on Christmas Day 2006.

After a relatively quiet post-invasion of two months, which gave the Ethiopian authorities a false sense of victory, Somali resistance began to rise. Surprised by its intensity, the Ethiopian forces unleashed their firepower on the city and its civilian population (Samatar 2008). Large swaths of the city were turned into rubble. Thousands of innocent people were killed, and over a million residents fled into the surrounding countryside without shelter, food, or water. Except for a few human rights voices, the so-called international community ignored the carnage (Human Rights Watch 2008). Over the next few months, the UICs' youth wing, Al-Shabaab, proved to be the most resilient among the resistance, and the Somali people rallied behind the *muqaawama* or *kacdoon* (uprising). By the end of summer 2007, the Ethiopian troops were pinned down in three locations, and their losses began to mount.

During the final weeks of the year, the UICs and affiliated groups controlled nearly 90 percent of the country, and it became clear to the United States that the Ethiopian invasion and occupation to quell the UICs resistance was doomed. US authorities took matters into their own hands and engineered a split of the Islamic movement into "moderate" and "extremist" camps.[15] US officials seduced Shariif Sheikh Ahmed, who was the head of the executive of the UICs, and those loyal to him, with promises. President Abdullahi Yusuf was forced to resign, and in a "political compromise," Shariif and his team took over the TFG. But Shariif and his group had not consulted with field commanders of the resistance,[16] and the military leadership of the resistance saw Shariif's maneuvering as a betrayal and the compromise as a Trojan horse for the United States and its Ethiopian allies. The field commanders and troops that had challenged the Ethiopian forces the most were mainly members of the Al-Shabaab wing of the UICs, and they immediately rejected the Shariif regime.[17] America's plot to split the resistance into two camps succeeded, and the US Department of State listed Al-Shabaab as a terrorist organization on March 18, 2008 (United States Department of State, 2008).

America and the European Union induced the African Union (AU) to establish a peacekeeping force in Somalia. The African Mission in Somalia (AMISOM) deployed in Mogadishu in 2007, funded entirely by the United States and European Union. Ugandan troops were the first to arrive and shared the Mogadishu airport with the occupying Ethiopian forces. The AU force passively watched throughout 2007 and 2008, as Ethiopian helicopter gunships took off from the airport and indiscriminately bombarded the city and its population (Human Rights Watch 2008). Other African troops, such as Burundians, arrived to bolster AMISOM. Contrary to the original mandate of AMISOM, which stipulated that the military of neighboring states would not be part of the AU forces in Somalia to prevent a conflict of interest, Ethiopian troops formally joined AMISOM in 2009, although they had never completely left the country after invading it. Similarly, Kenyan troops invaded the Juba region of southern Somalia on the pretext that Al-Shabaab was endangering its tourist-based economy (Boswell 2011), and the Kenyan government petitioned to join AMISOM after incurring huge and unsustainable financial costs.

Shariif's government, and those that came to power after him in 2012 and 2017, failed to fulfill the hope of the Somali people to create an independent and united Somalia. These governments practically became clients of the Ethiopian and Kenyan regimes, giving credence to Al-Shabaab's persistent claim that the authorities in Mogadishu were nothing but a front for those waging war on Muslims, and more significantly, opposing a free Somalia.

The most telling evidence to support this claim was the presidential election in February of 2017. Among the dozen candidates for the highest office, people looked for one they *thought* was not beholden to Ethiopia or Kenya.[18] When the winner was the candidate mistakenly believed to be a nationalist, people celebrated in Mogadishu and many parts of the country. But he had paid millions of dollars to buy MPs' votes, and the people's euphoria evaporated when the president handed over an anti-Ethiopian nationalist, Abdikariim Qalbi Dagax, to the Ethiopian authorities in 2017. The president was not the independent patriot he originally claimed to be, and in more recent years, became a second-rate partner to the regime in Addis Ababa.

AMISOM had success in removing Al-Shabaab's direct control over all major urban areas in southern Somalia, but the terrorist group controls the rural areas and perpetrates horrific violent acts in the capital at will—as in October 2017, when it slaughtered nearly a thousand people in a single explosion.

Al-Shabaab's resolve and resilience in the face of overwhelming military odds is due to five factors. First, AMISOM's conventional military strategy is plainly unsuitable for defeating a guerrilla movement like Al-Shabaab. Al-Shabaab is highly mobile and able to melt into the bush when confronted by AMISOM. For instance, in the Juba region of the country, most AMISOM forces reside in camps just on the outskirts of the regional capital, Kismayo. These troops are stationary and in defensive positions rather than being mobile and actively going after Al-Shabaab. Consequently, the terrorist organization can operate in the vast areas it controls, and make forays into the territories it does not control. AMISOM's unwillingness to adjust its strategy does not bode well for liberating the country.

Second, the failure of the European Union and United States to provide necessary resources and training for a unified professional Somali defense force that is accountable to its people, and that can take the war to Al-Shabaab, offers the terrorists a wide latitude for their operations.

Third, the deeply dysfunctional and sectarian Somali government lacks the credibility and necessary skills to galvanize the population in a tangible common purpose. It has equally failed to transform the security forces from clan militias into an integrated national force with sufficient resources to meet the national challenge.

Fourth, the government's subservience to, and dependency on, neighboring states, as well as the European Union and United States, all of whom do not have Somalia's best interests in mind, undermines its legitimacy with the Somali people.

Fifth, the regime in Mogadishu, and the Somali political class more generally, has failed to produce a coherent national vision and strategy that the public can support, and is willing to take risks for. Given these circumstances, the public cannot rely on the TFG for security, the consequence of which is that Al-Shabaab is able to collect "taxes" from the population, including from businesses in the capital.[19]

Although the vast majority of Somalis abhor Al-Shabaab's misuse of Islam as justification for its tyranny, they have come to realize that the anti-Al-Shabaab coalition of local, African, and international actors have so far offered only corrupt and divisive politics that have driven the country into a political cul-de-sac. Thus, most people consider Islam to contain the ideas and ethics that can provide the foundation for peace, which will enable Somalia to regain its sovereignty. Interestingly, while the population's attachment to their faith has gained strength, their view of the ulema has changed. They now see two types of religious men: those who are deeply invested in communal and faith issues, and those who use Islam as a cover for their fraudulent politics. The first group is held in high regard and has become the center of communal work among Somalis throughout the world. Whereas the rise of Shariif and his cohort to national political leadership in 2012, appears to have significantly discredited the second group. Somalis do not believe the alliance of international forces and local sectarian politicians, including Al-Shabaab, is the vehicle for restoring peace and enabling Somalia to regain its sovereignty and independence.

Conclusion

The rise of Islam as a political force in the lands of the Somalis coincided with the invasion of those lands by European and Ethiopian colonialists in the latter part of the nineteenth century and the early twentieth century. Since then, Islam and the ulema's roles in the country's political affairs have been contingent on the legitimacy of government, and the danger the Somali people felt. This chapter identifies five distinct periods that show the different roles Islam and the ulema played in the making of modern Somali society.

First, the ulema's foremost responsibilities in precolonial society were primarily as custodians of the faith and as peacemakers when conflict arose between communities. Second, when the colonialists invaded Somaliland, Somalis looked up to the ulema to lead the resistance to foreign domination. The British, Italian, and Ethiopian colonial authorities branded Somali leaders as terrorists, just as the dominant powers do today, demonstrating their incapacity to comprehend why free people resist domination. Third, the ulema reverted to its traditional role of dealing with ordinary faith-based communal affairs under the postcolonial democratic period. Its return to tradition was because the government of the time did not oppress its citizens or menace their faith.

Fourth, the ulema were semi-dormant for much of the military rule, but they took center stage in communal affairs, and then in politics after the state collapsed. Warlord tyranny produced dreadful living conditions and high levels of crime, which moved members of the ulema to create community-based sharia courts to restore some semblance of order. This development ultimately led to the fifth period: the rise of the UICs and the defeat of the warlords. Fragile and uncertain peace was restored to the capital and its vicinity, but the United States, European Union, and African Union preferred their own agendas and conspired to undermine this Somali initiative. The United States derailed the best chance for peace when it endorsed the Ethiopian invasion. Further, the US government defined elements of the UICs they considered moderate and radical, and helped the moderates gain power in Mogadishu. But this move split the ulema into two warring camps: those who occupied the seat of power in Mogadishu, and those left out in the bush. UICs members who opposed Shariif's subservience to the Ethiopian and Kenyan governments and his Western allies decided to take the war to Mogadishu, and in the process, inadvertently allied themselves with Al-Qaida (Sh. Ahmed Dheere 2018).[20]

The chapter's historical narrative challenges much of the literature that examines the genesis and role of Islam and the ulema in the modern history of the Somali people. Western powers, their regional allies, Ethiopia and Kenya, and opportunistic Somali political groups have failed to crush Somalis into submission. Somalis yearn for freedom and a just government of their own. They see Islam as the only thought that can offer an alternative political roadmap to the slavish subservience of national and provincial leaders to the so-called international community. They therefore strongly believe in Islam as a major source of political legitimacy, while rejecting Al-Shabaab's cruelty and nihilism.

Two viewpoints have emerged among the public regarding Islam and Somali politics. In the first, Islam becomes a vehicle for the ulema to attain state power and rule the country as a degenerate theocracy. In the second, Islam provides a civic foundation for the establishment of an accountable system of government, regardless of whether it is led by the ulema or others, comparable to the Tunisian model (Ghannouch 2016). No one can say which approach will carry the day, but it is likely the first approach will lead to a political and social cul-de-sac.

Finally, Somalis have become more religious (not necessarily spiritual) and conservative over the last thirty years of statelessness. The relationship between politics and Islam has shifted in such a way that it is not possible to think of Islam as a contingent force, because it has become the sole force that stands between the demise of the Somali people as a national entity, and their resurrection as a free political community. Meanwhile, for most Somalis, Wahhabi interpretation of Muslim ethos has lost its hegemony, particularly in the context of the corrupting influence of Arab money in Somali affairs.

Bibliography

Abib, Hashi. Interview, Ottawa, October 1996.

Abdullahi, Abdurahman M. *The Islamic Movement in Somalia*. Adonis & Abbey Publishers Ltd, 2015.

Africa Watch. *Somalia: A Government at War with its Own People*. London: Africa Watch, 1990.

Ahmed, Leila. *A Quiet Revolution: The Veil's Resurgence, from the Middle East to Africa*. Yale University Press, 2011.

An-Naim, A. *Islam and the Secular State*. Cambridge: Harvard University Press, 2008.

Ciise, Aw Jaamac Cumar. *Taariikhdii daraawiishta iyo Sayid Maxamed Cabdulle Xasan, 1895–1921*. Mogadishu: Wasaaradda Hiddaha iyo Tacliinta, 1976.

Bradbury, Mark. *Becoming Somaliland*. London: James Currey, 2008.

Bernal, Victoria. "Gender, Culture, and Capitalism: Women and the Remaking of Islamic Tradition in a Sudanese Village," *Comparative Studies in Society and History*, vol. 36 (1994): pp. 36–67.

Boswell, A. WikiLeaks: "U.S. Warned Kenya Against Invading Somalia." http://www.mcclatchydc.com/news/ nation-world/world/article24719194.html. 2011.

Cassanelli, Lee. *The Shaping of Somali Society: Reconstructing the History of a Pastoral People*, 1600–1900. Philadelphia: University of Pennsylvania Press, 1982.

Duhul, Yusuf. *Dalka Days: Documents from a Free Somalia Press*. London: Haan Publishing, 1997.

Ghannouch R. "From Political Islam to Muslim Democracy: The Ennahda Party and the Future of Tunisia," *Foreign Affairs*, vol. 95, no. 5 (2016): pp. 58–67.

Great Britain. *Correspondence Respecting Affairs in Somaliland*. London: Darling and Sons, 1910.

Harper, Mary. *Getting Somalia Wrong: Faith, War, and Hope in a Shattered State.* London: Zed Books, 2011.

------------------. *Everything You Have Told Me Is True: Living in the Shadow of Al Shabaab.* Hurst & Company, 2019.

Hess, Robert. *Italian Colonialism in Somalia.* Chicago: University of Chicago Press, 1966.

Human Right Watch. "So Much to Fear: War Crimes and the Devastation of Somalia," 2008, www.hrw.org/report/ 2008/12/08/so-much-fear/war-crimes-and-devastation-somalia.

Human Rights Watch. "Shell-Shocked: Civilians under Siege in Mogadishu," 2007, www.hrw.org/report/ 2007/ 08/13/shell-shocked/civilians-under-siege-mogadishu.

Hussen, Abdirazak H. Interview, March 21, 2006.

------------------------. Interview, Minneapolis, March 2002.

Ibrahim, Ahmed. "The Shari'a Courts of Mogadishu: Beyond 'African Islam' and 'Islamic Law,'" PhD Dissertation: The Graduate School, New York, 2017.

International Crisis Group. "Somalia's Islamists," Report no. 100, Washington, DC, 2005.

Interviews 9, 16, and 21, Asmara, 2007.

Interviews 1, 4, 5, Mogadishu, July 2006.

Le Sage, A. "Prospects for Al-Itihad & Islamist Radicalism in Somalia," *Review of African Political Economy*, vol. 28, no. 89 (2001): pp. 472–477.

Le Sage, A. and Kenneth Menkhaus, "The Rise of Islamic Charites in Somalia: An Assessment of Impact and Agenda," Unpublished paper, 2004.

Lewis, Ioan M. *Blood and Bone: The Call of Kinship in Somali Society.* Lawrence, NJ: Red Sea Press, 1994.

Lonsdale, John and Berman, Bruce. "Coping with Contradiction: the Development of the Colonial State in Kenya, 1895–1914." *Journal of African History,* vol. 20, no. 4 (1979): pp. 487–505.

Lyons, Terrance, and Samatar, Ahmed. *Somalia: State Collapse, Multilateral Intervention, and Strategies for Political Reconstruction.* Washington, DC: Brookings Institution, 1995.

Mamdani, Mahmood. *Good Muslim, Bad Muslim: America, the Cold War, and the Roots of Terror.* New York: Pantheon Book, 2004.

Menkhaus. Kenneth. "Political Islam in Somalia," *Middle-East Policy Council,* vol. IX, no. 1 (2002): pp. 1–12.

------------------------. "Calibrating Counterterrorism Strategy with U.S. Regional Interests in East Africa," National Defense University, Washington, DC, 2003.

Mustapha. Raufu. "Religious Encounters in Nigeria," A.R. Mustapha & E.D. Ehrhaes, editors. *Creed and Grievances: Muslim–Christian Relations and Conflict Resolution in Northern Nigeria.* London: James Currey, 2018, pp. 1–34.

Osman, Aden A. Diary, Mogadishu, June 15, 1965.

Osman, Mohamed. *The Scramble in the Horn of Africa: History of Somalia, 1827–1977.* Mogadishu: Somali Publications, 2001.

Rothberg, Robert. editor. *Battling Terrorism in the Horn of Africa.* Cambridge: World Peace Institute, 2005.

Sahnooun, Mohamed. *Somalia: the Missed Opportunities.* Washington, DC: United States Institute of Peace Press 1994.

Said, Edward. *Covering Islam: How the Media and the Experts Determine How We See the Rest of the World.* New York: Random House, 1981.

Samatar, Abdi Ismail. *The State and Rural Transformation in Northern Somalia, 1886-1986.* Madison: University of Wisconsin Press, 1989.

------------------------. "The Islamic Courts and the Mogadishu Miracle: What Comes Next for Somalia?" *Review of African Political Economy,* no. 109 (2006): pp. 581–587.

------------------------. "Ethiopian Invasion of Somalia: US Warlords and the AU Shame," *Review of African Political Economy,* vol. 34, no. 111 (2007): pp. 466–473.

. ------------------------. *Africa's First Democrats: Somalia's Aden A Osman and Abdiazak H. Hussen.* Bloomington: University of Indiana Press, 2016.

------------------------. Field notes, July 2006.

Samatar, Ahmed. "The Curse of Allah: Civic Disembowelment and the Collapse of the State in Somalia," Samatar A., editor. *The Somali Challenge: From a Catastrophe to Renewal.* Boulder: Lynne Reinner, 1994.

Samatar, Mohamed Ali. Interview, Minneapolis 2004.

Samatar, Said. *Oral Poetry and Somali Nationalism: The Case of Sayyid Mahammad "Abdille" Hasan.* New York: Cambridge University Press, 1982.

Scahill, Jeremy. *Dirty Wars: The World as a Battlefield.* London: Serpent's Tail, 2013.

Shiekh-Abdi, Abdi. *Devine Maddness: Mohamed Abdulle Hassan.* London: Zed Books, 1991.

Sh. Ahmed Dheere. Interview, Johannesburg, December 29, 2018.

Soguk, Nevzat. *Globalization and Islam: Beyond Fundamentalism.* New York: Rowman & Littlefield, 2011.

Somali Republic. *The Constitution of the Somali Republic.* Mogadishu: 1961.

Stith, Charles R. "Radical Islam in East Africa," *The Annals of the American Academy of Political and Social Science,* 632, no. 1 (2010): pp. 55–66.

Trimingham J., Spencer. *The Sufi Orders in Islam.* London: Oxford University Press, 1971.

Timacade, Abdillahi Suldaan. *Maandeeq.* Hargeisa, 1969.

United Nations Monitoring Group for Somalia and Eritrea, Report of the Monitoring Group on Somalia Pursuant to Security Council Resolution 1676, 2006, https://www.cfr.org/content/publications/attachments/Somalia.doc.

United Nations Trusteeship Council Eighteenth Session. Official Records, 703 Meeting 703, June 1956, p. 11, New York, 1956.

United Nations Trusteeship Council. Official Record, Eleventh Session, Meeting 415, June 9, 1952, p. 18, New York, 1951.

United States Department of State. Research memorandum, RAF, July 8, 1969.

United States Department of State. Airgram A-32, February 26, 1969.

United States Department of State. "Designation of Al-Shabaab," https://www.state.gov/j/ct/rls/other/des/143205.htm.

United Kingdom Archives. FO371/53526 and FO1015/51, 1949, Kew Gardens.

Endnotes

1   For a conceptual discussion of the colonial state's efforts to manage its contradictory character and functions, see Lonsdale and Berman (1979).

2   Appendix. All-Somali Conference on the Unification of Somali (Mogadishu, February 1947). The signatures includes elders of all major Somali groups. One of the most extensive petitions was drafted by the leader of the Somali National League, Mohamoud Jama Urdoh (Burao, October 18, 1948, FO371/53526). This petition for a United Somalia was signed on August 17, 1946, while the one opposed to the Bevin Plan was signed on September 11, 1946. Among the signatures of the first petition is Haji Ibrahim Egal, the father of the future political leader of the Somali National League. Michael Mariano became one of the leading nationalist in British Somaliland Protectorate, and later in the Somali Republic. Lewis Salool, who had a Somali father and an Indian mother, was "a native of British Somaliland and of a missionary Catholic family. Educated in Bombay, where he graduated with an MA LLB, practiced as a lawyer in Addis Ababa under Italian regime, and later in British Somaliland. He came to Mogadishu in 1945, as the Legal Advisor to SYL." (FO 1015/51)

3   Often, the distinction is made between secular and religious politics. My argument shares the analysis of An-Naimeen (2008) and considers no major contradictions between Islam and secular politics in Muslim societies.

4   The other Sheikh who occupied a senior position in the cabinet was Sh. Ali Ismail, who was the minister of Defense. Lastly the Speaker of Somali Parliament for several years was Sheikh Mukhtar Mohamed. None of these senior individuals' political practice was laced with Islam.

5   The Sheikh was concerned about the church in Mogadishu which was the center of the very small Catholic community (mostly Italians), and the few Somalis who were Christianized through orphanage centers.

6   I was imprisoned for three and half months for asking questions of the military commander in the village where I had worked as a teenager.

7   The UICs wrote a letter to the United Nations and the American Government declaring its intentions to cooperate with them in eliminating all forms of terrorism in the country, but they never received a response from either. It is clear from hindsight that some of the members of the UICs based in lower Shabelle had some knowledge of at least one of the suspects of the Nairobi embassy bombing, but they did not share that with the leadership in Mogadishu.

8   The CIA helped established a radio station for one of the warlords (Bashir Raage). Once the public found out who was underwriting the cost of the radio's operation, they labeled it as "Radio Sharon," after the late Israeli Prime Minister.

9   I met with the key EU and USA representatives in the Nairobi Peace process for lunch, and they admitted that they were very concerned about the dominance of warlord in the newly installed Transitional Federal Government. January 2005.

10 Given that Mogadishu-based warlords were opposed to the establishment of the TFG, as well as the UICs, their defeat created a fantastic opportunity for the UICs and TFG to collaborate in order to advance the peace. Unfortunately, this chance for peace was thwarted because of the TFG's subservience to Ethiopia and the West, as well as the narrow-mindedness of the UICs' leadership. The country is yet to recover from that calamity.

11 The irony was that both Mogadishu-based warlords who opposed the

TFG, and the TFG, were supported by the American government simply because they both opposed the UICs.

12 The author met Assistant Secretary of State Jendi Frazier in her office in Washington, DC, in September, at her request. Our meeting was fruitless, as she and her ill-educated Desk Officer on Somalia were such committed Islamophobes. At one point, the assistant suggested that the UICs must hand over its weapons to the Mogadishu municipality. Neither the Secretary nor her assistant were dumbfounded when I pointed out that there was no such thing as a Mogadishu municipality to take over the weapons. This showed how ill-informed policy-making was in the Department of State.

13 The popularity of UICs, and the enthusiasm of the population for the change, was such that far off regions in the country, like Somaliland and Puntland, felt the pressure and pronounced that they would use the sharia as the basis for governing the regions. It was also reported that many Somalis in various region of the country began to use the mosques to solicit money from the people in support of the UICs.

14 The author was occasionally consulted by the leadership of the UICs, but it soon became clear that the consultation approach was a sort of window dressing.

15 Interview 5 (2008). Senior members of the UICs in Asmara told me that Shariif Sh. Ahmed was acting in strange ways. Then Shariif told me to help mollify the concerns of members of the team. I told him that I could not do so, and that he must be candid with his team. Within a week after this conversation, Shariif flew into Nairobi, and from there, onward, he was no longer in contact with his team in Asmara.

16 The author had a telephone conversation with the chief UICs agent in Mogadishu, who told me how bewildered people were (*waanu yaabanahey dhamaantayo*) by Shariif's erratic and unprincipled moves. (October 22, 2008)

17 Mogadishu denizens were so excited about the defeat of the Ethiopian Army, the withdrawal of their troops out of the capital, and the rise of Shariif as national president. But many people in the city were deeply concerned about the split among the resistance, and I remember listening to a national broadcast over the BBC Somali Service, where an elderly women urged the two factions of the resistance to join forces and not to engage in war.

18 I was the Chair of the independent parliament appointed nation-

al commission to insure the integrity of the presidential election. I was able to speak with a wide spectrum of the population, and it was clear from the contacts that their hopes were "a president that was free from the shackles of the neighboring states, and that was serious about uniting the country."

19   In 2018, the Ministry of Finance introduced a sales tax, but the merchants in the Baraka market, the country's largest market, refused to heed this demand, as they complained that taxes collected in the city are used to provide security and salaries for the politicians, and not used to improve quality of life in the city. The merchants' claims are partially true, but what they did not say is that if they collect such taxes, Al-Shabaab will demand an equal amount, and the government will be in no position to protect them from such extortion.

20   Other militant groups predated Al-Shabaab, such as Al-Itixad. (Sh. Ahmed Dheere, Interview, Mogadishu, January 2, 2018)

4
Reframing "Somali" Piracy[1]

What I do argue is that there is a difference between knowledge of other peoples and other times that is the result of understanding, compassion, careful study, and analysis for their own sake, and on the other hand, knowledge—if that is what it is—that is part of an overall campaign of self-affirmation, belligerency, and outright war. There is, after all, a profound difference between the will to understand for the purpose of coexistence and humanistic enlargement of horizons, and the will to dominate for the purpose of control and external domination (Said 1979, p. xix).

The international strategy to curtail piracy along the Somali coast has been ineffectual (The Maritime Executive 2010) because the strategy overlooked the reasons for the piracy. In this chapter, I reframe the debate in a way that challenges the dominant manner of seeing piracy in the Indian Ocean. Contrary to the stereotype depicted in the Tom Hanks film *Captain Phillips*, there are several pirate types in Somali seas and the Indian Ocean—and not all of them come from Somalia—each driven by different logics. Somali pirates, who emerged after the Somali Civil War, operate from a failed state. In contrast, pirates in other Third World regions operate out of established states. Piracy off the Somali coast is, I argue, more than robbery on the high seas. I define Somali-based piracy as an outgrowth of that region's political economy and political ecology, and conflicts over resources. My more refined assessment of piracy in the region and critical appraisal of the moral economy of Somali pirates yields an understanding for devising an effective solution.

Somalia has been the prototype of a failed state for the last thirty-two years. The Somali state slowly disintegrated over a decade, and then collapsed in 1991. A horrific civil war engulfed the country starting in 1988, and the demise of the political order has produced an untold tragedy by consuming nearly one million lives and displacing over three million citizens. Somalia's political calamity became the worst humanitarian crisis in the world at the time (Mynott 2008, Gettleman 2007, Human Rights Watch 2010). The suffering continues in large measure because the politics that produced the civil war is poorly understood, as it is wrongly framed (Samatar 1992). Somalia's misfortune has not been confined to the misery of its people. For over two decades, the country has been infamous for the pirates that operate off its long coast (Hansen and Mesoy 2006). Piracy by Somalis has attracted increasing journalistic, and some academic, attention (Hastings 2009, Sorenson 2008, Draper 2009, Middleton 2008, Moller 2009, Murphy, 2009). However, much like the Lewisian interpretations of Somali culture and politics, these works frame the nature and dynamics of piracy along the Somali coast in ways that demonize and criminalize Somalis and ignore how Somalis are victims of foreign pirates (Schofield 2008, Phillips 2009).[2] This chapter *reframes* the piracy by answering four vital questions: What was the political context that made piracy possible? How did piracy along the Somali coast evolve? And what were the respective logics of various pirate types? Why did Somalis not more strongly condemn piracy along their coast despite its ill effects?

The first section of the chapter outlines two ways of framing piracy, and briefly describes modern piracy in the Third World. Section two sketches how political ambitions of factions of the Somali political elite, driven by a divisive and sectarian strategy, dovetailed with the interests of cold warriors, and how this toxic combination subverted the legitimacy of government, ultimately ruined the state, and prepared the way for piracy. Part three digs deeper into the essence of the piracy off the Somali coast since the late 1980s, and finds four types.

In the fourth section, I explain how the rise of some of the piracy is rooted in the population's moral economy, and why Somalis have been reluctant to heed the international community's concern about piracy. In the fifth section, I discuss international strategy to combat piracy, and why it has been ineffective for so long despite the presence of a large flotilla of naval forces stationed in the region. Finally, I offer an alternative view of piracy that provides a more reasonable way to deal with the problem.

Ways of Seeing Modern Piracy

Although piracy has been a problem on the high seas for centuries, its visibility has grown with the globalization of the last few decades (Lane 1998, Murphy 2009, Peet 2007, Ong-Webb 2007, Hansen 2008, Weldemichael 2019). In the most recent phase of globalization, pirates and other non-state actors take advantage of globalization's spread and tap developments in technology (Warren 2003). The development and spread of communication technologies and their relative cheapness accelerated the interconnectedness of economic operators, as well as both grassroots activists and criminals (Keck and Sikkink 1997; Held, McGrew, Goldblatt, and Perraton 1999). Pirates use speedboats and mobile communication facilities to operate near land and on the high seas. Globalization has also made more visible the contrasts between those living in wealth and those living in poverty and exposed to the harm done by sharp economic downturns on the livelihoods of the poor. The race for natural resources exploits populations worldwide who live near natural wealth, and the ensuing injustice engenders struggles. Finally, the proliferation of smaller, cheaper weapons in the hands of non-state actors, including criminals, diluted the "monopoly" that governments of Third World states had on instruments of violence. These global conditions dovetailed with local processes, and thus circumscribe the terrain from which modern piracy has emerged.

Mainstream scholarship postulates that modern piracy occurs where circumstances permit. It has identified five conditions considered to be necessary prerequisites for piracy: (1) the existence of favorable topographic environment, (2) prevalence of ungoverned spaces—due to legal dispute between states, or simply their absence, (3) the existence of weak law enforcement or little political will of governments in the areas to curb piracy, (4) a cultural environment that is not hostile to piracy, and (5) the availability of great rewards for piracy while the risks are minimal (Murphy 2009, p. 29–44).

Scholars outside this mainstream do not necessarily disagree with the aforementioned conditions, but they insist that modern piracy is partly induced by poverty, unemployment, and the temptations brought about by the proximity of wealth and poverty (Frecon 2007,

Ong-Webb 2006, Campo 2003). Others add that resource robberies by states, multinational companies, and other powerful actors create unbearable living conditions for local populations that compel them to respond to these predations in a manner that is culturally accepted (Ukiwo 2007, Watts 2006, Obi 2008, Harvey 2003). We think that these arguments form a distinct theoretical stance, the predation-resistance framework, distinct from the first group's, but the two approaches are not mutually exclusive. The predation-resistance argument is more insightful, however, because it interrogates how the necessary conditions were created and who created them. These conditions—with the exception of topography—do not occur naturally. For example, how did the ungoverned spaces come to be, and who was behind it? How were the piracy-friendly cultural environments produced? In addition, the predation-resistance approach deconstructs the totalizing notion of pirate, and unearths the varied motivations of actors involved rather than simply defining piracy as "unlawful depredation at sea involving the use or threat of violence, possibly, but not necessarily, involving robbery."[4] These are decisive questions that require analysis.

Southeast Asian pirates dominated global piracy for a long time. They were eclipsed by pirates operating from the Horn of Africa in 2007. The International Maritime Organization (IMO) tracks piracy incidence, and found that its frequency began to increase in the late 1980s (Murphy 2009, p. 62). Nearly all the increase in piracy has been in Third World waters. In the mid-1990s pirate attacks were few and confined to the coast of Latin America, the Gulf of Guinea, the Bay of Bengal, and the Strait of Malacca (figure 4.1). Piracy near the Horn of Africa was unknown before 1989.

The patterns of piracy off the coasts of East Asia and West and East Africa shadow global economic cycles and reflect the contestation over resources between the powerful and the poor. Piracy in East Asia, particularly in the Strait of Malacca, modest in scale in the early 1990s, began to increase substantially after the Asian financial crisis that severely hit Indonesia in 1997 (Friedman and Levisohn 2002). Less than 30 attempted hijackings in 1996, grew to 51 in 1999, and mushroomed to 215 in 2000. The number then stayed at over 150 incidents per year until 2005, and started a downward slide in 2006. This pattern suggests that the incidence of piracy is related to economic cycles.

Elsewhere, corrupt government officials and unscrupulous oil companies create horrific living and ecological conditions that force residents into piracy. Piracy occurs all along the West African coast, but the Niger Delta remains the epicenter of piracy in the region. (Watts 2007, Ukiwo 2007). Initially, piracy in Nigeria was concentrated in Lagos Harbor due to corruption and theft. However, it increased and spread as destruction of the communal and ecological life in the oil-producing Niger Delta grew, and as the resentment and resistance of the local populations increased (Idemudia and Ite 2006, Omeji 2005, Watts 2008).

From fewer than five hijackings in 1995, the industry grew considerably and reached a peak of ninety-three in 2003. Obi and Watts both argue that much of what is characterized as piracy in the region is, in fact, local resistance to destruction of livelihoods and the ecological depredation visited on the region (Obi 2008, Watts 2007). They also acknowledge the presence of a significant criminal element as well. In Latin America, particularly on the northwestern coast bordering Colombia, Venezuela, and Ecuador, and in the Caribbean, corrupt officials and drug dealers are implicated in much of the piracy in the region (Murphy 2009).

Whereas the upsurge of the East Asian piracy relates to the decline of the economic fortunes of the region, that in Nigeria is associated with the degradation of quality of life. Nigeria has two types of piracy: legitimate resistance of the local population to predation by the state and oil companies, and criminal entrepreneurial elements seeking monetary gain from piracy.

Both the Southeast Asian and the Nigerian cases illustrate that piracy is a more complex issue than many imagine. We cannot assume that all pirates are cut from the same criminal cloth. The predation-resistance framework provides a more fruitful way to examine the conditions that breed piracy, and that might lead to local resistance and criminal enterprises, and to investigate the nature of different types of pirates. We now turn to the Somali case and this complexity.

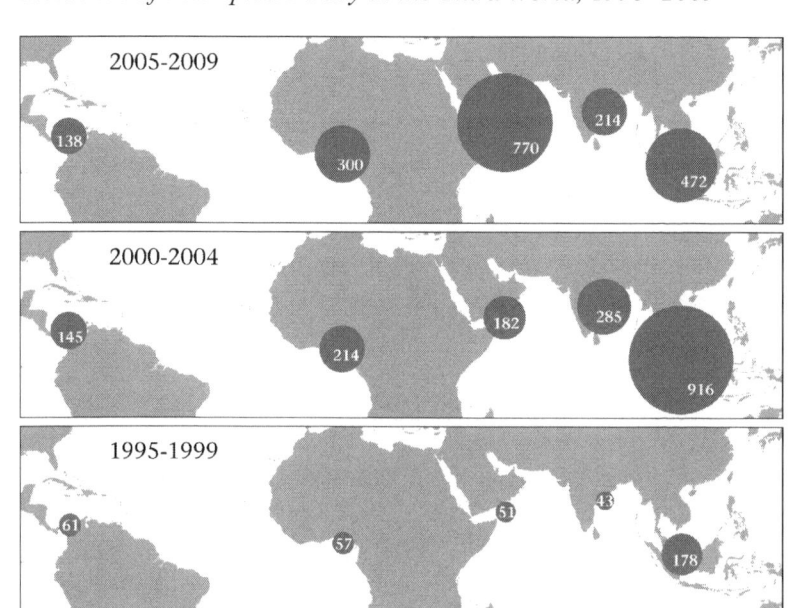

Figure 4.1[5]
Incidence of Attempted Piracy in the Third World, 1995–2009

Creating a Piracy-Friendly Environment in Somalia

It is my argument that the absence of a Somali national government is the principal factor that has created opportunities for piracy.[6] I contend that what brought the state down is widely misunderstood, and suggest that the interplay between internal and external forces destroyed the state and prepared the way for piracy. This section of the chapter examines the coalition of forces that created the necessary conditions.

Somalia became a sovereign state in 1960, and the nationalist movement led by the Somali Youth League was widely supported by the population. Somalis' enthusiasm for liberation included an unwavering commitment to the unification of the British and Italian colonies, and the liberation of Somali territories in Ethiopia, French Somaliland, and the North Frontier Districts (NFD) of the Kenya colony. There have been two political tendencies in the Somali body politic (Samatar 1997). One tendency had civic nationalism and institutionalized democracy as its core values, and the second was sectarian in nature and sought to use public power for divisive and private ends (see Chapter 2).

The tussle between the civic and sectarian agendas had dominated Somali political life since independence. Both groups advanced their agendas in ways that have had lasting effects on the country, and both sought allies inside and outside the country. The civics led the first two governments, 1960–1967, and had to contend with the constraints inherent in the three imperatives that guided their policies. First, they were mindful of the public's psychic and emotional attachment to liberation of the "missing" Somalilands, and the civics were themselves staunchly committed to Somali unity. Second, the country's constitutional commitment to non-alignment during the Cold War was deeply held by the leaders, who strove to maintain the country's neutrality in the East-West conflict. Third, the first Somali president, 1960–1967, who was resolutely loyal to the democratic system, appointed prime ministers he thought would be similarly loyal (Samatar 2016). The president and his supporters in government and parliament sought to institutionalize democracy by adhering to these three principles (Africa Report 1964), but the democratic principle was the toughest one to uphold. As they tried to keep the sectarian camp from gaining power, institutionalizing and upholding the rule of law alienated sectarian parliamentarians whose support was needed to advance the democratic agenda.

By contrast, the sectarian camp's guiding political principle was retaining power no matter what (*fortuna*). They had no enduring allegiance to the Constitution, and institutionalizing democratic governance was not a priority item on their agenda (Samatar 2016). Further, despite the country's formal affiliation with the Non-Aligned Movement, in practice the government, which the sectarian group dominated from 1967 to 1969, was decidedly pro-Western. Given the centrality of their commitment to endure in power, the sectarian camp saw the civics' attachment to democratic principles and institution building as a weakness they could corruptly exploit during elections.

For the first seven years of independence, the civics maintained a slim majority in parliament and controlled the executive branch. The government's commitment to building democratic institutions was recognized during 1960–1964 (Arraleh 2002). After the 1964 parliamentary elections, President Aden Abdulle Osman appointed a more activist prime minister, Abdirazak Haji Hussen, to push the agenda forward (Africa Report 1964). During Hussen's tenure (1964–1967), the civics made their most daring attempt to build democratic institutions. The prime minister appointed younger and more educated ministers, and demanded that ministers publicly declare their assets in order to inspire confidence among the population (Hussen 2001). Hussen then did the unthinkable by accepting the proposals of the UN-expert-led Public Service Commission, which recommended thorough civil service reform (US Department of State 1964). Implementing the policy entailed the dismissal of many senior civil servants for incompetence and corruption. The prime minister also sacked three ministers and one deputy minister for malfeasance (Samatar 2016). Finally, the regime honored the separation of powers among the executive, judicial, and legislative branches.

These progressive moves frightened a handful of sectarian members of parliament, who made several unsuccessful attempts to bring down the government through votes of no confidence (US Department of State, July 1964). The political tide eventually turned against the civic camp, in part, because of the displeasure of international superpowers with government policies. The Soviets thought the government was pro-West, despite the Soviets having trained the Somali military. America and the West were unhappy about the Soviet's military support to Somalia, and were affronted by the regime's willingness to talk with North Korea in early 1967 (Hussen 2001). Even so, the government was optimistic about its chance of retaining power in the June 1967 presidential election. But then the opposition left nothing to chance and promised appointments to some parliamentarians, disbursed cash to others, and assured four disgraced former cabinet members that the legal cases against them would be dropped (Abshir 2004). Consequently, candidate Sharmarke won the presidency by the narrowest of margins, and his victory marked the triumph of sectarian political culture.

Within a year of the new regime's inauguration, it was clear that deepening the institutional roots of democracy was not its priority. The 1969 parliamentary election exposed its corrupt agenda. The Soviets also realized that their man—the president—was not who they thought he was, because his regime aggressively pursued a pro-West foreign policy. President Sharmarke was assassinated by one of his police guards in October 1969, and the Somali military, which had been conspiring with the Soviets to engineer a coup, seized power in the dead of night (Patman 1990). And so the curtain fell on Somalia's promising democratic experiment.

The dictatorship exhausted the population's goodwill within a decade, and the regime intensified its brutality as it lost all manner of legitimacy. As if to reinforce the saliency of political expedience, the Soviets and United States switched sides in 1978. The Soviets saw the new military regime in Ethiopia as a worthy client, and the United States felt it had to support the Somali dictatorship to keep the balance.

A combined Ethiopian, Cuban, and Yemeni force defeated the Somali military in the 1977–1978 Ethiopian–Somali War. Meanwhile, the main opposition forces, the Somali Salvation Democratic Front and the Somali National Movement, adopted political tribalism to mobilize segments of the population. Government retaliated by engaging in a scorched-earth policy (Human Rights Watch 1990). These sectarian strategies from the regime, and the opposition, ultimately pushed the country over the precipice.

As the last vestige of public authority disintegrated, Somalia slid into chaotic civil war. Warlords in their rule surpassed the old regime's cruelty, and some used food as a weapon, which caused famine that consumed hundreds of thousands of lives. A US-led force of 35,000 UN troops intervened and opened the roads so food could get to the indigent population. Feeding the population was successful. However, the intervention lacked a political program to re-establish a government (Sahnoun 1994). An ill planned US attempt to capture one of Mogadishu's notorious warlords ended in the death of eighteen US Marines, which precipitated the withdrawal of all UN forces. Thereafter, Somalia remained a forbidden territory until the 1998 terrorist bombings of US embassies in Kenya and Tanzania. US intelligence established contacts with some of the Somali warlords to find the bombers, and after 9/11, the relationship between US. intelligence and certain warlords was cemented to assist the United States in its fight against "radical Islamists." But this approach backfired because Somalis rallied behind the Union of Islamic Courts (UICs), which defeated the warlords in 2006. US leaders were alarmed by the rise of the UICs, and impulsively endorsed Ethiopia's intentions to invade Somalia. The invasion and occupation by Ethiopia met with stiff resistance, which ultimately led to its withdrawal in 2008.

The political faction that triumphed in the 1967 presidential election subverted democratic institutions, and the military coup of 1969 completed the task. Then the military's naked political violence together with the opposition's sectarian strategy precipitated state demise. Its collapse imposed huge humanitarian costs on the population and created opportunities for warlords, who preyed on the local population. International community turned Somalia's troubles into a political football, and rapacious resource hunters invaded Somali waters.

The Nature of Piracy Along the Somali Coast

Whereas Asian, West African, and Latin American pirates operate under the gaze of their states, the Somali national government did not condone piracy along its coast. Not until the government began to disintegrate in 1989, were there instances of piracy in Somali waters, and incidence declined significantly in 2006, when the UICs dominated Mogadishu. State failure was the critical prerequisite for piracy in Somalia, which implicates the forces that contributed to state collapse by creating the necessary conditions.

Recall the earlier discussion of the five necessary prerequisites for piracy and how they are informed by addition of the predation-resistance approach. We now turn to examine the pirates who emerged from these conditions. A careful study of the evidence shows that four types have been operating off Somalia since 1989: political, resource, defensive, and ransom pirates.

Piracy along the Somali coast first appeared as the state began to crumble and was not tied to criminals who were in business for the loot. These actors were linked to the political struggles against the Somali dictatorship, and their first attack took place after much of the northern region became a civil-war zone in 1988. Hijackings that took place in 1989–1990 were politically motivated, and therefore must be considered political pirates. Their aim was to weaken the regime by blocking seaborne supplies from reaching areas controlled by the government. As such, Somalia's first pirates were members of an opposition political group known as the Somali National Movement (SNM), which was supported by Ethiopia. Here are two examples of political pirates in action, as reported by the International Maritime Organization:

> *The [SNM] warns all shipping agencies not to cooperate with the dying regime of Mogadishu, because they are not able to ensure the safety of ships and their crews against any dangers that they may be exposed to. For this reason, on December 5, 1989, the SNM Coast Guard seized a ship flying a Panamanian flag en route to Berbera. This is a major port still in the hands of the loyalist troops of the Mogadishu Regime.* (United States National Geospatial Agency, http://www.nga.mil/NGAPortal/MSI.portal)

Then the organization reported again, six days later:

> *Rebels captured the Italian ship Kwanda and her crew of 2 Italians and 14 Somalis without a fight, off northern Somalia, near the port of Zeila. She was carrying petroleum products from Djibouti. She was captured by rebels in speed boats armed with machine guns. No injuries were reported. The Kwanda was anchored and her cargo of petroleum was discharged by the rebels, 7 January 1990. Kwanda released by captors after 27 days. The Kwanda entered the port of Djibouti after being relieved of its cargo of 350 tons of fuel oil, food reserves, tools, and everything else that could be removed and sold. The crew were robbed of their money and clothes, and beaten.* (ibid)

SNM used all possible means to dislodge the military regime, and the regime reciprocated. Political pirates operated during the dying days of the regime and disappeared immediately after its collapse when their limited objective was achieved.

The second type of piracy appeared along the Somali coast after the political disintegration of the country in 1991. Resource pirates comprise two subgroups. One subgroup is companies from Asia, Europe, and Africa, lured by Somalia's unprotected, rich fish resources (United Nations Environment Program 2005, Nur 1998, Hari 2010).[7] The other is searching for unguarded territories to use as dumps for Europe's surplus trash and toxic waste (Hassan and Tako 1999, Mackenze 1992, Coffen-Smout 1998, UNEP 2005).[8] Despite the importance of the waste-pirate subgroup, I limit this discussion to the thefts of fish pirates.

Somalia's coast guard disintegrated when the state collapsed, and fish pirates seized the opportunity to loot Somalia's marine resources. Industrial fishing trawlers from Asia and Europe illegally exploit these waters, which contain Africa's third-richest fisheries (Chanda 2009). Estimates are that every year, some seven hundred foreign vessels loot fish worth anywhere from $150 million to $450 million (Hari 2010).

Fishing communities along the coast watch factory ships anchor short distances offshore for days at a time as they ransack Somali resources (UNEP 2005).[9] Some of the former government's coast guard decided to challenge the predators, and local fishermen later joined the fray. These Somalis, defensive pirates, are protecting their marine resources and not looting. One of the first incidents in which Somalis challenged illegal fishing in their waters took place on September 9, 1994 (US National Geospatial Agency):

> *The M/V Bonsella was approached by 26 bandits in a dhow presenting themselves as Coast Guard and using mortar fire to hijack the ship. The attack occurred three miles offshore Caluula, the northernmost point of Somalia in the Gulf of Aden. The hijackers used the M/V to chase other fishing vessels in an unsuccessful attempt to capture other ships. The hijackers told the master that they wanted to capture a faster vessel for further use in their patrolling operations. After six days the hijackers emptied the cargo and stole all the available money and then released the ship.*

Chapter 4

A day later, off the Somali coast in the Gulf of Aden:

a vessel had sheltered off the coast during heavy weather. At 1538 hrs. GMT, she was underway at a speed of 12.2 knots when an unmarked boat about 20 meters in length with a white hull and red superstructure, approached the vessel and began to fire without warning. The vessel under attack broadcast a mayday call, which resulted with the pursuing boat making radio contact, claiming to be the Somali Coast Guard. Assurances were made that the firing would stop and the boat followed for a short time before returning to the coast.

Other reports from the same organization reinforce the pattern:

*[October 9, 1994] BIMCO has received a report in which a Master described the hijacking of his ship which was finally released after six days. On September 9, 1994, whilst sailing from Djibouti to Mombasa, the ship was at position 12 00 90N 050 50 70E, when a dhow was spotted approaching the ship. As the dhow came alongside, many armed men could be seen on deck, one waving a red flag, ordering the ship to stop. Two mortar shells were fired at the vessel. The master was ordered to drop anchor, otherwise they would sink her. There were 26 men onboard the dhow, of which 11 boarded the vessel and identified themselves as the **Somali Coast Guard**, North East Region. They demanded the ship's manifest and ordered the master to proceed to Bolimook, near Cape Elfante. As the vessel proceeded, the intruders attempted to make radio contact with their base at Bossasso. The vessel anchored at Cape Elfante, at 11:00 56 50 N 050 37 00E. On 10 September, the master was told that the ship would be used to apprehend fishing vessels operating off the Somali coast without proper licenses.... On 11 September, the master was ordered to prepare the vessel's Zodiac for future use during pursuit operations. At 1325 hrs., the vessel sailed from Cape Elfante for Cape Guardafui, where she anchored at 11 51 00 N051 14 20 E.... On 14 September the captors demanded that the ship's cargo would be discharged into the dhow before the ship was released. If they were given any resistance, the crew would be killed and the vessels would be sunk. At 1300, discharging was complete. The captors then demanded cash from the master. However, when he claimed that there was no cash on board, the captors led him at gun point to the ship's safe, which they emptied.... They claimed that they needed*

the cash for stevedoring expenses at Bossasso. The master was ordered to sail to Djibouti.... The captors took the entire cargo and aid supplies, as well as almost all of the ship's stores and equipment. Fortunately no crewmembers were injured during the episode. (ibid. Bold is mine)[10]

But the biggest catch for the Somali operators came in December 1994, when defensive pirates landed a major catch. Here is how it was described by the official reports:

On 15 Dec. [Somali] pirates captured two fishing vessels belonging to the Somali Highseas Fishing Company (SHIFCO) outside Hurdiyo, Somalia. SHIFCO paid a US $1 million ransom for the two ships which were returned on 09 Jan. 95. (ibid.)

SHIFCO was a joint venture between Italian interests and the old regime that operated as a private Italian operation after 1991. The three cases described here were just two and a half miles from the Somali coast, and almost all the foreign trawlers fish in areas less than five miles from the coast—that is, well within Somalia's territorial waters.

Finally, lawlessness and the absence of a government in the country created excellent conditions for criminals of all sorts in and around the country. Some of these criminals recognized the superb looting opportunity provided by the more than thirty plus thousand merchant ships that annually ply one of the three most strategic waterways in the world, the Gulf of Aden, which connects to the Indian Ocean. Initially, these criminals mimicked the defensive pirates by claiming to be protecting Somali waters, but that veil could not conceal their true motivation—the search for ransom. In contrast to the limited reach of defensive pirates, the scope of *ransom pirates* spans a significant area of the western reaches of the Indian Ocean, well-beyond Somali waters, as shown in figure 4.2. These are the pirates who have attracted the world's attention, and who extort about $35 million to $60 million annually, in exchange for their victims.

Figure 4.2: Reach of Ransom Pirates

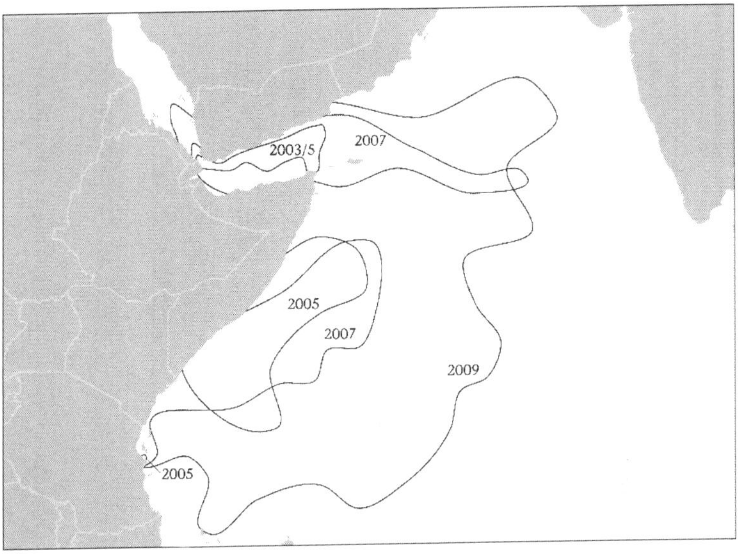

Understanding Defensive Piracy

Much reporting, and some analysis, have examined ransom pirates, but no systematic attempt has been made to understand the motivation of former Coast Guard members and fishermen for defensive piracy. Further, no effort has been made to appreciate why many Somalis are indifferent to the world's concern about piracy. This is in part due to accepting the assumptions embedded in the piracy literature that underscore the importance of a tolerant cultural environment to the development of piracy. Describing a cultural environment is not very useful unless it explains how and why such a culture developed. The conundrum that requires explication is Somalis' tolerance for pirates and their thinking behind it.[11] Embedded in the notion of defensive piracy, I suggest, are the core reasons for Somalis' indignation about the world's concern with ransom piracy (Ho 2009),[12] For most Somalis, defensive piracy symbolizes the population's feeble effort to protect the moral economy of their livelihoods.[13] From their perspective, it is not possible to separate defensive and ransom piracy from the depredation of resource piracy. Comprehending the logic of Somali reasoning requires knowing the nature of their moral economy.

The idea of moral economy was first noted by the British Historian E.P. Thompson, in his writing about the poor people's movement in England (Thompson 1971). Thompson points out that the struggles of the poor reflected their wish that the rich allow them to earn a minimum level of income. James Scott picks up the idea where Thompson left off, and applies it to the livelihood struggles of peasants in order to understand why peasants rebel (Scott 1976). He argues that rebellions are rooted in peasants' need for subsistence security. Scott's analysis aids in understanding not only the rationale behind defensive pirates, but also the population's tacit support for ransom pirates.

Scott's moral economy has three pillars: safety first, subsistence security, and an ethic that governs the peasantry's relations to authority. Precarious peasant life (Tawney, Quoted in Scott 1976)[14] obliges peasants to be *risk averse*, or prioritize safety, and to avoid opportunities that may yield greater gain but jeopardize a peasant's subsistence needs. Scott convincingly argues that risk aversion is a rational calculation rather than a preordained cultural trait. The second pillar of the moral economy is related to the safety-first principle and undergirds peasant need for a secure subsistence base. Subsistence security is at the core of peasant life. Peasants rebel against their overlords not because of the magnitude of what overlords extract from them. They rebel when such exactions endanger their subsistence security. Finally, emerging from the first two principles are moral and ethical guidelines, which are a set of expectations pertaining to the subsistence rights of the peasants and the obligations of the powerful. Scott's work shows that peasants rebel when (colonial) states oblivious to the moral economy of the peasant violate these ethical principles (Edelman 2005).

The essence of the moral economy argument is that peasants and the poor in general have a set of expectations that govern their sense of justice, and when those expectations are violated, they respond vigorously to protect their livelihood and their sense of fairness. In fact, these values are so much part of peasants' worldview that rebellion against infraction is seen as normal. In the words of Tawney, as a result of this worldview, the peasant radicals are astonished when overlords and others accuse them that their rebellion is disturbing the peace because they believe that they are "merely trying to get back what has been rightfully theirs" (Tawney cited in Scott 1976, p. 11).

Peasants and other subaltern groups do not rebel in all circumstances to obtain justice. When the forces of domination are stacked against rebellion, these groups engage in non-confrontational tactics to resist deprivation. Scott explores these other forms of resistance in Weapons of the Weak (1985). He illustrates that, when rebellion is not feasible for the poor, owing to the overwhelming power of the elite, peasants often turn to less visible ways of responding to the predations of the powerful, such as foot-dragging and feigning to register hiding their umbrage.

The combination of arguments in Scott's *Moral Economy of the Peasant and Weapons of the Weak* provides a useful framework for explaining defensive piracy and the Somalis' attitude toward ransom pirates. A moral economy interpretation of defensive pirates would indicate these actors are merely protecting their resources from stronger outside groups that are not bound by local ethics. It is not that Somalis object to fishing by non-Somalis in their waters, but because the fish pirates loot on such an egregious scale, it endangers Somali livelihoods. In the language of the moral economy, it is not the exploitation of the fisheries per se that offends Somalis, but the pirates' callous ransacking of resources without consideration to residents' livelihood needs that trigger the attack on foreign fishing trawlers. Local people's rage intensified as the international community began to talk about Somali pirates without ever acknowledging the resource pirates as the predators. In addition, labeling local fishermen who were defending their livelihoods as pirates, while depicting illegal foreign fishing trawlers as victims, enraged many Somalis. To add insult to injury, the international community exposed its duplicity when ransom pirates got involved. The robbery by ransom pirates is similar in kind to the deeds of fish pirates, but ransom pirates steal a fraction of what fish pirates take. Nevertheless, the world pays little attention to the resource pirates, and condemns only the Somalis as pirates.

Most Somalis resemble Tawney's radical peasant bewildered by the overlord's (international community's) accusations. They are astonished at hearing complaints of the troubles ransom pirates create for world commerce and security in the region. They think that Somali piracy is simply a justified response to the political and resource predation visited on their country. Somalis see the discourse on piracy as a clear manifestation of the double standards of the international system.

An Alternative Framework and Strategy

The international community was deeply troubled by the growth of piracy and its effect on trade in the strategic waters off the Somali coast (Sorenson 2008, BBC 2010, UN Security Council 2008).[15] NATO members and other concerned nations deployed their navies to patrol the area (Swedish Defense Agency 2009).[16] Despite the increased presence of foreign navies in the Gulf of Aden and the Indian Ocean, piracy increased substantially between 2007 and 2012 (Entous 2010, Murphy 2010).[17] Southeast Asia had the overall lead in the total number of piracy instances during the years under study, but the frequency of Somali pirate attacks was four times higher than Southeast Asia's in 2009.

The cost to companies with ships traversing Somali waters increased substantially. In addition to the $35 million to $60 million a year collected by ransom pirates, the cost of insuring ships has increased tenfold, and the cost of maintaining the naval presence of the European Union alone was estimated to be at least $450 million in 2009 (Hansen 2009, Giplin 2009, *Times Online* 2008).[18] Fittingly, the beneficiary of increased piracy, besides the pirates collecting ransom money and insurance companies collecting premiums, is Somali fishing resources. The risky nature of fishing in Somali waters has chased away some fish pirates, although diehards continue to take their chances (Channel 4 News, UK 2009).[19] The actions of ransom pirates offered a partial and temporary response to the plight of Somali fishing communities that have been ignored by the international community (Reuters, May 9, 2006).

Armed security personnel on ships and deployment of costly naval armadas did little to curtail resource pirates exploiting Somali marine resources (Entous 2010). In fact, resource pirates from at least two dozen countries have flourished under the full gaze of the international naval force. All fair-minded people would ask why the international community, which has such a powerful military presence in the area, was unwilling to push resource pirates out of Somali territorial waters.

The answer rests on the way the international community and its experts *framed* Somali issues. In the same way that some see Somali politics as motivated by some cultural traits and values, so are piracy's motivations confounded with unrelated circumstances. This Somali political framework ignores the generative forces that have shaped Somalia's destructive politics.

Similarly, those who have studied piracy along the Somali coast, and those who have attempted to contain and destroy it, have failed to understand the critical causal forces that made piracy possible. Among these foundational causes was how the Cold War intensified local and regional political conflicts, which had a large part in the demise of the Somali state in 1991.

As the evidence presented in the chapter shows, pirates did not operate along the Somali coast when Somalia had a national government, verifying the proposition that the Somali state was a bulwark against piracy. Given this evidence, one would think that the most effective strategy to eliminate piracy in the region would be to help Somalis rebuild their national government. The sense of this strategy has eluded the international community because its understanding of the causes of the Somali calamity is marooned in an antediluvian framework. Further, European and US powers' Somali policy is also subservient to their efforts to strengthen regional allies, such as Ethiopia and Kenya, which consider a progressive and united Somalia as an existential challenge.

Ransom piracy has declined significantly since the beginning of last decade, but resource pirates continue to plunder. This means that current strategy has had limited effect, and therefore, an enduring solution requires better understanding of the complexity of piracy. My analysis that differentiates pirates into four types provides the first global view of all the actors. Identifying the motivations for each type of piracy makes possible deploying measures that will demolish these incentives. The military strategy that was pursued ignored resource and defensive pirates and their contribution to the rise of ransom pirates. Defensive pirates emerged to protect their resources from global predators. Once global resource predators are eliminated, defensive piracy will vanish just as political pirates did. Resource and ransom pirates, goaded by the lust for booty and ransom, thrive in the lawless environment created by the collapse of the Somali state. Reversing lawlessness requires a political program that addresses the original factors that produced statelessness.

An anti-piracy strategy that addresses the motivations of all types of pirates, and has immediate- and medium-term goals, is necessary. In the medium term, a competent political and reconstruction program for Somalia is essential because, unlike piracy in other regions, piracy along the Somali coast was non-existent when the country had a functioning government. As further evidence, the incidence of ransom piracy declined when a semblance of popular authority in the country emerged in 2006, in the shape of the UICs.

Clearly comprehending the true causes of the country's political collapse is vital to avoid repeating the same errors that have borne poisonous fruit. International and regional sectarian-driven agendas will not work. A new alliance between the Somali civic movement and an international community genuinely intent on the country's needs can re-establish government in the country that will serve their mutual interests. I think that only such a partnership is the best hope to prevent further growth of resource and other forms of pirates.[20]

A more immediate undertaking is necessary for the international community to regain the confidence of the Somali people. Somalis are understandably infuriated by the devastation to their moral economy. They regard ransom pirates as no more criminal than resource pirates. Somalis believe the international community is, at best, unsympathetic to their cause, or worse, a major factor in the making of the Somali disaster. The international community must be more evenhanded in its treatment of pirates.

In the immediate term, sustainable security and peace in Somali waters and in the country depends on official UN recognition that resource pirates are part of the problem. Meanwhile, NATO countries and nations that have brought their navies to the Gulf of Aden and the Indian Ocean to protect merchant ships should also protect the Somali people's livelihoods and chase resource pirates out of Somali waters. Simultaneously, the international community can assist local people in rebuilding their fishing economy. A collaborative relationship will stimulate discourse between the international community and Somalis that could cut off ransom pirates from safe havens on land. The cost of achieving these immediate goals would be substantially less than that for the current approach to fighting piracy (Hansen 2009).[21] Folding the immediate- and medium-term approaches to piracy and lawlessness into a broader strategy has a better chance of securing the region and restoring peace and democratic order.

Reframing piracy along the Somali coast brings to the fore the concepts and analytic tools we use to explain political economy problems and the assumptions they are based on. Challenging the necessary conditions for piracy of mainstream scholarship, the chapter explains the genesis and timing of piracy along the Somali coast. Identifying the four types of piracy transcends legal diktats that circumscribe our intellectual vision. Power and historical-geographic context matter in coming to grips with the making of the Somali world—or any other world, for that matter.

Bibliography

Abshir, Mohamed. Interview, Minneapolis, October 2004.

Africa Report, Washington, DC. November 1964, p. 6.

Arraleh, Ali Said. Interview, Nairobi, May 2002.

BBC News. "The UN Backs Tougher Stance Against Somali Pirates," April 27, 2010, http://news.bbc.co.uk/2/hi/africa/ 8647928.stm.

Bustelo, M.G. "Somalia: The Explosive Combination of Illegal Fishing, Toxic Waste and Piracy," *Forum for a Safer Democracy*, June 4, 2009.

Campo, A. "Discourse Without Discussion: Representations of Piracy in Colonial Indonesia, 1816–25," *Journal of Southeast Asian Studies*, vol. 34, no. 2 (2003): pp. 199–214.

Chanda, N. "No Safe Harbor for Illegal Fishing," September 15, 2009, http://www.policyinnovations.org/ideas/innovations/data/000147.

Channel 4 News. "The 'Benefit' of Somalia's Pirates," October 25, 2009, http://channel4.com/news/articles/world/africa/theaposbenefi.

Coffen-Smout, S. Coffen-Smout. "Pirates, Warlords and Rogue Fishing Vessels in Somalia's Unruly Seas," February 1998, http://www.chebucto.ns.ca/~ar120/somalia.html.

Copson, R. *The United States in Africa*. New York: Zed Books, 2007.

Draper, R. Shattered Somalia," August 2009, http://ngm.nationalgeographic.com/2009/09/somalia/draper-text.

Entous, A. "US Admiral: Military Ships Cannot Stop Somali Piracy," Reuters, April 15, 2010.

Edelman, M. Bringing the Moral Economy Back in to the Study of 21st Century Transnational Peasant Movements," *American Anthropologist*, vol. 107, no. 3 (2005): pp. 332–345.

Frecon, E. "Piracy and Armed Robbery at Sea Along the Malacca Straits," G. Ong-Webb, editor. *Piracy, Maritime Terrorism, and Securing the Malacca Strait*. Singapore: Institute of Southeast Asian Studies, 2006

Friedman, J., and J. Levisohn. "The Distributional Impacts of Indonesia's Financial Crisis on Household Welfare: A Rapid Response Methodology," *The World Bank Economic Review*, vol. 16, no. 3 (2002): pp. 397–423.

Gettleman, J. "Humanitarian Crisis in Somalia is Worse than Darfur," *International Herald Tribune*, http://www.iht.com/articles/2007/11/20/africa/somalia.php.

Giplin, R. "Counting the Cost of Somali Piracy," United States Institute of Peace Working Paper, Washington, DC, 2009.

Hassan, M.G., and M.H. Tako. "Illegal Fishing & Dumping Hazardous Waste Threatens the Development of Somali Fisheries and the Marine Environment," Tropical Aquaculture & Fisheries Conference, Terengganu, Malaysia, September 7–9, 1999.

Hansen, S. "Modern Piracy as a Subject of Academic Enquiry," *International Relations* vol. 12, no. 18, 2008.

Hansen, S. and A. Mesoy. "The Pirates of the Horn: State Collapse and Maritime Threat," *Strategic Insights* vol. 3, no. 1 (2006).

Hansen, S. "Piracy in the Greater Gulf of Aden," *Norwegian Institute for Urban and Regional Research,* London, 2009.

Hari. J. Toxic Waste Behind Somali Pirates," 2010, Hiriraan.com.

Harvey, D. *The New Imperialism.* Oxford: Oxford University Press, 2003.

Hastings, J. Geographies of State Failure and Sophistication in Maritime Piracy Hijackings," *Political Geography* vol. 28, no. 4 (2009): pp. 213–223.

Held, D.A. McGrew, Goldblatt, D., and Perraton, J. *Global Transformations: Politics, Economics and Culture.* Stanford: Stanford University Press, 1999.

Ho, J.H. "Piracy Around the Horn of Africa," *Korean Journal of Defense Analysis,* vol. 21 no. 4 (2009): pp. 501–518.

Human Rights Watch. "Somalia: A Government at War with Its Own People: Testimonies About the Killings and Conflict in the North," New York, 1990.

Human Rights Watch, "Harsh War, Harsh Peace: Abuses by al-Shabaab, the Transitional Federal Government, and AMISON in Somalia." Washington, DC, 2010.

Hussen, Abdirazak H. Interview, Minneapolis, March 2001.

Idemudia, U. and U.E. Ite. "Demystifying the Niger Delta Conflict: Towards an Integrated Explanation." *Review of African Political Economy,* vol. 109 (2006): pp. 391–406.

Keck, M., and K. Sikkink. *Activists Beyond Borders.* Ithaca: Cornel University Press, 1997.

Lane, K. *Pillaging the Empire: Piracy in the America, 1500–1750.* New York: Armonk, 1998.

Lefebvre, J. "The United States, Ethiopia and the 1963 Somali-Soviet Arms Deal: Containment and the Balance of Power Dilemma in the Horn of Africa," *Journal of Modern African Studies,* vol. 36, no. 4 (1998): pp. 611–643.

Lemarchard, R. "The CIA in Africa: How Central? How Intelligent? Ray, E., Schaarp, W., Meter, K. Meter, and L., Wolf (editors. *Dirty Work 2: The CIA in Africa.* Secaucus: Lyle Stuart Inc, 1979, p. 16.

Mackenze, D. "Toxic Waste Adds to Somalia's Woes," *New Scientist,* Sept. 19, 1992.

Middleton, R. *Piracy in Somalia: Threatening Global Trade, Feeding Local Wars.* London: Chatham House, 2008.

Moller, B. "Piracy off the Coast of Somalia," DIIS Brief, January 2009.

Murphy, M. *Small Boats, Weak States, Dirty Money: The Challenge of Piracy.* New York: Columbia University Press, 2009.

Mynott, A. "Somali Crisis 'Worse than Darfur,'" BBC News/Africa, June 18, 2008.

National Security Council. "Countering Piracy off the Horn of Africa: Partnership and Action Plan," Washington, DC, December 2008.

Nur, A.H. "Somalia Putting Heavy Emphasis on its Fisheries," *World Fisheries,* vol. 37, no. 10 (1998), pp. 2–3.

Johann, Hari. "Toxic Waste Behind Somali Pirates," 2010, *Hiriraan.com.*

Obi, C. "Enter the Dragon? Chinese Oil Companies and Resistance in the Niger Delta," R*eview of African Political Economy,* vol. 117 (2008): pp. 417–434.

Omeje, K. "Oil Conflict in Nigeria: Contending Issues and Perspectives of the Local Niger Delta People," *New Political Economy,* vol. 10 no. 3 (2005): pp. 321–334.

Ong-Webb, C. "Piracy in Maritime Asia: Current Trends," Lehr, O., editor. *Violence at Sea: Piracy in the Age of Global Terrorism.* New York: Routledge, 2007.

Peet, J. "Modern Sea Piracy," *Pacific Maritime Magazine,* August 2007, pp. 24–26.

Rice, X. and S. Goldenber. "How the US Forged an Alliance with Ethiopia over Invasion," The Guardian, www.guardian.co.uk/world/2007/jan/13/alqaida.usa.

Sahnoun, M. *Somalia: The Missed Opportunities.* Washington, DC: United States Peace Institute, 1994.

Samatar, A. I. "Destruction of State and Society in Somalia: Beyond the Tribal Convention," *The Journal of Modern African Studies,* vol. 30, no. 4 (1992): pp. 625–641.

------------------. "'Leadership and Ethnicity in the Making of African State Models: Botswana Versus Somalia," *Third World Quarterly,* vol. 18, no. 4 (1997): pp. 687–707.

------------------.*Africa's First Democrats.* Bloomington: Indiana University Press, 2016.

Schofield, C. "Plundered Waters: Somalia's Maritime Resource Security," Doyle T., and Risoly M., editors. *Crucible for Survival: Environmental Security and Justice in the Indian Ocean Region.* New Brunswick: Rutgers State University, 2008: pp. 102–125.

Phillips, L. "The European Roots of Somali Pirates, *E U Observer,* April 21, 2009.

Scott, J. *The Moral Economy of the Peasant: Rebellion and Subsistence in Southeast Asia.* New Haven: Yale University Press, 1976.

---------. *Weapons of the Weak: Everyday Forms of Peasant Resistance.* New Haven: Yale University Press, 1985.

Sorenson, K. "State Failure on the High Seas: Reviewing the Somali Piracy," Stockholm: Swedish Defense Research Agency, FOI Somali Papers, Report 3, November 2008.

NSN Money. "The Real Cost of Piracy," http://articles.moneycentral.msn.com/Investing/Extra/the-real-cost-of-piracy.aspx. April 14.

The Maritime Executive. "Pirates Attack Two Fishing Boats Off Somalia," https://www.maritime-executive.com/article/pirates-attack-two-fishing-boats-off-somalia.

Thompson, E.P. "The Moral Economy of the English Crowd in the Eighteenth Century," *Past and Present 50: 1971*: pp 76–136.

Times Online, https://business.timesonline.co.uk/to1/business/industry_sectors/banking_and_finance/ article..., September 11, 2008.

Weldemichael, A. *Piracy in Somalia: Violence and Development in the Horn of Africa*. Cambridge: Cambridge University Press, 2019.

Ukiwo, U. "From Pirates to Militants: a Historical Perspective on Anti-State and Anti-Oil Company Mobilization Among the Ijaw of Warri, Western Niger Delta," *African Affairs*, vol. 106 (2007): pp. 425–436.

United Nations. *Humanitarian Situation in Somalia*, Monthly Analysis, Nairobi, April 2007.

United Nations Environmental Program. "The State of the Environment in Somalia," Nairobi, UNEP, 2005, p. 45.

---. "Environmental Problems of the East African Region," *Nairobi Regional Seas Reports and Studies*, vol. 12 (1982).

---. "The State of the Environment in Somalia," Nairobi, 2005, p. 33, http://english.aljazeera.net/news/africa/2008/10/2008109174223218644.html.

United Nations Security Council. Resolutions 1864, SC/9514, 2008, and United Nations Security Council Resolution 1851, SC/9541, 2008.

United States Department of State. Incoming Telegram, Department From American Embassy in Somalia, July 16, 1964.

United States National Geospatial Agency (NGA). http://www.nga.mil/NGAPortal/MSI.portal).

Warren, J. A Tale of Two Centuries: The Globalization of Maritime Raiding & Piracy in Southeast Asia at the End of Eighteen and Twentieth Centuries," Asia Research Institute, Working Paper 2, June 2003.

Watts, M. "Empire of Oil: Capitalist Dispossession and the Scramble for Africa," *Monthly Review,* vol. 58, no. 4 (2006): pp. 1–16.

Watts, M. "Petro-Insurgency or Criminal Syndicates? Conflict & Violence in the Niger Delta." *Review of African Political Economy,* vol. 34, no. 114 (2007): pp. 637–660.

Watts, M. editor. *Curse of the Black Gold: Fifty Years of Oil in the Niger Delta.* New York: Powerhouse Books, 2008.

Endnotes

1   A version of this chapter was previously published in *Third World Quarterly,* https://doi.org/10.1080/01436597.2010.538238. Permission to republish has been granted.

2   An exception to this line of thinking is Phillips, who points out: "As global powers ratchet up the naval pressure off the coast of Somalia and the European Union this week prepares to play host to a major international conference on the growing scourge of piracy, very little attention is being paid to the other 'piracy' in the area—the decades of European illegal fishing and dumping of toxic waste in Somali waters."

3   The United Nations Law of the Sea Convention of 1982, offers a slightly more restricted definition confining piracy to occur outside the jurisdiction of nation-state maritime borders. Earlier conceptions of piracy were not confined to such acts that took place outside the limits of maritime boundaries, or by criminal robberies in the high seas as private groups, or as some states were involved, such as the British, which commissioned piracies against Spanish ships. (Murphy 2009)

4   Data used to make the maps in the study were derived from the Anti-Shipping Activity Messages (ASAM) database from the US National Geospatial Agency (NGA). This data is freely downloadable from the NGA website, (http://www.nga.mil/NGAPortal/MSI.portal). The ASAM database includes incidents of specific hostile

acts against ships, and includes a location, an ID, a region code, a date, the type of aggressor, the type of victim, and a verbal description of the incident. Some of the records in the database were edited in order to fix obvious locational errors, and to rectify inconsistencies between an incident's location and its description. The regionalization for the study is not based on the region codes in the database, but were derived from the locations of the incidents. The maps were produced in the Cartography Laboratory in the Department of Geography at the University of Minnesota.

5   Mark Lindberg produced the two maps contained in the chapter.

6   A prominent feature of this ecosystem is a seasonal upwelling which gives rise to high levels of biological productivity, which in turn sustain rich fishing ground.... Surveys carried out in the 1970s estimated that the potential yield of marine fishery resources could range between 380,000 tons and 500,000 tons per annum.... More conservative estimates, however, suggest that the annual catch potential is likely to be between 180,000 tons and 200,000 tons per annum.... Overfishing has been noted in a number of sectors, primarily offshore—where trawlers from many nations ply the waters untroubled by any national maritime force" (United Nations Environmental Program 2005, p. 45; Nur 1998, pp. 2–3; Hari 2010). Hari notes that nearly $300 million of fish are stolen annually by international fishing companies from the Somali coast.

7   According to United Nations Environmental Program (UNEP), the absence of surveillance means that tankers routinely discharge oily ballast off the Somali coastline: annual discharges were once estimated at 33,000 tonnes" UNEP indicates that Tar balls are regularly found on certain sections of the Somali coast, above all high energy beaches in the western sector... Sewage and solid waste discharge from marine vessels is another unregulated activity. United Nations Environmental Program (2005: 3); http://english.aljazeera.net/news/africa/2008/10/2008109174223218644.html. See also The Canadian Broadcasting Corporation estimated that it cost $8 to dump a ton of toxic waste in Somali waters while it cost $100 a ton to bury it in America or Europe (Bustelo. June 4, 2009).

8   The United Nations Environment Program estimates that 700 trawlers have been illegally fishing in Somali waters, (2005).

9   ibid.

10 This assessment is based on interviews and correspondence with fif-

Chapter 4

ty-five Somali pirates from Eil, Haradheere, and Bossasso. (January 2009–December 2009)

11 This is one of the few articles that speak about "… grievances of the Somali people have to be addressed."

12 Interviews with four journalists who extensively covered the issue for local media. (Bossasso and Garowe 2004 and 2008)

13 Quoting Tawney's characterization of the precarious nature of peasant "… as that of a man standing permanently into the neck with water, so that even a ripple might drown him." (Scott 1986, p. 1)

14 Here is how Sorenson describes it "… new phenomenon occurred off the coast of Somalia and in the Gulf of Aden, Ships and *fishing vessels* were being attacked by pirates…. In response, the UN Security Council passed resolution 1816, and later in 2008, UNSCR 1838, which encourages the international community to actively participate in the management of security in the Gulf of Aden and off the coast of Somalia. The resolutions also stipulate the legal framework for actively targeting the pirates. (Sorenson 2008)

15 I was told that some of the naval intervention by the EU is partly designed to test their new naval equipment. (See also Swedish Defense Agency person, May 2009)

16 Admiral Mark Fitzgerald, Commander of US Naval Forces in Europe and Africa, is quoted as saying that "we could put a World War Two fleet of ships out there and we still would not be able to cover the whole ocean. (Murphy, *Somali Piracy: Not Just a Naval Problem*, 2009)

17 Shipping Insurances Cost Sours with Piracy Surge off Somalia(*Times Online* 2008). http://www.business.timesonline.co.uk/to1/business/industry_sectors/banking_and_finance/article…". (NSN Money 2009). This article estimates that the $30 million Somali pirates collect annually is "less than a percent of the total value of cars stolen in the US last year." (Hansen (009, p. 45, Giplin 2009)

18 According to Channel 4 (2000), "the increasing levels of piracy off the coast of Somalia have caused an unexpected spin-off, raising the levels of fish in the area…. The massive factory trawlers which used to drain their fish stocks have been scared away, and that means there is a huge bounty for local fisherman, as well as helping to restore the health of the marine eco-system." What is not reported here is that significant number of Somali fishermen have either abandoned fish-

ing, or are too frightened to venture into sea lest they be considered pirates by the naval forces in the area.

19   The regime in Mogadishu has signed a contract with China in 2018, which allows the fishing fleet of that country to ransack Somali resources without let and for a long time. In essence, this contract gives greenlight to resources pirates from China.

20   Hansen states: "In Somalia, the cost of one Norwegian frigate deployed for six months...[is] USD 30.1 million, [and that] represents pay for 100,000 Police officers for the same period." (Hansen, et. al., *Piracy in the Greater Gulf of Aden*)

5
Liberating Somali Studies and Somalia

Bad theory is like bad medicine; it kills.[1]

Corrupt politics and authoritarian rule instigated a prolonged civil war that shattered Somalis' lives for at least over three decades (1988–2022). Among the major consequences have been the premature death of nearly a million citizens, millions were displaced inside and outside the country, the environment and material infrastructure was destroyed, and a sense of national belonging was eroded. Recovering from all the material losses will be a daunting undertaking, given the dearth of immediately available resources, human and otherwise. The reconstitution of civic life, and the retrieval of a people's common humanity, will be the most formidable challenges, but they are key to human upliftment and an enduring human and eco-centered development. The indispensable first step in this expedition is to redefine the country's problems by reframing the nature of the Somali calamity—intellectually, politically, economically, socially, ecologically, and culturally.

This journey begins by identifying the major actors and the bad theories that produced the catastrophe. Three instrumentalist groups guided by their myopic visions have been the foremost drivers of the calamity. They framed and defined Somali issues and problems to prioritize political solutions that reflect their self-serving agendas. The first group, the dominant faction of the local political class, tribalized communal relations to maintain its grip on power. They insist that the country's administrative regions must be drawn along tribal lines (Samatar 2019), and that members of parliament and other political officers in key organs of the state must represent tribal groups rather than competing political agendas and civic ideas. Even more devastating is their insistence that genealogical identity must be the most significant criterion for determining the staffing of public service positions, and not professional skills and competence (a most glaring illustration of this is the current mayor of Mogadishu). Because of these diktats, each ministry has become the fiefdom of a sectarian group.[3] The "tribalization" of politics and civil service perpetuates dysfunctional public affairs, deepens communal divisions, prolongs conflicts, and profoundly undermines rebuilding competent state institutions by going against the very definition of statehood, which is anchored in such institutions' ability to serve the needs of the population effectively and impartially (Berman 1999).[4] The second group of culprits consists of cultural leaders, over the last thirty years, who lust after money, power, and recognition. Having joined forces with the first group, they claim to be the only authentic and legitimate authorities of "their cultural groups." They have become political kingmakers and hold significant sway in selecting political representatives and shaping the venue in which members of parliament are chosen. Politicized traditionalists have gained status in this environment, and use it to sell parliamentary seats to the highest bidders.[5] This mutuality between sectarian politicians and perverted traditionalists has completed the corruption of culture and politics.

The third group, major powers and other organizations such as the United Nations, the African Union, and the Intergovernmental Authority on Development, claim to represent the international community, and their intellectual consultants have consistently accepted and advanced discourses that frame Somali politics as quintessentially tribal or prehistoric. Their political and material stances have merged with the interests and agendas of the sectarian Somali politicians and perverted traditionalists. International actors pretend that the current course of Somali politics will *miraculously* morph into a democratic governance that will improve lives and protect the rights of all its citizens—despite three decades of evidence to the contrary.

These groups' interests and ideas left Somalis of civic political orientation leaderless and without a supportive international or African network. Moreover, the tough economic and security circumstances prevalent in the country inhibit the vast majority of the population from mobilizing for progressive change. Thus, it appears that the feasibility of an alternative political project in the country is dim, yet there is public hunger for national resurrection.

Rejuvenating civic life and mobilizing the population begins with de-ethnicizing political and social problems. Doing so entails recovering the political history of the country and introducing concepts that are rich enough to unpack the dialectics and complexity of that history, cultural change, and material life. Such an approach will open up possibilities for a more humane future. This book is an invitation to open-minded scholars, civic-oriented activists, and those who care about the fate of the Somali people, to rise to the challenge of redefining concepts and developing theories that illuminate a feasible civic political praxis anchored in an enduring moral foundation.

Reframing Thought and Practice

To do the impossible, you must see the invisible.[6]
Unsettling what has become the normal way of seeing Somali political identity and problems, and offering an alternative intellectual agenda, is the primary purpose of the book. Chapter 1 reviewed the dominant paradigm in Somali studies, and showed not only its conceptual prejudice, but also its inability to explain historical events and circumstances, or entertain alternative explanations. For scholars working in this paradigm, little difference exists between the *appearance* and *essence* of social and political phenomena. Scholars and writers working in the field treat the symptoms of social and political events and processes as their true soul. They ignore crucial factors that give meaning to specific social and political phenomena in historical, economic, political, geographic, and cultural contexts. Further, the remedies applied to the Somali catastrophe, prescribed by the dominant school of thought, deepened the disaster rather than ameliorating it.

The remaining chapters of the book expanded Chapter 1's meaning-making contextual analysis of the social construction of political and social phenomena to offer an alternative way of understanding the Somali conundrum without ignoring or fossilizing key elements of the people's cultural heritage.

Chapter 2 challenged established ethnic explanations of politics during the democratic era, and by extension, broader issues in Somali affairs. It did so by bringing back in the value-adding historical, political, and cultural contexts. Reframing politics this way gives individuals and groups agency that is not tightly bound to their genealogical roots, but that allows them latitude to select their political course of action from competing trajectories. Individuals from the same genealogical group or family might have contrasting political positions and advocate for competing political parties. This approach does not deny the significance of cultural values in politics, but stresses that, at best, such norms are contingent rather than necessary in the political dynamics in the country.

Chapter 2 identified two broad trajectories in Somali politics: civic and sectarian. Framing Somali politics in this manner liberates politics from the shackles of discredited functional anthropology and Orientalism. Thus, the social construction and political economic framework allows for contingency without determining a priori what will shape the political orientation of individuals and groups.

Chapter 3 took up the debate about the role of Islam and the ulema in Somali life. Once again, the establishment scholarship on Islam, as the late Edward Said illuminated, fails to contextualize the circumstances that induce religious leaders and the faith to play certain roles in the political and cultural life of the people at specific times. Because of Orientalist prejudices, scholars in this vein see only one dimension of political Islam as they cast their gaze from the vantage point of the Western power structure.

Chapter 3 showed how diverse historical and political contexts shaped the role Islam and the ulema played in Somali life over the *longue durée*. Five historical and political periods in Somali affairs have framed Islam's social and political influences. First, Islam and the ulema played cultural and peacemaking roles in precolonial times, with little relevancy to formal politics. Second, with the advent of the European and Ethiopian invasion of Somali territory, the ulema became the main sources of resistance, and consequently gained a major new political role in public life. After the twenty-one-year anticolonial war ended with British victory, some of the ulema resisted, whereas others succumbed to colonial pressure and assumed subservient roles in the colonial administrations, such as in Qadi courts.

Third, as Somalis agitated for independence, the ulema were barely visible in the liberation struggle, though political leaders were cognizant of the importance of Islam for the movement. Somalia's democratic constitution stated that Islam was foundational anchor to all laws, yet the ulema were barely visible in the political affairs of the new country. Despite the invisibility of the ulema, democratic leaders of the country recognized the centrality of Islam in Somali culture and identity, and thus ensured that government honored and respected Islam while maintaining an open democratic order. Thus, the ulema and the population did not see the democratic government as a menace, and religious and political leaders maintained affable relations.

Fourth, the military overthrow of the democratic regime, and its adoption of scientific socialism, changed the relationship of the state, the population, and the ulema. The combination of the despotic military rule, and the dramatic change it introduced into Islamic family law, without public consultation, prepared the ground for conflict. Relations between the government, on one hand, and the population and ulema, on the other, deteriorated, and the ulema became a political force for the first time since the British had defeated Sayyid Mohamed Abdulle Hassan in 1921.

Fifth, when the authoritarian regime fell, and the entire state edifice disintegrated in 1991, Islam and the ulema gradually gained political influence. A decade and half after the collapse of the state, the deaths of a million people, and political despair, compelled a segment of the ulema and an affiliation, the Union of Islamic Courts (UICs), to take control of Mogadishu with the full support of the population, in the spring of 2006. In a rash action, with terrible consequences, the African Union and the international community attempted to discredit the UICs as a terrorist group. Ethiopia, encouraged by this climate and material support from America, invaded Somalia and occupied its capital on December 26, 2006. In Mogadishu alone, the invasion displaced over a million people and killed nearly twenty thousand. Enraged by the cruelty of the Ethiopian military, Somalis from all over the world mobilized in support of the UICs, and gave the UICs both moral and material support. Because of these interventions, political Islam has been a major political force in the country ever since.

The UICs and associated militias went underground after the Ethiopian invasion, and the government of Eritrea gave safe haven to the political leaders of the UICs, while the military wing fought an intense and sustained guerrilla war against the invaders. Because the invasion became difficult to sustain, the United States co-opted some political leaders of the UICs. "Hardliners" split from the "moderates," and the latter then took power in Mogadishu. Meanwhile, the US Department of State designated Al-Shabaab, the youth wing of the UICs, as a terrorist organization. Since then, Al-Shabaab has resorted to indiscriminate violence in an attempt to dislodge regimes in Mogadishu. The United States' political agenda, carried out by Ethiopian and African Union foot soldiers and sectarian elements of the Somali political elite, has made Islam the foremost alternative political force in the country. Islam's role in politics and culture has had a sea change largely driven by the political developments in the country. Accordingly, rather than demonizing Islam and the ulema, it is more productive to understand the ways in which political circumstances (outside the faith) have shaped current practice.

Most views on piracy along the Somali coast suffer from the same myopic ideology and condemn Somalis for their "mischief" in the Indian Ocean and the Gulf of Aden. Chapter 4 demolished this superficial thinking. In contextually grounded analysis, I separate the bare "fact" of piracy from its complex essence. My alternative analysis of the problem starts with the conceptual premise that things are not necessarily what they appear to be. I examine data on piracy, using sources from the US Navy and the International Maritime Organization (based in London), to see why piracy became a problem only after the disintegration of the state. I then bring the political history of the country into the analysis to understand what made the state collapse, and discern links to global geopolitics. Such framing and analysis reveal four types of pirates rather than the stereotype that the literature, media, and political authorities around the world have focused on. This discovery provides the clearest manifestation of the vital role context plays in meaningfully explaining the nature of social and political problems.

Coda

The word *frame* carries at least two meanings in the English language. As a noun, it is a contextualization of an object to give it a particular focus, like framing a photograph. As a verb, it means to set a person up for failure, or as a target for harm. This book draws on the dual meaning of the term in confronting the dominant Somalist literature. Depicting Somali political culture as a fossil anchored in antediluvian identity (if it ever existed) has meant that Somalis' identities were singular and unmalleable. As the late I.M. Lewis asserted, "Somalis receive their fundamental social and political identity at birth" (Lewis 2001). Framing Somali political, religious, and other identities in this fashion has facilitated others in denying their humanity and responding to them in prejudicial ways that have been at odds with the reality of who they are, the nature of their culture, and the sources of their political ills. Defining them as a "tribal man," a "Muslim terrorist," or a "pirate" has had the effect of turning them into objects of alienation, manipulation worthy of abuse.

For example, the international community has deliberately ignored the billions of dollars of fish that the international fleet (resource pirates) have looted from Somalis. In contrast, the same international community has violently reacted to Somali defensive and ransom pirates who have hijacked fishing trawlers, merchant ships, and yachts valued at a fraction of the stolen fish. The failure to understand context in the dynamics of Somali cultural, political, and religious identity has produced wrong narratives, disastrous policies, immeasurable injustices, and awful human conditions at every turn.

If we are to reverse the Somali condition and realize the tremendous potential of the Somali people, we urgently need a total shift in thinking and practice. Somalis cannot afford to wait for the international community and their intellectual comrades to wise up. Civic-minded and genuinely pious Somalis must do more than pray and hope, and instead mobilize the population. Simultaneously, Somali scholars and their progressive associates from around the world need to do what the old Chinese revolutionaries said when their society was in peril: "*Fanshen*," or turn over, upend, the intellectual and political soil inside out, and embark on new and liberated Somali studies. Such liberated scholarship will inspire Somalia's freedom from the humiliation of the last forty years.

Bibliography

Berman, B. "Ethnicity, Patronage and the African State: The Politics of Uncivil Nationalism." *African Affairs,* vol. 97: pp. 305–341.

Lewis, I.M. Court Statement, London, 2001.

Said, Edward. *Orientalism.* New York: Vintage, 1979.

Samatar, Abdi Ismail. "Fate Worse Than Artificial Borders is the Insidious African Elite Politics: The Somali Case," *South African Geographical Journal,* vol. 101, no. 3 (2019): pp. 357–3

Endnotes

1   I heard this statement from Prof. De Janvry of the University of California, Berkeley, when I took his course in 1982. He wanted to underscore the critical importance of theory for the life of people and nations.

2   I had firsthand experience with this madness. I met a female student in Turkey who had just completed her MBA in financial accounting, but who has been unable to get the appropriate job with the Somali government despite the latter's desperate need for skilled young people. She asked me if I could be a reference for her, to which I agreed. I recommended her to the Central Bank of Somalia. She was told that she had the necessary qualifications, but must take an exam. She passed the examination and got a job. She then met with the second most senior person in the bank, who was responsible for placing new recruits. The responsible women asked her which clan she belonged. The young employee was shocked and evaded the question. She was subsequently assigned to a post with a salary lower than employees who had lower qualifications. The senior female banker found out a few days later that the new recruits belonged to the same genealogical group as her children. By this time, the young banker was disgusted and decided to leave the bank. She told me the story, and then I called an old friend who was a senior minister in government. I sent all her qualifications to the minister, and after a long pause, he informed me that the young women had all the requisite skills to work for him. I was delighted to hear this, and Ms. X started working for the minister. After a couple months, office gossip said that the new employee was a mentee of Abdi Samatar, although she did not belong to his clan.

Chapter 5 197

The group who considered the ministry to be their clan's turf began to connive against her since her genealogy was different than theirs. After enduring much pressure, she quit the job, although the minister told me that he was exceptionally happy with her performance.

3 Bruce Burman noted the dysfunctional effects this had on the relationship between the state and citizens. "For ordinary people, the central problem lies in their day-to-day contacts with local authorities and agents of the state, where they cannot expect disinterested competence and fairness. Instead, they expect, and mostly get, incompetence, bias, venality, and corruption. So long as this persists, they cannot develop the critical relations of trust in their dealings with the state, and will continue to rely on the personalized, protective ties of *clientalism*. Without displacement of decentralized despotism…limitation on the opportunities for accumulation and patronage through the state apparatus, and effective accommodation of the reality of ethnic pluralism in formal political institutions, there can be little hope of fundamental change moving more clearly towards *modernity*. (Berman 1999, p. 341)

4 I observed this firsthand in 2021, when I ran for parliament.

5 Professor John Adams of the Department of Geography, Environment, and Society at the University of Minnesota, shared this statement with me. He attributed it to an Egyptian Development expert who worked for the United Nations Development Program. Prof. Adams could not remember the name of the expert.

Index

A

academics 1, 7, 42
Achebe, C. 25, 50
advisors 100
Africanist 4, 25
Ahmed Guray 128
Allah v, 53, 73, 154
Amin, Samir 3, 4
anthropological gaze 29
Asad, Talal 20, 25, 28, 50, 54
assets 82, 166
auditor 88, 89
austerity 6

B

BBC 7, 8, 23, 35, 42, 157, 176, 179, 182
beasts in human form 77
birre ma gaydo 128
Borama conference 39
Borey, Omer 59
British 2, 5, 7, 17, 23, 25, 26, 27, 28, 30, 34, 36, 37, 38, 47, 53, 54, 57, 60, 61, 82, 91, 109, 112, 126, 129, 130, 131, 133, 149, 155, 164, 174, 185, 192, 193
British tribunal 7
Brown, Firth 4, 18

Burton, Richard 2, 27

C

cadaan studies 17
Capitalism 21, 23, 151
Catastrophe 23, 53, 154
central committee 31, 78, 80, 98, 99, 100
Christmas Day 2006 145
CIA 94, 109, 141, 156, 182
civic agenda 26, 143
civil service reform 87, 108, 166
clean elections 69
Colonialism 52, 129, 152
consultants 6, 7, 10, 43, 128, 190
corruption 6, 40, 41, 67, 80, 88, 90, 95, 117, 120, 122, 130, 136, 138, 163, 166, 190, 197
cultural and social homogeneity 44

D

Dahirie 82
Dalka 90, 91, 92, 109, 151
Daud, General 87, 121
dependency theory 3
Dhuhul 91
disciples 28
division of labor 88, 91, 92
donors 6, 7, 15, 16, 141

199

E

Egal, Mohamed Ibrahim 39, 61, 65, 74, 80, 114

election 11, 31, 59, 61, 63, 64, 68, 69, 70, 71, 72, 73, 82, 89, 93, 94, 96, 97, 100, 101, 102, 103, 104, 106, 108, 113, 116, 120, 121, 122, 136, 147, 157, 166, 167, 168

Encyclopedia Britannica 3

Ethical 80

Ethiopia 8, 13, 29, 32, 71, 72, 87, 91, 119, 120, 128, 129, 130, 139, 142, 144, 145, 147, 150, 156, 164, 167, 168, 169, 177, 181, 183, 193

EU 8, 9, 33, 34, 52, 156, 187

F

fairest election 72

family law 138, 193

fragmentation 29, 32, 33, 46, 47, 72, 134, 139, 144

frame 7, 10, 11, 31, 124, 160, 190, 194

framing 6, 10, 45, 49, 160, 194, 195

functional anthropology 2, 8, 192

G

genealogy 7, 26, 31, 34, 35, 45, 46, 55, 65, 107, 108, 133, 144, 197

golden handshake 70

Goulet, Dennis 3

Grimslid 18

H

Haley, Alex 2

Hashiish 94

Hirabe, Ali Mohamed 77

Hussein, Jirde v, 99

Hussen, Abdirazak 31, 32, 53, 73, 74, 75, 76, 77, 78, 79, 80, 81, 82, 83, 84, 85, 86, 87, 88, 89, 90, 92, 94, 95, 96, 97, 98, 99, 100, 102, 103, 104, 105, 106, 107, 108, 109, 115, 116, 117, 118, 119, 120, 121, 133, 135, 152, 154, 166, 181

I

IGAD (Intergovernmental Authority on Development) 8, 9, 141, 145

imagined Somali futures 26

IMO (International Maritime Organization) 162

international community 6, 41, 141, 144, 145, 150, 160, 175, 176, 177, 178, 179, 187, 190, 193, 195

International Monetary Fund (IMF) 105, 136

Iowa State University 3, 18

Ismail, Haji Bashir 87, 99

Issa, Abdullahi 65, 77, 115, 120, 133

Italian 5, 26, 30, 36, 37, 38, 47, 54, 60, 61, 77, 82, 93, 100, 102, 117, 126, 131, 132, 133, 134, 149, 152, 155, 164, 169, 172

Index

Italy 1, 29, 60, 83, 132, 133

J

Jama, Mohamoud Issa 76, 79

K

Karti iyo hufnaan 81

Katanga Group 63

Kenya 6, 8, 17, 22, 23, 43, 115, 139, 140, 141, 147, 150, 151, 152, 164, 167, 177

L

Lewis, I.M. 2, 3, 7, 8, 22, 24, 25, 27, 28, 29, 30, 31, 32, 33, 34, 35, 36, 37, 42, 43, 50, 52, 54, 55, 56, 107, 124, 152, 155, 195, 196

Lords of Poverty 6, 21

M

Marxism 5

Marx, Karl 4, 25

merchants of misery 6, 7, 8, 10, 17, 141

military regime 5, 33, 39, 55, 126, 137, 167, 169

Ministers fired 89, 90, 93, 95, 117, 171

Mukhtar, Sheikh 64, 99, 109, 113, 156

municipal election 68, 70, 73

Museveni, Yoweri 9

N

Neoliberal 6

NGOs 5, 6, 7, 10

Norway 13, 14

O

old orthodoxy 25, 44

opening shot 2

Osman, Aden Abdulle 31, 53, 62, 63, 64, 65, 66, 67, 69, 70, 71, 73, 74, 75, 76, 77, 79, 80, 82, 86, 88, 89, 90, 92, 93, 94, 95, 96, 97, 98, 99, 101, 102, 108, 109, 113, 114, 115, 116, 117, 118, 119, 120, 121, 129, 134, 135, 136, 153, 154, 166

P

pirates 159, 160, 161, 162, 163, 168, 169, 170, 172, 173, 174, 175, 176, 177, 178, 179, 184, 187, 188, 194, 195

defensive pirates 147, 168, 170, 172, 173, 174, 175, 178, 195

ransom pirates 168, 172, 173, 174, 175, 176, 178, 179, 195

resource pirates 170, 178, 183

police 69, 70, 71, 72, 88, 89, 100, 101, 103, 105, 106, 114, 119, 121, 122, 167

political class 7, 48, 73, 107, 148, 189

political earthquake 86

Political Economy 21, 23, 50, 152, 153, 181, 182, 185

political ethnicity 41, 43
political tribalism 6, 40, 133, 167
political war 81
politicized genealogy 26
power 5, 6, 7, 15, 17, 28, 29, 32, 43, 44, 45, 48, 54, 59, 70, 77, 81, 91, 93, 98, 100, 103, 105, 106, 107, 108, 121, 122, 123, 129, 137, 138, 146, 149, 150, 165, 166, 167, 175, 189, 190, 192, 194
public service 6, 59, 80, 83, 88, 98, 137, 138, 189
Public Service Commission 91, 92, 106, 166

Q

Quranic 6, 127

R

rain and fog 66
referendum 62, 63, 68, 71, 77, 107, 112
Rome Conference 1

S

Said, Edward 17, 23, 123, 192
Samatar, Mohamed Ali. 138, 154
scientific socialism 5, 138, 193
Scott, James 174, 175, 183, 187
Scunthorpe 4, 18
sectarian 6, 32, 35, 44, 48, 59, 60, 62, 68, 76, 92, 108, 126, 133, 134, 135, 137, 138, 139, 142, 144, 148, 160, 165, 166, 167, 168, 178, 190, 192, 194
shared values 45, 128, 139
Sharia 133
Sharmarke 32, 62, 63, 65, 66, 67, 69, 73, 74, 75, 76, 77, 78, 79, 82, 87, 93, 94, 95, 96, 97, 98, 101, 102, 103, 104, 105, 106, 108, 114, 115, 117, 118, 120, 121, 136, 166, 167
Sheikh Mukhtat 61, 64, 67, 80, 99, 102, 109, 113, 134, 145, 155, 156
Shir 27
SNL 132
Somali consultants 7, 10
Somali democracy 27, 44, 49, 72, 138
Somali News 81, 82, 85, 109, 117, 118
Somalinimo 132
Somali Reconciliation Conference 8
Somali studies 2, 7, 8, 19, 26, 27, 49, 50, 107, 191, 195
Soviet Union 5, 106
Sproul Plaza 18
Supreme Court 65, 69, 76, 102, 103, 104, 105, 122, 136
SYL 31, 47, 60, 61, 62, 69, 70, 71, 72, 73, 74, 76, 77, 78, 79, 80, 87, 94, 98, 99, 103, 104, 114, 116, 120, 121, 122, 132, 133, 136, 155

T

Third World 3, 159, 160, 161, 162, 164, 183, 185

Thompson, E.P. 174, 184

Timacade 47, 53, 137, 154

Transitional Federal Government 12, 141, 156, 181

Tusmo 19

Tutu v

U

Ulema 133, 137

UN 6, 9, 10, 11, 12, 13, 24, 55, 82, 83, 133, 166, 167, 176, 178, 179, 187

Union of Islamic Courts (UICs) 141, 168, 193

United Nations 6, 35, 42, 60, 132, 154, 155, 156, 170, 184, 185, 186, 190, 197

United States 1, 8, 18, 67, 93, 94, 106, 110, 114, 123, 124, 125, 139, 140, 145, 146, 147, 148, 149, 153, 155, 167, 168, 169, 180, 181, 183, 184, 194

University of California, Berkeley 4, 18, 196

University of Iowa 1, 19

University of Minnesota 14, 16, 19, 186, 197

University of Pretoria 19

University of Wisconsin–La Crosse 2, 18

V

violence 36, 37, 46, 70, 71, 134, 138, 143, 145, 161, 162, 168, 194

vote of confidence 66, 67, 74, 76, 77, 79, 104, 118

W

wadaad 127

Walter Reed Hospital 74

War 35, 41, 51, 54, 60, 132, 141, 151, 152, 153, 159, 165, 167, 177, 181

warlords 8, 9, 32, 126, 139, 140, 141, 142, 143, 144, 145, 149, 156, 167, 168

weltanschauung 7

Western 5, 28, 43, 84, 93, 123, 124, 125, 142, 144, 150, 165, 184, 192

winds of change 28

World Bank 1, 6, 180

X

X, Malcolm 2, 3, 21

Y

Yama v

Yasin Nur Hassan 74, 99, 101, 120

Z

Zoope 75, 95, 96, 102, 103, 111, 120, 121, 136